THE AX BOOK

The Lore and Science
of the Woodcutter

This book is gratefully dedicated
to
LLOYD WARREN SIMPSON,
a native son of
Dixmont, Penobscot County, Maine,
for whom
just recognition is long overdue.

THE AX BOOK

The Lore and Science of the Woodcutter

D. Cook

(Formerly published as
Keeping Warm With an Ax)

Illustrated by
S. Lawrence Whipple

Alan C. Hood & Company, Inc.
CHAMBERSBURG, PENNSYLVANIA
www.hoodbooks.com

ACKNOWLEDGMENT

To my wife, Mary, without whom
this book would not be,
and
to Steven A. Young of Concord, Maine,
whose informed editing has done so much
for its content

The Ax Book
(Originally published as *Keeping Warm With An Ax*
byUniverse Books)

Copyright © 1981, 1999
by D. Cook
All rights reserved.
Printed in the U.S.A.

ISBN 0-911469-16-8

Published by Alan C. Hood & Company, Inc.
Chambersburg, PA 17201

www.hoodbooks.com

Copies of *The Ax Book* may be obtained
by sending $25.50 per copy to:

Alan C. Hood & Company, Inc.
P.O. Box 775
Chambersburg, PA 17201

Price includes postage and handling.
Quantity discounts are available to dealers
and non-profit organizations.
Write on letterhead for details.

Library of Congress Cataloging-in-Publication Data
Cook, D. (Dudley), 1921-
    The ax book : the lore and science of the woodcutter / D. Cook ; illustrated by S. Lawrence Whipple.
        p.   cm.
    Reprint. Originally published under title: Keeping warm with an ax. New York : Universe Books, 1981.
    Includes bibliographical references and index.
    ISBN 0-911469-16-8
    1. Axes. 2. Fuelwood. I. Cook, D. (Dudley), 1921- Keeping warm with an ax. II. Title.
SH441.H7 1999
662'.65--dc21   99-052674

Contents

Diagrams

Foreword

If you know one thing well and set out to explain it clearly and completely, you may find yourself explaining many things. You may find the pamphlet you sat down to write has become an encyclopedia. Hence the old story of the simple cobbler who proposed to write on fixing shoes. Once fairly started, he found he couldn't write about fixing shoes without writing about hammers, benches, pegs, and awls; he had to touch on leather, as well, on tanning, on cattle, and on the anatomy of the human foot and leg. In the end, he had written a book about everything. The cobbler had become a philosopher.

There is something of this same feeling about *The Ax Book*, here revised and reissued following its original publication in 1981. It is a book about axes that is also a book about saws, fuel, wood, trees, forestry, steel, history, geography, morals, and much else. Its author, Dudley Cook, of Waterboro, Maine, tells the reader a certain amount about himself. He has evidently worked in the woods a good deal, having learned to use an ax and the other tools of the woodsman as a boy growing up in a small New England town in the 1930s. He doesn't say whether, in writing *The Ax Book*, he found he had taken on a longer journey than he had expected; but if so, he was equal to the task, and his reader is the gainer by the bargain.

Every page of this book is endowed with the confident, unfakable authority of real experience. To be sure, the author knows his subject through study as well as practice. He knows the history of the ax (and of the crosscut saw) and the history of the lumber industry, both in the northeastern United States and in other parts. The reader benefits from Mr. Cook's learning as well as from his experience. But it's in his practical instruction and advice that *The Ax Book* is most impressive and most helpful. You are in the company of a man who knows his subject backwards and forwards. You might say the author has forgotten more about chopping wood than the rest of us will ever know—except that Mr. Cook has apparently forgotten nothing.

The Ax Book tells you how to use an ax safely and efficiently for every task it can perform, especially in connection with cutting firewood: felling trees, trimming them, sectioning them, splitting them. The author isn't afraid to compare the ax with the chainsaw in this work, and he explains the use of the latter tool as well. He discusses the parts of the ax and their care. (The reader who has some small experience of axes quickly learns that, compared to his own, Mr. Cook's ax is shorter, lighter, and much sharper.) The author also gives a thorough account of the woods saw, its care and use; his chapter on the forgotten art of jointing, beveling, setting, and sharpening these saws is one of the most remarkable in the book. He has chapters on selecting, handling, storing, and burning cordwood; and he has reflections and reminiscences on ax work from Maine to the South Pacific. On whatever topic, his writing is consistently simple and clear. You can't write that way about what you don't know. When this author tells you how to accomplish some complex maneuver—in felling a leaning tree, say—you know he has done it himself or has seen it done.

And yet, a disclaimer is necessary. As the author cautions: "Trees will not fit completely into books, not by a good bit." For the reader who aims at real understanding of the ax—understanding on a par with the author's—*The Ax Book* is a guide to experience, not a substitute for it. Mr. Cook knows that, too. He is the guide every reader seeks: honest, clear, patient, humorous, and demanding. What is possible to learn about using an ax from a book, his book will teach.

CASTLE FREEMAN, JR.
Newfane, Vermont
September 1999

Introduction

Before America gave serious attention to a shortage of energy, Eric Sloane, noted historian and illustrator of Americana, wrote, "Perhaps the tool least regarded in America is the axe." Since that was published in *The Second Barrel* (1969) our mode of living has accelerated. So in an age of lasers, cloning, and space probes, devoting an entire book to use of the ax requires explanation.

Numerous omens hint that broad change is coalescing as we watch. Not all the signs are rainbow-hued, certainly not shifting patterns of international strength, economic confusion, or knowledge that fossil fuels cannot forever spout from ceaseless fountains; most of all, not the pandemic loss of faith in who we are, whether we can influence our destiny or even survive. There is no turning back the clock. Who made time has His own cycles. Perhaps in the refining of megalomania, some of our ways will become more simple rather than more complex.

Several sentences after the quotation above, Eric Sloane stated, "Yet a century ago, the axe was the most important implement in America." To those who are unafraid to enjoy life, I believe that knowledge of the ax still can be of use, and should be passed on.

1

The Tool of Necessity

Don't sneer at the ax. Its genealogy may be better than your own. There is no need to be afraid of it either. You can easily learn to use it. And as things seem to be shaping up, perhaps you should learn.

For uncounted generations, the ax was man's best tool. Early man did just about everything with it. He dug tasty roots, chopped fuel and building materials. He caught running food and took care of troublesome neighbors, the latter two often simultaneously. Our more recent forebears cleared land, built log cabins, and kept warm by means of their axes. In our climate, to live in the woods, a man had to have an ax.

It is true that we do not have quite the same manner of living today. But before feeling too superior, check what you have been paying lately to keep warm. If your winter fuel bills seem to have cancerous growth of some sort, maybe relearning the ax could be profitable to you. It can certainly be enjoyable.

The modern tree-felling ax is an efficient instrument perfected during a long history. Man's first tool was undoubtedly a club or hand-held stone. But somewhere in the past millennia, some of our cleverer ancestors put a club and a stone together to make an ax, and a whole new era began. Men could hit harder and cut deeper.

When metals were discovered, metal striking tools would have been among the first applications. The resemblance between the later, more skillfully formed stone axes and the earliest known bronze specimens is remarkable. Bronze axes probably more than 3,500 years old have been unearthed from ancient Ur in what is now Iraq. A double-bitted ax found in Crete dates back to 2000–1700 B.C.

That axes became weapons was only natural evolution. As well as for chopping up roots, an ax was useful for chopping down enemies. History can be viewed as a compilation of peoples who repeatedly resorted to this sort of activity. Much early and classical artwork depicting warriors shows axes carried as weapons. The weapons themselves were sometimes bits of art. As with swords, the battle-axes of chieftains were often chased in silver and gold. As armies grew, there were whole formations of axmen. Even development of the many forms of the sword did not entirely supersede the ax. The ill-fated Harold II, king of Saxon England, apparently wielded a mighty two-handed ax. But at the Battle of Hastings in 1066, Harold lost. England fell to William the Conqueror and the Normans.

With the settlement of America, the ax emerged as the prime tool of necessity, even before a gun. In a land of forests, the trees had to be cleared so that crops could grow in the sunlight of open fields. So the first Americans made it their business to destroy as many trees as possible. What they accomplished is as amazing as, from our viewpoint today, it is dismaying. But for families that had to bare the soil to plant seed, it was "Root, hog, or die!" Their work in eliminating whole regions of forest, leaf, limb, trunk, and root, surpasses any effort that a labor union could conceivably have a nightmare about today.

Indispensable as the ax was, it alone was insufficient means to accomplish that gargantuan land-clearing task. Usually the great trees were "deadened" with the ax, which gouged the life-giving sapwood in a girdle about the trunk. Left to die so as to burn better, or just to rot eventually, trees would stand for years as ugly monuments to the energy of man. Meanwhile, with the fallen leaves or needles no longer blocking the sun, crops could be sown among the stumps and the branching towers of wood.

That depressing spectacle was particularly noticed by new travelers through American frontier areas. The desolation surpassed anything within their experience. As late as 1840, Alexis de Tocqueville, a French observer, described such a scene: "All the trees seemed to have been suddenly struck dead. In full summer, their withered branches seemed the image of winter." But for the settlers who lived there, this stage was necessary to make the land productive. For largely, food came from field crops, not from the forest.

Nor was the work of the axman finished with killing the trees, even if they were to be soon burned. For you could not plow through roots. The stumps had to be laboriously split apart if possible, then grubbed out or back-breakingly pulled out down to the rootlets. Stumps moved easier if they rotted for a few years, but however done, it was a stupendous task. All across the eastern half of North America, this process was repeated wherever forest gave way to farms. In any area, the entire cycle took years to complete. Only among the painstaking Pennsylvania Dutch was it commonplace to convert a plot of ground from forest to root-free cropland within one year.

To the early settlers, shelter was also vital. In the bitter winters, shelter was often an even more immediate need than food. Some of the first shelter arrangements were only caves or brush lean-tos. But with the plentiful trees, houses built from criss-crossed logs notched together at the corners soon became common merely because the materials were available everywhere for the cutting. The ax was indispensable. To fell enough trees to make a cabin for his family, a man had to have an ax. Contemporary drawings and accounts of the early cabins describe a feature common to virtually all of them, the tapered and hacked-off butts of each log. These were cut with axes. There was no other way to procure the abundant trees for either fuel or construction.

Even for so rough a job as making a crude cabin, a good saw would be an excellent tool of choice. But the settlers had few saws at all, let alone good ones as we know them, and of woods saws, none at all. Steel was both scarce and dear in North America, even down into the 19th century. Prior to modern methods of manufacture, not only were saws more difficult to make than axes, but a saw that could cut the same timber an ax could cut also required more steel. Nor could saws be as easily maintained. And bad as a dull ax is, it will cut if the man swinging it is man enough to keep going. A dull saw without any set to the teeth just about cannot work at all. It can even get stuck in a cut so it will not budge. Even to get the saw out of your way, you may have to use an ax.

With available materials, frontier woodsmen could sharpen an ax far easier and better than they could sharpen a saw. And axes were not so vulnerable to damage and were more easily carried. Consequently, on the frontier and in the early farm settlements there were almost no saws. These came later with the traveling artisans and the mills.

The first type of metal ax used in North America was undoubtedly the "trade" ax, a poll-less ax with a narrow but flaring bit. Most trade axes were probably of French manufacture, though they were used in the New World trade with the Indians by both Spanish and English certainly, as well as the French. These axes were already scattered among the Indians before there were any English settlements in North America at all. Since an iron ax was such a revolutionary tool to the Indians, their desire for the metal ax guaranteed its spread, for the Indian tribes were at war with one another much of the time. Captain John Smith found trade axes among the Indians near Jamestown, Virginia, in 1607. Over two generations previously, Hernando de Soto, the Spanish explorer, had found trade axes among the Indians of what is now southeastern United States.

The probable origin of these earliest noted trade axes was the even earlier arrival of white traders to the New World in the years following Columbus. Some of the first were Portuguese, but they were followed by the French. Many returned for fish but soon entered the fur trade also. That the trade ax was one of the more popular items of exchange was demonstrated by its spread among Indians who were far from any contact with the whites. Later English traders in the Hudson Bay region even left that ax pattern, modified somewhat, the name Hudson Bay. It was the trade ax pattern that still later was also made in the smaller and popular tomahawk size.

By the time the English colonists were established, they soon had reason to notice the distinctive axes the Indians carried. Under primitive conditions, the Indian ax or tomahawk was a small tool with its stone head lashed to a forked, or split and lashed, stick. Living without metals until the coming of the Europeans, particularly the irreplaceable iron for tools, the Indians seldom attempted to cut or use the heavy construction timbers favored by the white men. But forest life required a cutting tool. The lighter, more portable tomahawk served for the less demanding cutting and hacking the Indians needed it for. Like our own ancestors, the Indians also used the tomahawk for hacking people as well as tent poles. This way of living was part of Indian existence. To save their own skulls, they had to smash others.

The tomahawk was one of the most efficient weapons the Indians had. In reliability, effectiveness, and ease of use, the tomahawk was superior to the bow and arrow, even if not as long-ranged. Being most vulnerable, the skull was the foremost tomahawk target. With the sometime encouragement of white allies, it is not unlikely that this fact could have helped the grisly practice of scalping become a victory symbol. Even in our serene society, exultant spectators have been known to swarm to the field after a victorious football game and literally tear opponents' goalposts into splintered souvenirs.

In some manner and degree, we are all influenced by whomever we encounter. During the settling of North America, the harsh life of the frontier whites did not differ

Early North American Ax Types —
Diagram 1

All were substantially straight-handled.

8"

The "Trade Ax" - First ax commonly used in the New World. Mostly of French make. For almost 200 years "trade" axes were used for barter with the Indians by traders of all European nations. Much prized by the Indians, "trade" axes rapidly became widespread. De Soto even found them among Indians of interior Southern U.S. in 1540. A later, one-handed model of similar design was smaller, the deadly tomahawk.

9"

Anglo-American Ax was a development of English design. Its bit had a pronounced flare and there was the beginning of a poll.

9"

the German Ax had a strong resemblance to the Trade Ax, but had slanted bottom to the eye area & was somewhat larger. Was used in Pennsylvania area.

7"

The American Ax was squat, rectangular, and had a distinct poll. Despite its ugly lines, the American Ax gave more to modern ax design than other early models. After the Revolution, axes of this design were even being exported to Europe.

poll

greatly from the Indians' way of life. Forest living required a cutting tool, and to those on the move, the light Indian ax made sense. Soon white trappers and fighting men carried tomahawks of the new, reduced-size trade pattern, and even ones edged with steel. So to the accompaniment of their guns, the implacable white men used tomahawks just as the Indians did. The primitive Indians were powerless to stem the never-ebbing tide of whites. By this century, few Indians were left, scattered across the continent in desolate reservations. Their tomahawk pattern has survived. You can still find a modern version, usually with longer handle, in some northern stores. It is variously known as a "cruising," "trapper's," or "Hudson Bay" ax.

We know very little about the development of ax design in North America. Since each of the English colonies was separated from the others, they developed distinctive differences. After the ubiquitous trade ax there were three distinct patterns during the colonial and post-Revolutionary periods: the Anglo-American ax, the German ax, and the American ax. (See Diagram 1.) Although modern ax design is descended from all three of these prototypes, most axes were both shorter and broader and resembled the American ax more than the Anglo-American or German patterns. The standard American ax was well established by the late 1700s, and later than that was even exported to Europe.

Need for the ax did not vanish with the end of the frontier. As America grew, so did its demand for the same kinds of valuable timber and fuel that the first settlers had so diligently destroyed. Local woodlands did not regenerate soon enough even to meet local needs. As the margin of virgin forestlands retreated, lumbering became ever more distant from the settlements. It was no longer the work of the farmer. To the isolation and hardships of lumbering came the professionals who lived by their axes. In later years they became known as lumberjacks.

Lumber was not all that trees were sought for. Until coal came into general use in the decades after the Civil War, wood was the principal fuel for heating, cooking, furnishing charcoal for the early iron smelters, potash for soap, and fuel to fill the ravenous fireboxes in steam engines used by industries, steamboats, and trains. It was 1895 before the annual quantity of coal consumed exceeded that of wood fuel.

The ax felled trees, and the men who swung the axes were the stuff of legends. Did Paul Bunyan ever use a *saw*? If he did, nobody noticed, because with a single swing of his great ax he could fell the tallest tree, and some of the originals were pretty sizable. Almost to the 20th century, the ax was still the first tool of the woods.

Today, timber harvesting is mechanized. Modern machines shear whole trees off with giant jaws. Chain saws are also popular, and not only in the woods. Nearly every suburbanite has his chain saw to trim the shrubs on either side of his front door. These are all very efficient. They are also costly. They also require fuel to operate. To cut the wood to keep you and yours cozy on frosty nights, you do not need that kind of investment. You do not need to pay budget-breaking rents, gas, oil, coal, or electric bills, either. If you are man enough, and you have a woodlot available, all you need is your ax.

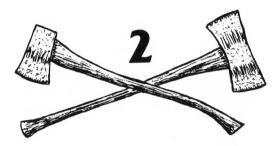

Ax or Chain Saw?

Watching the marvelous parade of energy sources developed since 1895, when wood was cast aside, has more recently seemed like a nightmare game of hide-and-seek. One result is already clear. Wood is again an eagerly bid-for fuel. You can buy it or, if you are among the lucky ones, you can cut it. If you will be able to cut your own firewood, what tool will you use?

Any wood-cutting tool depends upon what you need it for. If you will sharpen a toothpick, take a jackknife. If you work for a paper company that needs a half million cords of wood, maybe you will drive a monster woods harvester that cleaves off trees like jackstraws. If you need firewood for yourself, you will want something in between. Will it be ax or chain saw?

We can settle one thing right away. If you want to be fashionable, buy a chain saw. They are in. The chain saw is the delight of the suburban putterer. He is much aware that wood is energy and is a precious fuel. Whenever one of his shade trees has a dead limb he will cut it off in two pieces to store in his breezeway before he goes to Florida for the winter. It is pretty tough to beat a chain saw for that. An ax does not make noise enough to inform the neighbors that its owner is in on the energy thing too. To fit with the riding-lawnmower set, you must have a chain saw. To chain-saw salesmen, this the best selling point of all.

If you are serious about heating your home with wood, the easiest way is to buy the wood. But bought wood is expensive, and you will get small satisfaction out of that system. If you cut your own wood, it will probably be with either ax or chain saw. There are other tools, the one and two-man manual saws, for instance. Ordinarily though, these are not used without an ax, but either ax or chain saw can be used alone without the assistance of other tools. Because ax and chain saw are otherwise dissimilar, comparing them is essential to a clear understanding of what they can or cannot do.

If cutting your wood appeals to you from the cost angle, then you will be also interested in what initial investment you must make in tools. Considering only the bare-bones ax or chain saw without auxiliary items, a chain saw currently costs about eight to over thirty times as much as an ax. The variation depends on size and quality, the real bargains often not being the cheaper ones. Electric chain saws with independent power source for operating in a woodlot would price them out of reasonable comparison. There are essential

auxiliary items also. With an ax, you must at least have a hand-sharpening stone. For the chain saw, minimum operating equipment includes at least a gas can, chain adjusting tool, file and file holder, a depth gauge, and a flat file. One ax stone will outlast many saw files.

Maintenance costs are almost entirely one-sided because, barring damage, an ax needs only to be sharpened. A chain saw needs gasoline just as a lawnmower does, and considering how small a chain saw is, surprisingly often. On a routine basis, a chain saw must also have two different oils, two-cycle oil to mix with the gasoline and bar-and-chain oil for the chain lubricant reservoir. As I write this, gas rationing is not yet a problem for chain-saw users. That is a plus.

Maintenance time is an irritating necessity for any tool. Both ax and chain saw must be kept sharp. Time needed for sharpening might be the same for both ax and chain saw, perhaps fifteen minutes for each day's work. Beyond that, the chain saw must be fueled, filled with oil, and rather often have its chain adjusted. An ax does not.

That is only part of the maintenance story. As anybody who has tended machinery knows, the more complicated the machine, the more "down time" for repairs. And if your source of service or repair parts is not nearby, you can somehow spend a lot of time just going back and forth. With luck, your friendly repairman will have your saw ready for you to use. Though one of the worst aspects of chain-saw repairs is down time, the other is the cost of parts and service. It does not take many repair bills to equal a substantial portion of the original cost of the saw. The need for servicing does not all stem from breakage or abuse either. Some major items, the chain for instance, must be replaced from time to time just because of wear. If you are an attentive mechanic, you will succeed in making your chain saw run better and longer. Not everybody has that kind of ability. To use an ax, you do not need it.

An ax is obviously more portable than a chain saw. You will begin to appreciate that when you wander a short distance from your vehicle, as you might when cutting selected trees. Suppose you carry everything for continued cutting during the day. Toting only an ax, you will have one item of four pounds total and a hand stone that slips easily in the pocket. If you are a chain-saw man, you will likely have twenty or more pounds in four separate items, the saw, gasoline, chain oil, and the tool for adjusting the chain. That is with a light saw. With a large chain saw, run the weight up to suit. Now suppose you take a couple of other knickknacks such as a thermos bottle, a lunch, a measuring stick, and maybe an extra item of clothing. How many hands do you have?

On firewood up to 4" in diameter, a good axman can just about keep up to a chain-saw operator in the woods. For small sticks, the advantage lies with the ax, and on bigger trees, the chain saw would have a time advantage. To clear working area brush, the ax is far superior. A chain saw snagged in brush can easily kick back. For limbing the average firewood tree, the ax is almost as fast, and on smaller trees, faster. You can move easier with the ax. It is not only lighter, but being smaller also, it is far handier to wield.

Compared to the chain saw, the ax is virtually noiseless. Chain-saw noise is finally beginning to be recognized for what it is, a menace to hearing. Continued operation without good ear protection can irreparably damage the auditory nerve endings. Unfortunately, this type of damage cannot be later compensated for by hearing aids of any design. So no matter how bothersome ear protectors are, you should always wear them when operating a chain saw.

Any cutting tool is dangerous. But in no way is an ax as treacherously surprising as a chain saw can be. Improperly used, both ax and chain saw can strike at your legs. But an ax will not leap at your face as a chain saw can when the top edge hits a branch. Nor will you ever feel quite so complacent with a chain saw again if you witness a broken chain mangle a man's hands. Reasonable precautions reduce these dangers, but the potential for accident is always waiting in the wings. Being simpler, the ax is safer.

To have your chain saw stuck in a cut so you cannot move it without additional help sounds ridiculous. It should never happen, but when you are cutting larger trees it can easily occur unless you are a canny operator. To extricate the saw, using an ax, a peavey, another saw, or a long prybar or crowbar may be necessary. Having one of these available represents even more baggage to lug around with your chain saw. An ax seldom gets stuck badly. If it does, a thump on the handle or knocking the poll with a stick or rock will knock the ax harmlessly free.

Pinched and stuck saw incidents can cause expensive repairs. A chain-saw bar is tough, but it can be damaged by both pinching and your own frustrated efforts to pull it loose. The chain can likewise suffer pinch damage, particularly with the heavier hardwood trees that make the best firewood. And the rest of the saw is not nearly as rugged as the chain and bar are. The saw chassis and motor can be put out of action by anything from being dropped to a bit of dirt in the gas line. Suppose the ultimate damage occurs. A tree falls smack on your cutting tool. If the tool happens to be an ax, at worst you will have to get a new handle. If the tool is a chain saw, get a new saw.

Today, a sad advantage of the ax lies in the fact that it is less likely to be stolen than the chain saw is. The greater cost and popularity of expensive chain saws make them prime targets of break-ins and burglaries. Let the fancy paint wear off your ax handle and no modern thief will touch it. He would not know how valuable a tool it is.

Using an ax requires you to work. Whether you see that as an advantage or not depends on your vigor and disposition. Whatever details of description may have been different, nobody ever depicted Paul Bunyan with dull eyes, flabby muscles, and shortness of breath. The demands of the ax created a hero of different cut. Skilled use of the ax requires far more of both mind and body than the unskilled observer can believe or understand. If through your skill with an ax you can protect you and yours from the cold, you may find this as strangely satisfying as anything you have ever done.

There are those still living who have seen a man, his only tool an ax, cut and stack two cords of wood in a day, a skill level contemporary men are unlikely to attain, or even challenge. Yet in December 1986 *Yankee* Magazine printed that Edward Moote of Weathersfield, Vermont, in an ax exhibition born in a wager, on September 26, 1908, had chopped, split once and stacked *five* cords of white pine in less than twelve hours.

Was the story true? *Yankee* stated that its author had gleaned his sources from the Vermont Historical Society. I was unable to verify that. But vast disparity in human accomplishment is indisputable. It was possible for some men to chop two cords a day. As told, Moote's conditions had been ideal. Possibly he did chop five cords. What is worth remembering here is the awesome power of an ax when swung by competent hands.

It must be admitted that anybody can learn to use a chain saw skillfully far sooner than he could attain comparable level of skill with an ax. This undeniable advantage of the chain saw is considerably offset by the chore of maintaining it. Learning that well is something else. In general, the more you can do for yourself, the better. That may lead to maintaining a young machine shop also. The simple ax asks none of this suffering.

We must keep the comparison honest. A chain saw can cut a volume of wood, such as a large tree, a heavy log, or several logs piled together much easier and more quickly than an ax can. The leverage of this fact is tremendous. Nevertheless, it should not be viewed as overwhelming. An ax can cut anything that a chain saw can cut, and for light work, is quicker.

In common with all saws, a chain saw can cut at right angles to a log with virtually no waste. This is another tremendous advantage, one that can only be noted without fighting it. A skilled axman can hew almost exactly to a line. But he needs room to cut. The waste on the off side of the line will be great.

At the work site, with your chain saw fueled, full of oil also, repaired, adjusted, and ready to go, the chain saw requires less exertion to use than an ax does to cut the same amount of wood. If you don't mind being out of shape, this is an advantage. Mind you, the feat of actually reaching the work site with a chain saw and all its paraphernalia may be another matter.

For purposes of gathering firewood, the ax and chain saw are really complementary. I cut wood for my own use and use both of them. I seldom take the chain saw to the woods, but occasionally do. I dislike wasting much of the heavy pieces by chopping. I stack the wood I cut in lengths that are as long as convenient, then cut down through the pile as you would slice a loaf of bread. You cannot do that with an ax. Splitting the short lengths after cutting, I use an ax. Doing that with the chain saw would not only take forever, but would waste much wood and make a general mess. Both tools have their advantages.

But in the current popularity of the chain saw, the ax is overlooked. That does not make sense. Not today. Just the necessity of using gasoline to operate the chain saw makes learning how to use the ax look sensible. I have no apology for not advocating the "easy" way of gathering firewood. I know that the "easy" way is not always easy, especially for home warmth. Many other signs and portents indicate that the "easy" choice may not always be affordable or, conceivably, even available.

If I were to be isolated and could have just one cutting tool, I would choose an ax. It would outlast, and therefore outcut, any other woodcutting tool.

3

First Blood

I don't remember when I first hankered after an ax. Certainly it was before the age of chain saws. I could not have been too old when a doting aunt gave my older brother a shiny Boy Scout hatchet complete with brown leather belt sheath for Christmas. She gave me a carpenter's saw. Children are transparent little beasts. Even now I remember keen resentment roiling my craw because I had not been given a hatchet also, or that the gifts were not transposed. I liked the saw well enough. I still have it today. But that did not stop my wanting the hatchet. The tomahawk image of that belt sheath was not lost on me either.

Being devious—"sneaky" is more accurate—it did not take me long to try out that hatchet. My brother cleverly kept closer watch over me than my parents did, so I had to be circumspect about where I practiced. The woodpile behind the barn offered relative security. When sure that nobody was lurking about, I reached the woodpile unseen. Tearing off the leather sheath, I raised the hatchet over my head and swung fiercely at a large stick on top of the woodpile.

Something resembling a nick appeared in the heavy bark. Incredulous, I swung again. A second mark appeared. Angrily, I kept hacking until my arm was tired. I had only fuzzed the surface of several firewood sticks. They were probably oak. Anyway, I gained small satisfaction in attacking them. What I had wanted to do was make big chips pop out as my father did with his ax. But not even a small chip jumped out for me. I crept back to the house, hiding the hatchet behind me. After that, my goal became a full-sized ax.

Any edge tool always seemed fascinating. When I had one, my choicest possession was invariably a knife. With a jackknife you could make a bow and cut arrows. You could make acorn and willow whistles and hack off sassafras roots to chew. If there was somebody to play with, you could always play Jackknife.

Some people have termed Jackknife "mumbletypeg," but I don't claim to have explanations for everything. Nobody ever called it anything but Jackknife when I was playing it. It was one of those sexist games that girls could only monitor from a distance with a disdainful adoration reserved for the more hardy and skillful players. In a formal progression, you had to flip an open jackknife standing point down off various locations on your body so that it would stick upright in the ground. When you missed, it was the next player's turn. It

could be hard on a knife if you hit a rock head-on. On the other hand, it was easier to tolerate having the tip against your flesh if that tip was dulled or broken off. Shooting from the chin or top of the head was the worst. There you could gain a moral victory over the bigger boys by not using the thumb as a cushion. Of course arguments were endemic. I don't ever remember finishing an entire game of Jackknife without controversy of some kind.

The principal drawback to jackknives was that they were small enough to be easily mislaid. Somewhere in the half-grown stage I was proud of counting the number of jackknives that I had lost. It was eighteen at one time. Since my mother normally was more available than my father, I often tried to enlist her in these emergencies, though complaining about her system of finding things.

"Look where you last had it," she would tell me.

This was always too much. I would cry, "That's what I don't know!"

"Think," she would answer. "Think."

Using her system, I did find just one lost jackknife, perhaps because it had bright red celluloid handles. It was under a couch. The only other one of my boyhood knives that ever turned up I found myself without any help. It would have been better if I had not found it.

The discovery was quite accidental. Some of my older sister's friends were playing hide-and-seek on a summer afternoon. There were older boys playing also, and it was a privilege for me to be able to join them. A row of large trees fronted our property and I had hidden behind the huge trunk of the last one in line. As I lay on the root hummocks, I was delightedly amazed to find directly in front of my nose one of the better knives that I could remember losing, a genuine stag-handle Boy Scout knife.

Then I recalled crouching in the same spot the previous winter. The trees along the road were sugar maples. In the late winter, we could get sugary icicles from breaking off a low-hanging twig. The next day, the icicles' little sugar tips were ready for harvesting. These were sweet-tasting, but they only titillated. I wanted more.

My father would not hear of tapping the trees. He had never done it. "They're too valuable!" he said. Then he added, "Don't go breaking those branches, either!"

That left me to find my own solution. Later, I went to the last tree in line. Hiding behind the trunk, I attempted to gut the tree so a fountain of delicious maple syrup would pour out. You had to drill a hole. I had known that. But that last tree happened to be an ash, not a maple. I had not known that. With the drilling ability I had then, there was destined to be little difference. The fountain did not flow. I could not even make a hole. For some reason, forever forgotten, I had deserted the knife there also.

Now, waiting for action from hide-and-seek headquarters, I tried stabbing an ant with my recovered delight. I missed. The belt-punch auger was still open, rusted solidly in the position that I had left it. There was a cry from my flank. I had been discovered. With the knife in my fist I sprang to my feet to run for the goal, the gigantic cherry tree on the far side of our house. I never made it.

Somewhere en route, the open belt-punch proved that it still worked. The tip struck my opposite wrist, puncturing the artery. From running and excitement, my blood was up, you could say. I remember screeching in our backyard at the arc of liquid red spurting from my wrist as high as my forearm was long.

My father stopped that. From nowhere, he appeared to put his big thumb over the hole and we went off to the family doctor who sealed it up somehow. So life went on. The incident did not end knives for me, but it taught me not to run with them open.

My first ax came from Sears, Roebuck. I was about fourteen. I had saved my own money doing outside work, and my father reluctantly gave permission. He needed his own ax himself, and I could help with the firewood if I had one of my own. I studied the Sears catalog, finally selecting their "best Michigan Pattern" single-bitted ax weighing four pounds. It was a great day when that arrived. To a skinny kid, that four-pound ax seemed like something to swing. It was. When it came down, it had a lot of authority. To keep swinging it took a lot of wind. I had not used a full-sized ax before, let alone a four-pounder, and there was a lot to learn. I still did not know why keeping the blade sharp was so important. Because operating our old foot-pedal grindstone was such a chore, one day I went to the woods without touching up the blade. In the bright afternoon, I had no idea that I was starting another lesson.

Back in our woodlot, a solid old chestnut top lay prostrate for the taking. It had been there for a long time obviously, but chestnut kept well. It was not the best firewood, but it would certainly burn. The butt of that top had been cut long before with an ax. It was a wasteful cut, the end tapering off in a long wedge. I cut the limbs off and the trunk in half, leaving a couple of long sticks too heavy for me to carry out to the path. Chestnut split well. I decided to halve or quarter those sticks lengthwise.

The vertical side of the wedge-shaped butt seemed an obvious target. The four-pounder could easily start a crack in clear chestnut. Under other circumstances that might have been true. What I did not figure on was how a dull ax could skip through an angled surface that was also powdered with age. Nor did I stop to figure about protecting myself from a ricochet. I swung. Surprisingly, the ax did not lodge in the butt. At the same time my left foot felt as if it had been thumped. The ax was clear. It was also clean. What had happened? There seemed to be no mark on my foot. Had the back of the ax somehow knocked me in passing?

Revelations can come in waves. In my case, they now came with the shocking gush of blood welling freely from the side of my boot. On the inner edge of my foot, a clean line sheared entirely through leather boot sole, welt, and into the upper. The four-pounder had not been too dull for that. I attempted a tentative step. The foot began to throb now, but it worked. Throttling the treacherous ax, I hobbled home.

"Oh! Ah!" said my mother as I trailed smears into the kitchen. "I knew it would happen!" I remember thinking that if she had known it, why had she not told me so that I could have avoided it? I did not say that, though.

There was another trip to the old family doctor. Fortunately there was no major damage. Even so, years passed before the red scar at the base of my big toe could stand the pressure of a close-fitting shoe. Many times since, it has been a good reminder of how to place my feet when chopping.

The Hurricane of '38

After dissecting my foot, it was some time before I did any more ax work. With the initial mending over, I had to get a new and looser pair of boots. That hurt, and not only on the foot. The cobbler claimed that it was not possible to repair the ax slice in the old boot. He also sold new boots.

In the spring, I returned to several lawn-mowing jobs I had "to earn college money." As summer approached, I had the good luck to gain another customer who had lawns that took a day and a half to cut. Luck comes in globs. The new job was on the main street. I gained advertising exposure that I had not enjoyed before. After several weeks, one of the oldest trucks in town stopped by me as I mowed the roadside strip of lawn on the new job. I knew the driver. It was Lloyd, man of all work at Wiswall Sanatorium up the street.

"How'd you like a steady job?" he asked me.

He did not seem to be joking. But what he implied was almost too much to hope for. "It would be great," I said.

He scanned my mowing as if to see whether I had left any ridges. "I could use some help," he said. "Come around after work today. Maybe I can get Doctor Wiswall to try you out."

The Depression was still on, and Wiswall Sanatorium did not have a reputation for being loose with money. I tried not to think too much about it until I had finished that lawn job. Then I sought Lloyd out in the workshop of the Sanatorium's big garage where he was sharpening a lawnmower. Past the ever-present cigar stub in the corner of his mouth he said, "Doc says that I can try you. Can you come tomorrow?"

I quickly assured him that I could and would and went home ecstatic. At fifteen years old I was already assistant to the handyman at Wiswall Sanatorium! And the pay was twenty-five cents an hour! I came back the next day and the next and kept coming. Soon it became understood that I had a full-time job whenever I was not in school. As it turned out, I kept working for Wiswall Sanatorium on that basis until I left for the Marine Corps in World War II.

Helping Lloyd, I did everything that needed to be done from mowing more lawns and shoveling snow to clearing plugged plumbing and fixing locks. I learned a lot there. Lloyd had a lot to teach.

His name was Lloyd Warren Simpson. He had grown up on a farm in Dixmont, Maine. By nature, he was generous and kindly. I never saw him overtly angry, even on occasions when most men would have been. Physically he was a bull and tremendously strong. Though not tall, he weighed over two hundred and fifty pounds, his outstanding feature being his belly. It was enormous. His belt had to make a swooping dive beneath the belly to fasten somewhere below, so his belt buckle always faced downward. But that belly was like a rock. I had several times seen him let Doctor Wiswall's half-grown son hit the belly as hard as he could. Each time Lloyd only grinned as the boy backed off moaning how his fist hurt.

The Sanatorium had a half-dozen buildings set off by lawns and connected by winding drives through patches of woods. Occasionally a tree encroaching on a drive or other open space had to be removed. Anything to do with the trees interested me. As I loaded the brush into the old truck, I would watch in fascination as Lloyd did the ax work. His movements were deliberate, but whatever he struck seemed to fly apart, usually on his first stroke.

"Don't try to be quick with an ax," he said. "Just make up your mind what you want to hit. Then do it." That was clearly his system, and he had the heft to put the system into effect. Though I did not appreciate it at the time, his ax was something special, too. When he chopped, there was a minimum of both blows and chips. But to me, his chips seemed like pie plates.

In the autumn of 1938 I was seventeen. I don't remember whether I went to school or worked on 22 September. But I do remember the humid stillness of the air and a sallow sky I had never seen before. Gradually a breeze arose, dispelling the stickiness, and it persisted, its welcome puffs becoming continuous movement. Soon it raised dust in gusts and sent premature dead leaves flying from beneath the trees. But instead of gusting and dying away, succeeding gusts of wind were increasingly strong. Eerie patches of darting yellow opened overhead and then as quickly vanished into a swirling murk. Live leaves flew after the dead ones, and then twigs. Still the wind kept gathering strength, and branches joined the litter that was everywhere. By late afternoon, the manic power of the wind was frightening. The cumulative roar of its awful might seemed to come from a long way off. Hearing anything else was difficult. All about, the lashing trees streamed frenziedly before the wind as if in agony at their tearing.

I could scarcely stand unaided. Even then I had not

thought of that storm as a hurricane. Down South and in the tropics they had hurricanes, but not in New England. In our front yard the two blue spruces were bending dangerously sideways. These were my father's pride and joy. They were not too tall but were bushy and beautiful in an area where spruce was not native. Leaning against the wind, I brought rope from the barn. Climbing up through the thrashing bristles, I secured the upper sections of the two trees to each other and then to a post of our front porch. For whatever reason, the spruces did not succumb. Afterward I always wondered why the additional strain on our poor front porch did not pull it down.

Beside our driveway were five huge cherry trees each at least a foot and a half at the butt. During the height of the storm, I saw the second tree from the end give up and lie over against the last in line. The end tree partially rebounded, its branches in wrenched clusters. But on the windward side from below, a pythonlike section of root cracked, curling from the earth as if it were a whip. The end tree lurched, then as a unit both giants toppled together in a muffled thud that was scarcely noticeable above the wind.

Soon after that, I fled inside from the flying debris. Darkness came early and nearly completely. The electricity was long gone, and even within the house, the surging buffets of wind prohibited candlelight. We were lucky that we had a couple of the kerosene road lanterns to give a darting yellow shield against the fearful power outside. The old house creaked in seeming to lift before the wind, settled back, and then strained again and again. Occasionally there would be a crash, and we would all look at each other with wide eyes glittering in the lamplight, trying to identify from the sounds what more had been torn away.

By eleven that night the worst was over, though there were still diminishing winds until four in the morning. Everywhere there were fallen trees. We lost all but one of the line of cherry trees, part of a chimney, some shutters, and other miscellany. Along the street, the great maples, including the ash tree behind which I had found my rusted jackknife, were still standing, as was the tremendous cherry tree that was the traditional goal for hide-and-seek. We were lucky.

In the morning, with the emergency under control at home, I departed with my ax for Wiswall Sanatorium. It was not easy to get there. Downed trees and pole lines were everywhere. With axes and saws, several crews struggled to clear the road and repair damage.

Although the Sanatorium buildings were mostly intact, the grounds were a shambles. In keeping with the easiest scheme of outdoor decor through the years, many great white pines had grown up to shade the lawns and provide screening between buildings. Fully half of these beautiful trees were flattened or lodged at crazy angles against each other. Many trees blocked the drives. Others had fallen against buildings, ripping siding and roofing. A few had broken off, but most were uprooted, raising huge barriers of roots and soil.

Left to my own devices while Lloyd received orders from headquarters, I set to hacking off branches overhanging doorways and paths so traffic could pass from building to building. Lloyd nodded when he appeared. "That's good," he said. "But trim the logs. We'll have to pile them later. They

won't roll with a lot of stubs sticking out." Then he handed me a saw, a one-man crosscut that I came to know well. "Do the big ones with this," he said. "And don't pinch it in the scarf or you'll take the set out of it."

It took weeks for the Sanatorium to return to normal. And more than two years passed before those hurricane logs were finally hauled off for a fee. Nobody would pay for logs then. They were a glut. You had to pay to get them removed. A few foresighted operators stored logs in ponds. Logs kept far better in water even though many became waterlogged and sank. I remember hurricane logs being dredged from pond bottoms as much as ten years afterward.

It was exhilarating to work on those hurricane windfalls. I kept hacking where it seemed needed and watched Lloyd's work with open admiration. When he struck a limb, it came off clean. Except on the larger ones, he seldom used more than two strokes. At the second, if not the first stroke, the whole limb would fly off into the air. I tried to imitate him. That was not easy. After letting me hack away and discover things for a few days he said, "Did you ever try a lighter ax?"

At seventeen, I was still skinny, but implying that I was not strong enough for my four-pound ax nettled me. "Oh, this is just right for me," I said.

I might have saved my breath. "Your handle should be shorter," he said. "In limbing, there's no room for a long handle. And for you, your ax probably shouldn't weigh over three pounds."

Seeing the look that must have been on my face, he asked, "How much do you think mine weighs?"

I had wondered about that. He had told me it was a Snow & Nealley ax from Bangor, Maine. Its shape was different from my ax and judging its weight was difficult. From the cuts he made, maybe his ax weighed ten pounds for all that I knew. "I don't know," I said.

"Three and three-quarters pounds. If I were to swing this all day, it would be all I'd want." My eyes widened. He said, "I have a three-pounder, too. You try it after dinner. You'll see the difference. It's what you should have."

Using Lloyd's three-pound ax was a revelation, and I immediately had a new goal in axes. Soon afterward I had one of my own. Mine was a Cock-o'-the-Woods made by Emerson & Stevens of Oakland, Maine. It did not come hung, so Lloyd helped me select a straight-grained handle. He also hung the ax on the handle for me as I watched to see how he did it.

"This is a good ax," he said. "I like it even better than my light one maybe. You see. You'll do better with this."

He was right again. The pleasure of using that lighter ax made days go fast. I could swing it more often, and not becoming winded so quickly, I was able to strike truer. Before long, I too was able to scale chips out from my deepening cuts instead of just making a lot of fuzz.

But bodies are different. Neither then nor later was I ever able to match the skill with which Lloyd could use an ax. He could cut a butt or square a timber that was nearly as level and smooth as a table top. With seemingly casual guidance, his ax could repeatedly sink in over 3" to the stroke along an even advancing line for the side of a cut, or remove a paperlike slice from a horizontal surface by slewing the ax down almost flat so that it rebounded, ringing like a muffled bell. When I first saw him cut to a line with his ax, I began to laugh as I compared my ineffectual hacking to what he could do. He looked at me calmly. "If you'd had all the practice with one of these things that I have, maybe you could do it, too," he said.

Though he made little of it, Lloyd took pride in his work. I particularly remember a hurricane pine lodged high on a second-story roof. Because it lay between two dormers, it was impossible to pull off sideways. Dragging it directly away from the building would further damage the roof and endanger two large windows below. Shortening the trunk from the butt end could be dangerous work. Besides, if the tree jackknifed when partially cut, the top would also rake the building. The job could be done with scaffolding, but just erecting that would be both long and costly. Although I followed Lloyd to look the job over, most of these finer points did not register with me until afterward.

To my surprise, Lloyd cleaned the leaning trunk of branches at a point at least 7' above the ground. Chopping that high up would not be easy. Chopping accurately through the 12" trunk there would be even worse. He measured off the distance with his ax and began cutting, knocking out the kerf wood in thick chunks. Halfway through, he stopped. I had seen only two of his blows go wide of the mark, neither of them by much. The tree still had not moved.

Then Doctor Wiswall appeared. He looked worriedly at where the trunk was leaning upon the edge of the roof. "I made them get clear of those windows inside," he said. "Can't you do this some other way?"

"It's got to go, now," said Lloyd. "Another wind would fetch it down. Somebody could be hurt." He ducked smoothly under his cut to the far side of the trunk.

"Well, I hope it's something soft that hits those windows!" said Doctor Wiswall. His voice had an edge.

I also went to the far side of the tree to watch. Without answering the Doctor, Lloyd measured his distance again, then inhaled deeply. As he loosed the breath, he swung the ax. From there on, it was a succession of blows, right and left. The top plate flew off, then smaller ones. But the entire tree shuddered. It was jackknifing at the cut.

Lloyd's last stroke seemed almost a lunge, his massive arms straightening upward so that the entire bulk of his body appeared to propel the ax. The blow hit the flat middle of the incomplete notch, not at a slant, but perpendicularly. It crashed through, bursting the fibers that it did not cut. And somehow, Lloyd also turned half aside as a bullfighter

might. The heavy butt log thumped to earth immediately beside his feet. Miraculously, the new butt of the top swung away and in toward the building as the crown of the tree rose in an arc off the roof. For the barest instant before it fell, the entire top hung vertically as if planted. As the new butt hit the ground with a jolt, the crown shook. Then tipping outward away from the building, the whole length crashed to earth beside where Lloyd stood waiting for its return.

By completely severing the trunk so high, Lloyd had given the butt of the top section space to plunge into. The top had pivoted on the overhanging gutter, swinging the crown up and almost entirely off the roof. The only damage was a patch of two split shingles just above the foundation, where the new butt had ended its swing, and the original dent in the gutter-edge of the roof.

Doctor Wiswall stared at the still-quivering top, at the virtually unharmed building and finally at Lloyd. He wore a broad grin. "What luck!" he crowed. "I could have sworn those windows were goners!"

"It's practice," said Lloyd. The remark seemed irrelevant.

Doctor Wiswall studied everything a second time, expressed surprise again and left. As he disappeared around the corner I said, "He doesn't know that you made it happen, does he?"

Lloyd shrugged. "Why should he?" he said. "He's a doctor."

"He ought to know what you did!" I cried. "I never saw anything like that! That isn't just practice! That's engineering!"

"Engineering?" said Lloyd. He relighted his cigar stub, his head cocked to the side to keep the smoke out of his eyes. "Maybe you could say that. But you're wrong about the 'practice' business. To do anything with an ax, you got to have more than just steam. You got to use your head, too. Of course Doc don't understand. He couldn't unless he was the one doing this. You, you're only beginning to understand. Right? That's what I meant by 'practice.' "

I just looked at Lloyd. He was right, of course. There was nothing more to say because both Lloyd and Doctor Wiswall considered that Lloyd was only doing his job, no matter what was involved. So I said nothing and joined Lloyd in limbing the two logs. But even now, I have never forgotten the bald astonishment on Doctor Wiswall's face as he watched the crown of that tree swing up from the roof.

5

The "Right" Ax

The "right" ax is the one you can do the best cutting with. The variety of axes was greater a few generations ago because more work was done with axes then. Earlier North Americans not only used axes to fell trees. They also had special axes to split wood, hew logs into timbers, shape ribs of ships, split out rail slots in fence posts, cut turf, divide stone, slaughter cattle, and harvest ice. Each separate type of ax differed in design, size, shape, and weight depending upon its origin, purpose, era of manufacture, and who would swing it. Any current list of axes would also include the distinctive fire ax, but not the ground-digging pickax. The latter only digs in pointed thrusts, as sometimes represented when one speaks of "my old battle-ax!"

To cut firewood, you need a felling ax. Assuming that you can find a store that sells axes today, you may find that the only ax in stock will be the regular wood-chopping, or felling, ax. And that will likely be in only one size and pattern. It was not always that way. The ordinary hardware store where I bought my three-pound ax in 1938 was a long distance from timber country, yet that store stocked three different single-bitted ax patterns in each of several different weights. Today, you may have to shop around a bit to have any choice in selecting an ax, but the effort may reward you. Because in truth, all felling axes are not alike in either their characteristics or the work that they can do for you.

All axes used in colonial and post-Revolutionary America (Diagram 1) performed yeoman service in their respective eras, yet all appear awkward today. Compared with modern axes, they are. The unceasing search for greater efficiency kept bringing numerous changes in ax design. The relative isolation of scattered smiths servicing separate settlements, even as late as the 19th century, fostered diverse development. In the 1800s, this proliferation of ax design was adopted bodily by the growing edge-tool industry that gladly produced any design of tool that would sell. One company once produced up to three hundred different ax patterns and weights. Even in 1969, the Mann Edge Tool Company of Pennsylvania made seventy patterns of axes, though their greatest volume was in only twenty patterns.

Possibly, innovation in ax design in North America has been an exception. Certainly ax design has demonstrated marked conservatism down the centuries. A 1919 ax catalog of the Collins Company showed axes made for export to South America in patterns that bore more resemblance to the famed "trade" ax than to patterns that were popular in the United States in 1919. Obviously, the export axes were preferred in South America. Late 19th-century axes found in England were not greatly different in appearance from an iron ax dug from an Irish burial mound that predated the birth of Christ. Perhaps most striking is the similarity of the double-bitted ax from ancient Crete to our modern double-bitted axes in spite of the passage of more than thirty-six hundred years.

Webster's New Collegiate Dictionary shows six patterns of representative modern American single-bitted felling axes. All are shorter and cleaner-lined than earlier axes. The modern axes also have more resemblance to one another than the earlier types had to one another. The differences are becoming fewer.

If the quest for efficiency has brought considerable uniformity to current ax design, it is interesting to speculate on where continuous development would have led if the advent of saws, particularly the chain saw, had not throttled further attention to axes. That is, what sort of ax could you cut the most wood with? How should it be made? This is a prickly subject, but there are certain design features that do bear on how well an ax can knock wood apart. Listing a few of these may convince some present-day ax manufacturer that an ax of optimum design would sell better because it would be demonstrably superior in cutting wood.

We should appreciate that manufacturers have problems, too. They can protect their reputations better by selling axes that are relatively proof against abuse, such as slamming into a steel wedge, into a piece of granite, or even straight into some knots. Any of these can be good tricks for chipping a corner or a half-moon out of the blade of the ax. Today, rather than try to educate a public that may buy only a few axes anyway, the manufacturers take the protectionist way out by offering axes that really do stand up to rock-cutting pretty well. If you happen to want an ax keen enough to chop much wood, you have to grind down the edge for yourself. Used on wood, your results can surprise you.

To speak of the ax intelligently, you should know several terms that are shown in Diagram 2. The cutting portion of the ax is called "edge," "blade," or "bit." These are often used interchangeably. The blunt opposite end of the ax is the "poll," yet it is often spoken of as simply the "back," or "heel," of the ax. Length of the ax is measured from the

Ax Nomenclature

Diagram 2

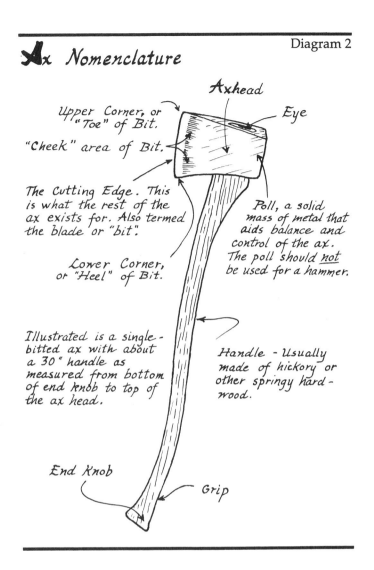

Axhead

Upper Corner, or "Toe" of Bit.

Eye

"Cheek" area of Bit.

The Cutting Edge. This is what the rest of the ax exists for. Also termed the blade or "bit".

Poll, a solid mass of metal that aids balance and control of the ax. The poll should *not* be used for a hammer.

Lower Corner, or "Heel" of Bit.

Illustrated is a single-bitted ax with about a 30" handle as measured from bottom of end knob to top of the ax head.

Handle - Usually made of hickory or other springy hardwood.

End Knob

Grip

center of the blade to the rear edge of the poll. Unless otherwise stated, the width or breadth of an ax is the distance between the upper and lower corners of the blade. The hole for the handle is the "eye" of the ax. Length of handle is normally measured from the top edge of the ax, so that the measurement includes the total length of wood.

An efficiently designed ax will have a keen cutting edge thin enough to sink into the wood it hits but be thick enough to keep from chipping or breaking off or folding over. This type of cutting edge is also naturally dependent upon the quality of its steel. Weight of the ax should be matched to the man who wields it. The bit should be rather straight, with little curve and rather broad—that is, relatively long from corner to corner of the bit. This broader blade in conjunction with a somewhat shorter length overall for the entire ax head will give the efficient ax a more blocky appearance than is usual for most axes today. The overall proportions must ensure rigidity, relative unity of form (as opposed to the hewing, or broadax, design as shown in Diagram 48 for example), and freedom from cumbersomeness. The handle, which must not be too stiff, must be hung so that it is aligned with the cutting edge. (See Diagram 45.) Length of the handle will depend upon the user and the type of work to be

done. There are good reasons for each of these features. When you understand why they are necessary, you will know what to look for in selecting the ax that is best for you.

How heavy an ax you should use will depend upon your native strength, what physical condition you are in, and, particularly, what you intend to chop. Where you live will probably also make a difference, because different notions are prevalent in different regions, even concerning how heavy an ax should be. Some of these concepts may be sensible and some not. Where I now live in Maine, most stores carrying axes stock them only in the three-and-a-half pound size, as if that were best for everybody. Yet many people learning to use an ax, or who will use one only occasionally, would do better with an ax a quarter to three quarters of a pound lighter. A small difference in ax weight can make a big difference in what you can do with the ax. A light ax is not only easier to swing, but easier to swing accurately. And control, not power, is the real secret of chopping wood. You may have to try more than one ax before you really know how much weight you can control without becoming fatigued. You'll learn faster if you start light rather than heavy.

Even in this century, the difference in the weight of axes manufactured in the United States and Canada for general chopping purposes has been surprisingly large, ranging at least from one to eight pounds. That does not mean that axes for general chopping that light or that heavy made sense, but only that somebody preferred them for some purpose. When I bought my first ax in 1936, our Sears, Roebuck catalog listed only axes weighing three to four pounds. Snow & Nealley, a well-known Bangor, Maine, ax manufacturer, made axes as light as one pound in 1948, but their heaviest felling ax was only four pounds. At that time, nothing heavier was needed for the trees in the Northeast, where most axes used were considerably lighter than that.

Heavier trees took larger axes. When the great trees in the Far West and the Pacific Coast areas were cut by hand, ax handle lengths reached forty-two inches and the axes were in proportion. An American Ax & Tool Company catalog of 1907 listed felling axes in weights from three to six pounds. For those who prize Yankee prowess, though, it is humbling to note that some of the export axes destined for South America mentioned before were offered in weights up to *eight* pounds. Although the patterns seemed archaic, those axes all seemed designed for chopping and felling. I can find no record of eight-pound axes ever being used for felling anywhere in the United States or Canada. Whether those eight-pound axes were an indication that the South Americans were more powerful than the Yankees or not, I am not qualified to state. If they were, they never proved it during the ax era by beating the United States in timber production.

A vital feature of any ax is the quality of its steel. Its bit must be hard enough to keep sharp and tough enough to resist breaking under the repeated impact of years of hard use. Axes used to be formed of malleable iron with a narrow cap of steel forged on for the bit. Today, though, most axes are formed of one piece of cast steel. When you use the ax, you will soon find out whether the steel in the bit is too soft or too brittle. In buying an ax, buy the best available. That is the best insurance for being certain that the ax is made of quality steel and is properly tempered for chopping.

In considering the "right" felling ax, two other types of axes must be mentioned. One is the double-bitted ax, the subject of Chapter 7. The second category is that of one-handed axes so excessively light and short-handled that they are generally called hatchets.

Without question, hatchets have their uses. A carpenter's hatchet is a marvelous tool for rough fitting an occasional board or timber. A shingling hatchet is just about indispensable for laying shingles in good time, especially poor shingles. I use a hatchet regularly to split light kindling. If you have years of experience behind you, you may prefer a pet hatchet for pruning. If not, you had better not start now. A hatchet can be used for trimming brush or blazing a boundary line through woods, though for these uses it is inferior to several other tools, including a full-sized ax. But none of these uses is procuring firewood. If you are thinking of cutting firewood, do not think "hatchet" at the same time.

Because of how it is held and swung in one hand, a hatchet is far more dangerous than an ax. The average, general-service hatchet, being too often used by too many, is also too often too dull. So there is grave tendency to swing the light tool fiercely to compensate for its ineffectiveness. The necessity to hit hard enough to cause the light head to penetrate also requires power-laden strokes. That increases the likelihood of either missing a small target altogether or cutting completely through the target with a large residual of uncontrollable force behind your swing. Then, because of the short handle, your legs are too near and too vulnerable. Another result is even more common. As the hatchet passes through the expected stopping point, it can easily slip out of the one-handed grip. A hatchet can fly many feet that way. If you think you need a hatchet for its light weight, consider the merits of a heavy knife, a saw, or even a light long-handled ax instead. Any one of them is safer than a hatchet.

The Efficient Ax

For those who may be interested in an efficient design of felling ax, a sketch of a representative efficient ax is shown in Diagram 3. Although this depicts an ax weighing three and a quarter pounds, only minor design difference need be made for similar axes up to a half pound lighter or heavier. The reason for this is that the thickness of the rear half of the ax in the vicinity of the eye and poll areas can accommodate considerable variation in weight without affecting the size of the sketch in the two principal dimensions illustrated.

At its extremes, ax weight certainly affects ax design. A five-pound ax cannot be as small as a two-and-a-half-pound ax of the same pattern. The heavier ax must be more cumbersome, for some dimensions must swell. As one example of how this could hurt efficient design, suppose that the additional weight of a heavier ax were all hidden in greater thickness overall. At some point, the ax could become so thick that it would no longer cut well.

For the efficient ax, the cutting edge should be only slightly curved from corner to corner. It should not be straight, either, but almost. Many axes are designed with a pronounced curvature of blade. Many older axes still cut even though their bits have been ground away until they are almost half-round. Why then should an efficient ax need an edge that is almost straight? The principal reason is that any shearing action (as distinguished from sawing) that is not backed up with another blade as scissors are, is best done with a straight-edged cutter. Do you cut bread, sausage, or cheese with a half-moon knife? If you did, you would scarcely know where you started and where you stopped. The same principle applies to chopping wood.

An excessively curved cutting edge has its uses, but not on an ax. Wood will grip any ax driven into it. The ax with a curved bit will be gripped tighter than one with a straighter bit. This is because the curved bit, with less cutting edge to impact (and absorb energy) immediately, will carry its thick upper section more deeply into the cut. In trying to close again, the sides of the cut will grip the thickest blade in the tightest grip. The extra tug to withdraw the ax may not be great, but every needless expenditure of energy is frustratingly stolen from useful effort that can bring home more wood.

As shown in Diagram 3, the cutting edge should be straightish but not absolutely so, as that would leave the corners unacceptably pointed and beg breakage. Even on a new ax, there should be a slight rounding of the corners for their protection. A large rounding gets back into the problems of a curved bit. With use, the corners tend to get rounded all too soon anyway. And to prevent breakage, the corners should never be ground too thin, either.

Diagram 3

An Efficient Single-Bitted Ax

Being shorter than most axes, the bit of this pattern will deflect less when the chopper's swing wobbles. Because this pattern is inherently more accurate, it is more efficient.

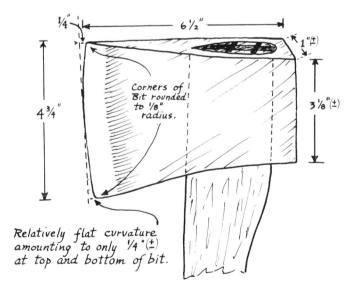

1/4" — 6 1/2" — 1"(±)

4 3/4"

Corners of Bit rounded to 1/8" radius.

3 1/8"(±)

Relatively flat curvature amounting to only 1/4"(±) at top and bottom of bit.

Dimensions of this or any pattern of ax would necessarily change with its weight. Relative proportions would remain approximately the same.

15

Another reason for not having a perfectly straight cutting edge also concerns freeing a stuck ax. This seldom happens in felling, but it can happen if you drive an ax into the face of a stump or the butt end of a large log. With a curved blade, the curve can act as a fulcrum for force exerted to free the ax, such as when you give it a thump on the handle. If the ax can move at all, the blade can seesaw on the hump of the curve. Any movement will help extricate the wedge-shaped body of the ax. It will work itself outward at each thump. So the curve in the bit does not need to be large for this purpose. A slight curvature is sufficient to begin the withdrawal. To understand how this works, imagine planting your beloved on the far end of a seesaw. You would be able to lift her by sitting down yourself, and possibly by only pressing your hand down on the plank. Now then, suppose she squatted on your end of the seesaw and you attempted to lift the whole business? Dainty as she might be, you would not find the new arrangement so easy. That would be similar to trying to extricate a lodged ax that had a perfectly straight edge. There would be no fulcrum in the middle.

The breadth of the ax blade, its length of cutting edge from corner to corner, should be as long as feasible. However, there are limitations. The first consideration is how much any increase in breadth will affect total weight, which must always remain suitable for the user. Second, the blade must be kept strong enough to resist breakage. If, with a constant weight of head, the blade were extended too far laterally, corner trouble would always be just around the corner.

Two other limitations to excessive width of blade are insufficient rigidity and being overly cumbersome. But mindful of these, an ax blade should be every millimeter as wide as it can possibly be. The ax shown in Diagram 3 is a reasonable compromise with all four limiting factors. A manufacturer that can make a broader blade adequately supported and sufficiently strong for years of chopping, yet keep the total weight within usable limits should do so.

In chopping wood, every wild stroke represents not only one more bit of work that remains undone, but also one more spurt of energy stolen from the finite supply available for that day's work. In trying to be accurate, you can miss on either side of your swing. You can also "overshoot" or "undershoot." In every aspect of the inaccuracy problem, the broad, relatively straight-edged ax is superior to a narrower ax with a curved bit.

Sight is important in guiding each of your chopping strokes to where you hope it will hit. If you question this, try chopping with your eyes blindfolded and see how accurate you are. Just armor your feet and legs first. For the tiny but critical corrections your muscles make during each swing, your eyes must gauge how much correction is needed. Of course a movement such as an ax stroke is more complicated than it seems. A major source of guidance while the stroke is in progress is also the sensory perceptions within your arms. But you must also be aware of the ax bit, extended beyond the arms, and what its position is as it descends. Just as it is easier to be accurate with a rifle than it is with a pistol, your eyes can sense position and direction better from a relatively broad, straight ax bit than they can from a narrower, more curved bit. Considering only this, the broader and straighter the bit, the more useful it is for maintaining lateral accuracy.

Some of the old broad, or hewing, ax designs were surpris-ingly light, and their long bits were ideal for guiding by eye. But they were otherwise ill suited for felling. Not only were they too cumbersome, but their flared blade ends lacked the straight-back support needed to withstand the heavier impact of felling and bucking wood. The cutting edge of the felling ax must be more intimately supported on its base. Also, the length of the cutting edge must not exceed proper proportions to the vertical width of the ax at the eye. The cutting edge can be the longer of the two, but if by too much, rigidity will suffer.

The broad, straight-edged bit cannot give much protection against your overextending or underextending your stroke, but the relatively straight line of the bit will dig in for a uniform depth along its entire length at each stroke. This permits your next stroke to hit on line a full bit's length beyond (or back, if you are cutting backward) and so extend the cut at the same uniform depth again. Naturally you would overlap each stroke in line just enough to ensure that no gap of uncut wood would be left between successive strokes.

The problem of leaving subsurface humps of uncut wood between strokes becomes worse in direct proportion to how rounded the bit of your ax is. With the use of an ax whose bit has become virtually half-moon from use and sharpening

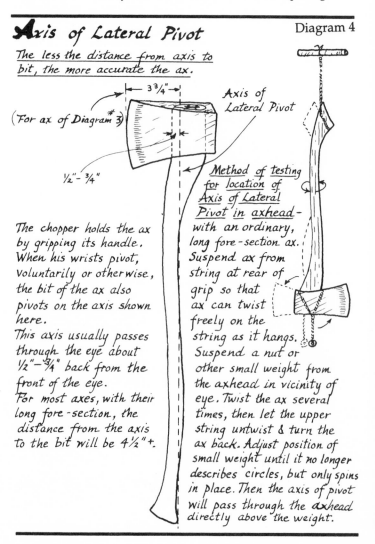

Axis of Lateral Pivot   Diagram 4

The less the distance from axis to bit, the more accurate the ax.

3¾"

(For ax of Diagram #3)

Axis of Lateral Pivot

½" – ¾"

The chopper holds the ax by gripping its handle. When his wrists pivot, voluntarily or otherwise, the bit of the ax also pivots on the axis shown here.
This axis usually passes through the eye about ½"–¾" back from the front of the eye.
For most axes, with their long fore-section, the distance from the axis to the bit will be 4½"+.

Method of testing for location of Axis of Lateral Pivot in axhead— with an ordinary, long fore-section ax. Suspend ax from string at rear of grip so that ax can twist freely on the string as it hangs. Suspend a nut or other small weight from the axhead in vicinity of eye. Twist the ax several times, then let the upper string untwist & turn the ax back. Adjust position of small weight until it no longer describes circles, but only spins in place. Then the axis of pivot will pass through the axhead directly above the weight.

over the years, abutting strokes that seem to form a continuous cut on the surface can bypass regular peaks of uncut wood underneath. The overlying chips will not split out until those subsurface peaks are cut through. And your ax cannot dig deeper until the top kerf wood has popped off. With such an ax, you can form a continuous, uniformly deep cut only by making numerous and tiring extra strokes. With an ax having a bit that is not quite so badly curved, the problem becomes one of depth rather than continuity of cut, but the remedy will be the same, many extra strokes. It makes no difference that the midsection of a curved bit may in fact sink deeper on each stroke than any part of a straighter bit can. The chips will not release from any given depth until all their fibers are severed. The straight-bitted ax can do this with fewer strokes than the ax with a curved bit.

It is not only the breadth of the bit that gives the ax in Diagram 3 a blocky appearance. It is also the shorter overall length of the entire head from the cutting edge to the back side of the poll. The ax of Diagram 3 measures only 6½″ from bit to poll. For most axes, an overall length of 7¼″ to 7½″ is usual. The additional 3/4″ or more in length of most axes does not add to the poll, but lies in an elongation of the bit end of the ax. This is a mistake.

The worst harm of this extension is neither its addition to weight nor cumbersomeness, but its doleful impact upon accuracy. There being no comparable mass of equal length at the hind end of the ax, the unbalanced extension magnifies lateral wobble. When you chop, where your strokes hit will depend upon how you face and hold your arms. But as you follow through on each stroke, some of your later "fine tuning" adjustment will be made in your wrists. But as golfers also know, wrist movement is not always easy to control. It is all too easy to pivot slightly to either side involuntarily. And as your wrists and hands turn the handle of the ax, down at the far end of the same shaft, the bit of the ax will obey, pivoting the same number of degrees in the same direction. If you have good control, all will go well. But wobble only a little bit and you will squander precious time and energy hitting either side of your mark instead of sinking deep into the cut along the line you had aimed for.

The axis of lateral pivot of most single-bitted axes is not in the center of the eye but farther forward, on average, about 1/2″ to 3/4″ back from the front end of the eye of the ax. You can verify its position in your own ax by suspending the ax from a light string tied to the rear side of the end knob on the handle. Then after twisting the ax a few turns, observe the axis of pivot as the ax untwists while hanging from the string. You can locate the axis easier by attaching a hanging bit of string from the axhead, with a nut, or other small weight, at its end. As the ax rotates, adjust this lower string until the nut no longer describes circles, but only spins in place. It is then on the axis of pivot which will pass through the axhead directly above where the nut and its string are hung. This is the same axis that your ax will rotate about if you let your wrists turn while you are chopping.

For most single-bitted axes, the distance from the axis of pivot to the bit will measure about 4½″, and in some cases, more. For the ax shown in Diagram 3, this distance is about 3 3/4″. This difference affects the chopping performance of the two axes. Assuming a modest wrist-pivoting movement of only 5°, the 4 1/2″ bit would deviate from its mark by .39″,

while the 3 3/4″ bit would deviate by only .32″. The difference of .07″ is about as thick as a man's leather belt or 25-45 numbered book pages, the latter depending upon whether they are light or heavyweight pages.

Slight as it may seem, this divergence represents a substantial disadvantage for the ax of the longer fore-section. Suppose that the chopper is skilled enough to hold his deviant wrist-pivoting to only 5°. Not every chopper is capable of this. Using the ax with the longer fore-section, he will suffer a comparative disadvantage of missing his intended line of cut at each stroke by a margin amounting to the thickness of a medium piece of leather.

You can appreciate this penalty best by swinging the ax yourself. It means that each time you swing, you must cut off a slice of hardwood across the grain that thick from the top to the bottom of your cut before the residual momentum of the axhead can finally be used to add new depth. Robbed of power, each stroke does less useful cutting. The end result will be making many extra strokes to perform the extra work.

Not every stroke would hit 5° wide of the mark, of course. Some strokes would fall on line with no error and no extra slice to cut through. Yet for each of those, you could expect an equal number of strokes having even greater dispersion with even fatter slices to laboriously gouge out. An ax of

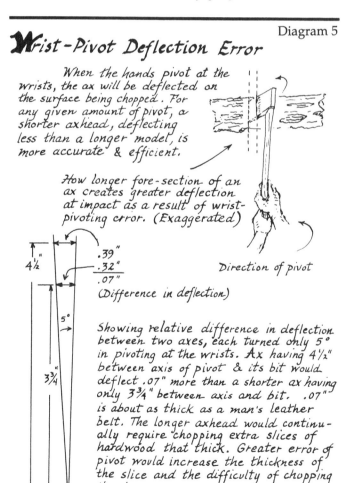

Diagram 5

Wrist-Pivot Deflection Error

When the hands pivot at the wrists, the ax will be deflected on the surface being chopped. For any given amount of pivot, a shorter axhead, deflecting less than a longer model, is more accurate & efficient.

How longer fore-section of an ax creates greater deflection at impact as a result of wrist-pivoting error. (Exaggerated)

4½″
.39″
.32″
.07″
(Difference in deflection)

5°

3¾″

Direction of pivot

Showing relative difference in deflection between two axes, each turned only 5° in pivoting at the wrists. Ax having 4½″ between axis of pivot & its bit would deflect .07″ more than a shorter ax having only 3¾″ between axis and bit. .07″ is about as thick as a man's leather belt. The longer axhead would continually require chopping extra slices of hardwood that thick. Greater error of pivot would increase the thickness of the slice and the difficulty of chopping it out.

shorter fore-section is no cure-all for the chopper's inaccuracy, but it keeps him from having to pay such a high penalty for it.

Inaccuracy of any cause being the enemy of efficient work, the chopper needs all the help he can get. Most of the fault will be in himself and he can purge himself only by practice. But it is idiotic not to use efficient equipment also. To reduce pivoting wobble as much as possible, the fore-section of his ax should be as short as feasible.

Could the ax shown in Diagram 3 be still further improved by reducing its fore-section even more? Possibly, but there would be a limit somewhere. Consideration must also be given to how long the entire blade must be to maintain a cross-section thin enough to chop efficiently while increasing its thickness to the 1" or more needed at the eye region to enclose the handle. Within that limit, the business end of every ax should be just as short as it is possible to design it.

The relatively short ax shown in Diagram 3 depicts proven ax design, so there is nothing novel about it. But unfortunately, neither is it common. Emerson & Stevens, the company in Oakland, Maine, that made axes of this design, went out of business in 1965. The age of chain saws, gasoline, and work without sweat had come to full flower.

A good ax must have a good handle. Of the number of features affecting handles, four must be listed as conditions for an efficient ax. The bit of the ax must be in line with the handle. The length of the handle must be suited to the user and the work to be done. A total length of about 30" will accommodate most requirements for cutting your own firewood today. Beware of too stiff a handle. It is both less efficient and excessively tiring to use a stiff handle for long. It will pound you to pieces. Last, the ax must be "hung" so that the center of the bit faces the work. All of these items will be examined more in Chapters 23 and 24.

The Double-Bitted Ax

The double-bitted ax is two axes in one. There is no back end to a double ax at all. On each end is a full, sharp bit. If one bit gets dull, you can flip the ax over and use the other end instead. Only a straight handle can satisfactorily accommodate chopping in opposite directions, and double-bitted axes have straight handles. The tested utility of the double-bitted ax was formerly reflected in its widespread use. To be usable, an ax had to be sharp, and any ax becomes dull from use. Why not carry two blades for the weight of one? Among professional woodsmen, beginning gradually after the Civil War and up to the advent of the chain saw, general acceptance of this logic solidly endorsed the double-bitted ax.

The double-bitted pattern had been familiar in military use as far back as ancient Egypt. When the tree-felling double was introduced into Pennsylvania from Maine in the decade before the Civil War, it was resisted at first as a "backstabber." Obviously, the double-bitted ax was no child's toy. But its steady climb to popularity in the mid-19th century lay with those who could learn to live with its disadvantages in exchange for its superior performance. It was a production ax, not a family dooryard tool to behead the Sunday dinner chicken. Two separate blades meant two different bits to grind and keep sharpened, but doing this by night gave an additional keen edge for use in the woods the next day where time and performance meant money.

One bit was frequently reserved for felling and the other for limbing. The felling bit could be thinner so it could bite deeper into the clear, straight grain of a tree trunk. The limbing bit would routinely encounter the incredibly dense knots and would need a coarser bevel back away from the cutting edge to prevent the bit from chipping.

When logs were hauled by oxen and horses, the chore of clearing woods roads often required cutting low stumps and even roots. With rocks lurking everywhere beneath the snow or humus, or even projecting above them, cutting roots was an ugly job for a sharp ax. Some teamsters reserved one bit of a double ax just for cutting roots. On such work, the bit would soon be unable to cut anything else anyway. As a solution, it beat carrying two axes. I have never heard of double-bitted axes deliberately manufactured with one keen and one heavy bit. Probably the bit reserved for the dirty work was the bit that had encountered some misfortune first, substantially disqualifying it for the primary role of being a felling ax. That done, continuing the dull bit in that role would protect the one remaining sharp edge left available.

Identifying the proper bit for the job was not difficult. An axhead frequently becomes marked with the distinctive scars of use, unfortunately including a chipped bit or broken corners. Rust, manufacturer's markings on the head, roughness or unusual grain on a single side of the handle

The Double-Bitted Ax

Diagram 6

Always straight-handled, it is two axes in one.

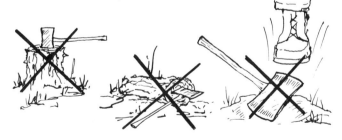

The most efficient and versatile of all axes, it is also the most dangerous ax!
You must not leave the double-bitted ax exposed so that somebody (perhaps you) will be hurt.

While working, safeguard the double-bitted ax:

would also be used to identify the proper bit in an instant without the user's having to examine the edge closely each time. A bit of paint or stain or stamping one side of the head or handle would serve the same purpose.

A double-bitted ax may be 2½" longer overall than an average single-bitted ax and nearly 3½" longer than the efficient ax of Diagram 3. An ax of this additional length is certainly more cumbersome, yet, in use, it is surprisingly accurate. Why? The question is interesting, because for a double ax, the distance from either bit to the axis of pivot is comparatively long, about 4½" to 5". As noted in the last chapter, single axes with a long fore-end are less accurate. Does not the same principle apply to a double?

For starters, the answer has nothing to do with weight. For formerly, at least, double axes were available in any ordinary weight just as the single-bitted models were. A major portion of the answer apparently lies in the similarity of the double ax on either side of the axis of pivot. It has no built-in tendency to wobble, because both bits, both ends of the ax, are of equal length and equal weight. One end cannot pull the other out of the intended line of cut. A second factor may be less implausible than it seems. The broadside silhouette of the double ax is nearly half again as large as the outline of comparable singles. This greater image is easier to be visually aware of during the descending stroke and therefore easier to guide on and to make continuing corrections by right up to the instant of impact. For doubters, remember that blindfolded accuracy will never match eyes-open accuracy. Nor does visual correction seem to consist solely of locating the line of cut.

The third factor seeming to grant greater accuracy to the double ax is not a positive advantage of the double ax at all, but an inherent disadvantage of the single, and not in the axhead, but in its gracefully curved handle. Simply stated, that design of handle promotes inaccuracy. That item is also examined further in Chapter 23.

For pure capacity to cut wood effectively, the double-bitted ax is superior to any single-bitted ax designed to date. Concerning this, B. S. Mason, author of *Woodcraft,* states, "[The double-bitted ax] is easier to handle and use than any other. Once accustomed to it, the single-bit seems clumsy and awkward. The weight of the double-bitted head is in line with the cutting edge—it swings truer and bites deeper." Without being quite so literary, the professionals of the woods in the age when timber was cut by hand almost unanimously agreed that the double-bitted ax was king.

Although the double ax became the primary tree-felling tool after the mid-19th century, it never stamped the single-bitted ax out of existence. The underlying reason was probably that innumerable occasional ax users did not care to have such a specialized cutting tool as the double. They were undoubtedly afraid of it, and with good reason. But there were lesser reasons also why the single-bitted ax kept farm and household popularity.

All modern single-bitted axes have had a well-developed poll, that heavy, flat-faced rear section. Because the poll area is not hardened and can be easily deformed, it is a truism that the poll should never be used as a hammer. But because of its availability, convenient weight and shape, the poll is often used as a hammer just the same. It can be irritating while using the double ax not to have the poll handy for such

harmless purposes as setting or loosening felling wedges, or sometimes even wooden splitting wedges, butting off a dry or punk stub without unlimbering the force necessary to chop it off, knocking a stick out from underfoot, or adjusting the face of a woodpile. For splitting wood, a double ax is a real handicap because you cannot reverse a stuck chunk to slam it down with the poll underneath. None of the other chores is done as well with a double, either.

But absence of a poll was insignificant compared with the innately dangerous nature of the double ax. Through necessity and long practice, the professional woodsman learned to live with this. The farmer and the small woodlot man never quite did. You can trace this trend today in the axes displayed by the stores stocking them. There will be at least several single-bitted axes for every double, and not unusually, no doubles will be stocked at all.

Carrying an ax sounds simple. It is. At the same time, in the woods not everything underfoot is always smooth as a sidewalk, not even a modern sidewalk. Tripping and falling are ever-present possibilities where there are trees overhead and their roots underneath. To fall with any ax is potentially dangerous. To trip carrying a double-bitted ax is far worse. The cutting edges face two opposite directions and both are deadly. Carrying the double-bit demands continued conscious attention to where and how you place each foot. The double ax from Maine was probably branded the "back-stabber" when it first arrived in the forests of Pennsylvania about 1850 because of the multiple hazards of carrying the double over the shoulder as well as stabbing one's partner on the backswing. The shoulder carry could easily result in a sharp corner of the double ax dropping down into the carrier's back. It was another case of two edges being more difficult to watch than one. Then or now, ax sheaths have never been popular because they are one more item to tote and perhaps be lost. But for carrying a double-bitted ax very far they are eminently practical. A sheath can also protect the ax, and that is not unimportant.

On the job, the double ax demands slightly more clear working room than the single does for the safety of one's partner on the job. The rear of a double ax is a bit longer. But of course there is more to it than that. It is true that the backswing of a single ax can knock a man silly, but the same arc of the double ax really can stab.

When laying aside an ax in the woods, it is almost instinctive to drive it into the nearest stump or log. It will stay there until you want it. In all likelihood, the location will be in plain sight where you and others are aware of it, and, if necessary, you will move it to protect it, as from moving logs or even falling trees. And because the location of a single-bitted ax will usually be in plain sight, you will not need to thrash around searching when you need it again. Finally, that sharp edge is taken care of. Encased in the wooden sheath of stump or log, it can cut nobody, not even if some inept fellow falls flat upon it. And for the same reason, the single's keen cutting edge is securely protected from rocks or tools that might dull it.

With the double-bitted ax, everything is different. Even working alone, you violate all common sense if you treat the double similarly. Driven into a stump or log, either vertically or horizontally, the double-ended bit is a terrible gouge waiting to be fallen upon or unsuspectingly lunged into. The danger is too great to risk. Somehow, you are always aware of the single-bit's flat poll. Its broad innocence catches the eye and you remain aware of it even though it is harmless. That is not true with the double, whose honed edge gliding nakedly up into nothingness has an inconspicuous quality that is the essence of treachery. You can bumble into it yourself even though you were the one who drove it into the log. For your partner, your responsibility is commensurately greater. You must not drive the double-bitted ax into anything that holds the opposite bit rigidly up or out.

So unless the double is continually sheathed whenever you set it down between chopping, an impractical absurdity, it must be left either flat under a log, or merely leaning loosely against something in a location where nobody will reasonably fall into or upon it. For the chopper, this means return to the entire train of recurring safekeeping problems that the stump location eliminated when using the single-bitted ax. Only sufficient desire would make a man adapt himself to these irritations. Among the professional woodsmen, that desire once was to cut more wood. Their livelihood depended on it. The double-bitted ax's extra bit assured constant availability of a sharp cutting edge. The superior handling qualities, balance, and accuracy of the double ensured that the sharp edge could be used with greater effect. It still can.

Swinging an Ax

An ax swings even when you carry it. Though you can reduce the movement somewhat with a shoulder carry, that position is clear mark of bravado, ignorance, or both. The safest method of carrying an unsheathed ax is to grip it just beneath the head, with the bit pointed outward. Then if you stumble, you are prepared to throw the ax aside, or at least to keep the bit from pointing inward toward some part of your body. If you are reasonably alert (if completely alert, you would not stumble), your hands will tend to break your fall and can carry the axhead beyond where any other part of your body will land on it. The problem with a double-bitted ax is that one bit will always point either near or toward you, no matter how you carry it. If you stumble with one, if possible, throw it away as you fall. Even in such an insignificant item as this, you can assess the toughness of the men who for generations cut timber with the ax. Danger was their life.

When you arrive at where you will chop, the first chore is to clear the area. You will not be able to improve the ground a great deal, although anything loose that might roll or slip under your feet should be thrown aside. But up above is of critical importance. Completely clear away everything within the arc of your swinging ax. Everything must go down to the smallest branch, for even twigs can deflect your swing. The less obvious branches are the ones to worry about. Seeing the others, you will have disposed of them already. Measure carefully where your full swing will reach, particularly on the backstroke. Your ax need only snag a small branch there to plunge disastrously wide of your mark. And the error will not be away from you. It can draw the descending bit straight into your leg or foot. For so much tragedy to lurk in so slight a cause may seem unlikely, but it is not. By the time you are aware that your swing has been snagged, it is usually too late to redirect its strike.

You are fortunate if you can walk away from one of these incidents. Yet they are so easy to prevent. Clean all obstacles, down to the last dangling leaf, from the reach of your ax in all directions. If something is too large to clear out—another tree, for instance—move to a more open spot. Once you have cleaned your area, leave your feet in place. If you have to move, make sure the new location is also cleared before chopping a stroke.

You may not be able to improve your footing much, but make sure that your feet cannot slip. Beware when in ice, snow, mud, or even dry leaves. Avoid sticks, logs or rocks that can give way or roll beneath you as you swing. Where possible to choose, the ideal lateral chopping height is about even with the top of your ankles. Chopping either higher or lower is increasingly difficult. This height will vary with the length of your ax handle and your own proportions. Of course, to be able to choose the chopping height as a matter of personal, as opposed to technical, choice is not common. In most cases, you must accommodate yourself to the height of whatever must be cut and wherever it lies. On chopping a log of any size for example, you would ordinarily stand upon it above your kerf, even though that would not be the best footing. If the log tends to roll, first chock it with a smaller piece wedged beneath the curve of the log.

A reminder of accuracy is worth repeating. It is laying every stroke of the ax where it should be laid that will cut more wood. The power of the stroke is of less importance because power will be of no help if the blow goes wide of the mark. Properly placed, the mere weight of the falling ax will ensure some depth of cut. And as you guide the bit, you inevitably add the considerable force-in-motion of your body to your follow-through and the power of your blow. With every stroke, concentrate on the exact line you want to hit. Too great emphasis on either power or speed can spoil concentration upon accuracy. When you master accuracy, then apply as much power and speed as you want—accurately.

In chopping, a right-handed man normally keeps his left hand at the bottom of the ax handle, the right hand grasping the handle nearer the top to lift the ax, and then sliding back down the handle to join the left hand as the stroke descends. For horizontal strokes, the hand movements are similar, and in chopping left-handed, these hand positions would be reversed.

Aim the total descending stroke from its beginning, directing the entire swing of your arms and body smoothly downwards to your mark. Avoid making corrections in the wrists, for that complicates attaining accuracy. Yet you should not lock your wrists, for wrist action adds immeasurably to the force, and therefore the whip, of the total swing. The wrists move independently of the total swing, but in the same plane. This is important to understand, for what is necessary for accuracy is to keep the wrists from pivoting side to side. You can learn to do this.

The whipping action given by the wrists accelerates the speed of the descending ax. Because the ax is heavy, considerable strength in the wrists is required to overcome its inertia. A lighter ax can often be more effective than a heavier model for a particular user. If he can give the lighter ax more whip, he will likely hit with greater effective force than would be possible for him to do with a heavier ax. Naturally, an ax can be too light also. You should try several weights, beginning with the lighter models. A three-and-a-half-pound ax has been considered "average" weight. But if you chop only occasionally, a three-and-a-half-pound ax may be uncomfortably on the heavy side.

In theory, perhaps both hands should be kept in place gripping the bottom end of the ax handle. Doing so, it is possible to take quicker strokes because you are freed of the necessity to slide the upper hand up and down along the handle. However, the upper hand is frequently needed to help raise a suddenly heavy ax aloft for another stroke. It is another instance of when the weight of the axhead can be important. It must be right for the chopper.

A right-handed man will normally find it most convenient to cut on the right side of a tree as he faces it, and vice versa for the left-hander. Yet there are many reasons why you cannot always chop on the side or in the position you might prefer. The ground may rise or fall away where you wish to stand, or a tree you want to leave standing may interfere with your swing. And for most trees of any size, you will likely have to chop on both sides anyway. The upshot of this is that you must become reasonably skilled in chopping either right-handed or left-handed. Not learning to chop on both sides is to handicap yourself. Sooner or later, probably sooner, you will encounter a tree or log that you are unable to chop except by attacking it left-handed (or right-handed). So practice whenever you can. Do not cross your hands. Practice in the normal manner until you are proficient in chopping to either side.

In one sense, no technique for using the ax is more important than emphasis on safety. If you maim yourself, nobody can swing your ax, either well or poorly, and certainly your wood will not get cut. There are hazards in lumbering by any method, but as far as your handling an ax is concerned, the primary danger is in striking yourself while chopping. There are other ways you can do this besides snagging branches.

To keep from slicing yourself, first make a distinction between lateral and vertical chopping strokes. The lateral category includes all diagonal strokes also. Vertical strokes are those that descend with no lateral movement at all, not across your front anyway. We will speak of them after looking at the lateral strokes.

Felling a tree is an example of lateral chopping. Some of the felling strokes will be made horizontally, but most will be diagonal. No matter what else happens, your ax must not swerve from or through its intended target and continue on to sink into you. In theory, you might prevent that by halting your stroke in mid-swing. But to accomplish anything useful while chopping, you must follow through on every stroke as if you really mean to gash the point you aim at. Unfortunately for your safety, once you launch a stroke like that, you cannot exert a different control over it in time to stop an unexpected deflection or continuation past its target. Both of these threats can too easily become real.

So to be safe, you must find a different system of protecting yourself. The only workable system recognizes that striking sideways at anything in front of you, or striking toward yourself, can always end with a blow hitting you. Avoiding that malign possibility means prohibiting all frontal or frontally directed strokes (except vertical ones). This translates into the rule: "In lateral chopping, strike only at targets lying *past* your front in the direction of chopping." "Your front" must include everything forward of you in any facing you make, bounded on the sides by a pair of parallel lines running forward from the outside edges of both of your feet.

Obviously, changing this frontal zone is a mere matter of shifting your feet. Simple perhaps, but most effective. For when your feet change position, so do your body and arms, and therefore also the arc of your ax. You are safe hitting beyond the frontal zone on the side you chop toward, for if you strike through the target, ricochet off it, or even miss it, the residual force will dissipate harmlessly to the side, or upward as with a golf swing, but not into you. The swing cannot hit you because its direction takes it *past* you before it ever encounters the target. Once your swing has already passed you by, no amount of deflection at the target can turn the ax back on you as long as your hands grip the handle.

Where a target lies in relation to the frontal zone is a matter of your assessment. You will ordinarily stand with your target in comfortable range, immediately outside of, and abutting, the frontal zone boundary on the side toward which you are chopping. (See Diagram 7.) The boundary line will extend forward along the outer edge of your foot on that side. The direction of the boundary is determined by its companion and parallel boundary running forward from the outer edge of your other foot. It makes no difference how your feet are turned because you can have only one "front."

When you are conscious of the importance of proper facing, positioning yourself to chop any target safely will require no measurements, sightings, or other stupidity. You will know when a target is forward of your feet or not. If you do not know, you had better go home before you cut a foot off.

But are formal rules really needed for so simple an operation as chopping safety? The answer to that is, "Maybe, and maybe not." It all depends on who you are and how much you know. When I notched my foot with my new four-pound ax years ago, I had never heard of the frontal zone rule. Splitting that slanted butt that lay in front of me seemed at the time to be a lot simpler proposition than it turned out to be. I cannot remember now whether that butt ever got split. But I do remember the sight of it before I swung my ax. It was dead in front of me. Being ignorant, I swung and shortly thereafter wished that I had not. Perhaps spreading a few facts around can keep other choppers from being hurt.

Intelligent tree-felling with an ax is not just dogged hacking, but execution of a plan. After choosing what direction you want your notch to face, you cut it into the tree. At the rear fold of that notch, where the top and bottom meet, lies the line-of-cut. It should be straight and level. An extension of the line-of-cut drawn on the ground toward you should coincide with your frontal zone boundary on the side you are chopping toward. As you chop, each stroke will deepen the line-of-cut. As required, then, you should adjust your footing so that you always abut the line-of-cut extension.

Diagram 7

Don't Chop Yourself!

For all sideways or diagonal chopping strokes, strike only at targets that are <u>past</u> your front in the direction you are chopping.

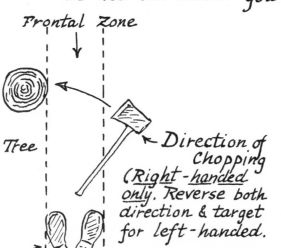

Frontal Zone

Tree

Position of Chopper

Direction of Chopping (<u>Right-handed</u> <u>only</u>. Reverse both direction & target for left-handed.

Your feet are most vulnerable. Boundaries of your "front" are the parallel lines running forward from outside edges of feet.

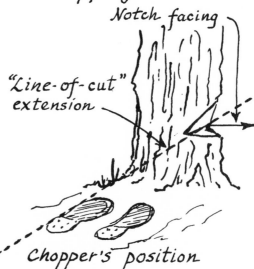

Notch facing

"Line-of-cut" extension

Chopper's position

When felling a tree, stay on notch side of "Line-of-Cut" extension.

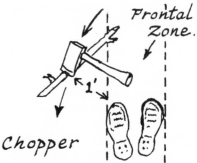

Tree

Area cut out by notching.

Notch facing.

Frontal zone boundaries.

Line-of-cut extension.

Chopper

Line-of-cut extension coincides with Frontal Zone Boundary on the side you are cutting <u>toward</u>.

Frontal Zone.

Chopper

Cut small sticks and other <u>unsupported targets</u> that lie on the ground a foot or so beyond the frontal zone boundary. Then, with your stroke aimed rearward, the ax will cut through swinging <u>up-ward</u> — not into the deck.

Diagram 8

Vertical Chopping

"Vertical Chopping" includes those strokes that can be performed _only_ _within_ _the_ _Frontal_ _Zone_.

There are three types:

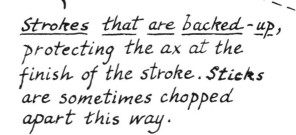

Frontal Zone

Strokes _that_ _are_ _backed-up_, protecting the ax at the finish of the stroke. Sticks are sometimes chopped apart this way.

Strokes _that_ _are_ _not_ _backed-_ _up_. This is dangerous work. The ax that goes up will also come down.

Chopping _done_ _beneath_ _the_ _level_ _of_ _the_ _feet_. This is the common way to chop a log apart. You stand on the log, cutting halfway in from each side.

In this position, each stroke will hit the line-of-cut perpendicularly and with greatest force. If you moved out away from the line-of-cut extension, you would hit with less force, for each stroke would have passed the peak of its power. Simultaneously, such strokes would tend to strike only on the top corner of your bit, forming a more saw-toothed line-of-cut that could require extra chopping to clear.

If you crossed over the line-of-cut extension, your strokes would be foreshortened, striking before they had attained full power. That would be harm enough, but there would be much more. With any part of your body past the line-of-cut extension, you would either be changing the facing of your notch into the tree or violating the frontal zone rule. Of course hitting the middle or far side of a large tree, your ax would most likely bury itself there. But that would not necessarily be true of the near corner of the same kerf where the ax could skip up and out to bury itself in you.

Chopping point targets is often more dangerous than chopping larger ones. Common examples are twigs, small branches, undergrowth, and light sticks lying unsupported on the ground. Being light, all these can be hard to cut. Many have frustrating resilience, bouncing away from the edge of the ax. You could bend over to hold each for cutting, but it saves time and energy to part each of them in a single, swift stroke. With a sharp ax, precise accuracy is less important. Be positioned properly and check for anything that could snag your ax in its swing. Then swing with snap. With a bush, for instance, aim low, but so your follow-through will arc upward. You will see the bush flop over and lie down.

Cutting unsupported sticks lying on the ground is often safer when they are removed a foot or so beyond the frontal zone boundary to the side that you chop toward. The reason is that these sticks are best cut by a stroke so nearly vertical that its termination would come too near your feet unless you strike farther to the side. Like golf swings, such strokes just skim the surface of the ground. They are at the peak of their power when hitting and are already heading upward. Unlike golf swings, though, these hits are executed to the chopper's side and directed toward the rear. It is a common stroke in splitting stovewood chunks when working the whole pile.

Vertical chopping strokes that have little or no lateral movement across your front are exceptions to the frontal zone concept because they are performed *only* in the frontal zone. There are three types of vertical chopping: that which is backed-up; that which is not backed-up; and that chopping done beneath the level of the feet.

The most familiar backed-up vertical chopping would be cutting a stick laid on a stump or log. The backing must be solid, sound, and broad enough across to stop the ax in the event that it cuts through the stick. In chopping into a backed-up stick or chunk, deflection of the ax is quite common if the target is hit off-center or if it flies apart. Your posture should be similar to that when splitting chunks of wood on a block: your arms extended for maximum reach

and force at the instant of impact. Then if the ax is deflected and misses the block, it will swing to the side or into the ground, but not back at you, for your extended arms will keep it sufficiently distant from your body.

Many things are possible. If you have little concern for what may happen to your ax, it is possible to view a stick lying on the bare ground as backed-up enough for vertical chopping. And it could be, but when you cut through, your ax will get a faceful of grit, or even rock. This may be an acceptable trick with a splitting ax, since such axes get to looking pretty much like battle-axes anyway, but you had better treat your felling ax more kindly. Another interesting feature of a vertical chopping stroke against a stick on the surface of the ground is that one end of such a stick sometimes flies upward—and occasionally, both ends. You will be lucky if your face is not in the way.

Vertical chopping that is clearly not backed-up is inherently so dangerous that it is seldom used, and when it is, one hand is usually held halfway up the handle for greater control. However, when lopping off an overhead limb from a standing tree, for example, you might be required to grasp the handle normally for maximum reach. This requires caution. The higher you chop, the more effort it takes and the greater the risk of your follow-through going all the way down. Down is where you keep your feet. All high, overhead strokes that miss or pass through the target will return the ax to your legs and feet. Factors tending to increase this are an overheavy ax for the job, a too-powerful stroke, and fatigue. Overhead strokes can be controlled, but gauge your strength. Hit only with the force you need. Before you strike upward, be sure you are capable of controlling the ax when it comes down.

The third type of vertical chopping, that of chopping beneath the level of your feet, is the common way of cutting a log. Standing sideway on top, you chop first into one side of the log, then into the other, until it parts at the middle. For all except the final stroke, perhaps, it is much similar to vertical backed-up chopping. Any stroke (except the last) that wanders sideway will bury itself in the log. At the moment of impact, your arms will be fully extended for maximum force, so it is your back that controls depth and keeps your feet safe. To cut nearer your feet, you straighten slightly. To cut farther beneath you, you lean over more. Your feet would not normally be directly over the kerf anyway, but would straddle it. At the final stroke, the ax might cut entirely through to the opposite side. As concerns safety, it would matter little. A backward stroke through your legs can go nowhere.

A final risk consideration for swinging an ax is enough light. Chopping in darkness, or even at dusk, is a lunatic trick. Not only are you unable to see branches that might snag your ax, but you will also be unable to see the surface you are chopping well enough to be certain of either your work or of your position and safety. Chop with enough light to see clearly, or go home.

Felling Trees — Preliminaries

In *Timber Cutting Practices,* a book aimed at professionals, Steve Conway states, "Cutting timber is an art, not a science . . . felling always involves a certain amount of guesswork. The more experience a feller has, the better his guess will be." The more you know about felling trees, the more likely you are to agree with these statements. Felling is both exacting and dangerous. To do it well, there is no substitute for experience. The reason for listing some relevant items about felling here is to help you interpret experience sooner.

Where you begin operations in the woodlot will largely depend upon how you will get the wood out after you cut it. If making roads or trails of any variety will be necessary, one early decision you must make is to determine where these will be most needed, where they will be the least harmful to the soil and to other trees, and where they will be the easiest to clear or construct. At this stage, be aware of where the trees you want to cut can be safely felled to facilitate removal, to avoid breakage, and to protect other trees and young growth.

Unless you intend to clear the entire lot, you should be selective, picking only mature and cull trees. You can often get adequate wood just by a cleaning operation, taking the broken or deformed trees, or cutting the less promising specimens from a clump so that the better growth can develop faster without interference. Perhaps you will want to mark the trees to take beforehand. You can blaze these with an ax. But if for some reason you later change your mind, you might wish you had used a painted mark instead. Spray cans are handy for this purpose.

Trees come in all sizes. When they are too big to push over by hand, every one is dangerous, for it is big enough to injure you in falling. First decide where you want your tree to fall and whether you can make it go there. This depends on many things, for with sufficient equipment, any tree can be felled in any direction. Whether you have sufficient equipment available to you is another matter. Some trees can be pretty difficult to control.

Using timber industry terms, the path that you want to drop a tree into is the "lay" of the tree. Few trees rise perfectly vertical, and the direction the tree naturally leans toward is called just that, the "lean" of the tree. However, for felling purposes, the lean is always considered in relation to the lay. The principal direction that the tree leans toward on the lay side of the tree is termed the "head lean." If there is also a lesser direction of lean, that is known as the "side lean." For instance, a tree might lean downhill, but also a little to one side. Naturally, felling into your lay is easiest when you pick the lay to coincide with the lean.

Lean and Lay

Diagram 9

The "lean" of a tree is its divergence from the vertical. Its direction affects where the tree can be felled.

The "lay" of a tree is the bed or path you want the tree to drop into when felled.

Lean is always expressed in relation to lay. The major direction of lean is the "Head Lean." The lesser direction (in relation to lay) is "Side Lean." Both must be assessed accurately to have the tree fall into the lay.

Amount of side lean.

Amount of head lean

Lay

To be sure of amount of lean, make a plumb bob with a rock on a string — or use your ax.

27

The larger the tree, the more urgent it is that you know exactly how it does lean. For every tree will fall about as it leans unless you somehow force it to fall elsewhere. You must know with precision how much lean a tree has and in what direction so that you can determine what actual lay is possible. In judging lean, use of the unaided eye can be deceiving. On less obviously leaning trees of good size it is wise to use a plumb bob. A stone on a string will do. With the stone dangling just off the ground, hold the string out high at arm's length and you will have a taut sighting line to determine how much a tree tilts from the vertical. Check for side lean also. Though the string and stone are better, you can use your ax for a plumb bob. Suspend it edgewise at arm's length, holding the end knob of the handle between the tips of thumb and finger, and sight along the side of the handle.

The right lay for any tree is where you think best after considering a number of items including: direction of lean, direction and force of the wind, ease of subsequent removal, avoiding other trees or obstacles, reducing destruction of desirable young growth, grade of the area, composition of the soil, preventing trunk damage, subsequent ease of bucking, maintaining clear access routes, disposition of slash, and perhaps even depth of snow or bearing strength of ice. Experience teaches how to sort these factors out. For most trees and locations, a man familiar with timber will merely glance and say, "There," to indicate the lay. But do not be fooled. The man who can make a sound judgment that easily for a large tree carries a computer in his head. He gives due weight to every convoluted factor using a mental program written by long experience.

You will probably pick a lay that is free of hollows, stubs, stumps, rocks, or other trees that your tree could hit in falling. If not, clear the lay or change it. Occasionally you may have to reconsider your lay or even your felling priorities, as when an obstructing tree must be cut first, or even a third tree taken to give a clear lay for the second. Use every precaution to prevent your tree from lodging in another. Clearing a lodged tree is a time-consuming mess. It is also needless exposure to danger.

To prevent damage to the trunk, it is desirable to select a lay that will support the tree evenly as it hits the ground. The larger the tree, the greater the chance of breakage if the lay is across a hollow or the trunk hits a ledge, stub or stump before the top section strikes to cushion the impact. For firewood purposes, breakage is not the disaster that it would be if you were felling the tree for lumber. But breakage usually causes waste wood in some manner and should be avoided whenever possible.

The first on-site chore before chopping is to clear the area. This is necessary on both sides of the tree because you will chop on both sides. Whenever you shift position, check again that nothing will cause you to slip or stumble that you are not aware of and that nothing can snag your ax. Another pre-chopping chore is to clear an escape route for yourself. If you do not feel confident of where the tree will fall, make as many getaway paths from the stump area as you need. This is nothing to be delayed until the tree cracks. When hurried, it is too easy to trip on a branch or flounder in deep snow. Because a tree can kick back—that is, also plunge backward as it falls—your escape path should not be directly rearward. Nor should it be anywhere on the front side of the tree in the direction of fall. Diagonally back of the tree, clear a path away from where you will finish cutting. A dozen yards or so is enough for most trees, and the path need not be fancy, but get it clear ahead of time. And remember your tools. They also can break. But as concerns your ax, laying it in some harmless spot may be better than carrying it off while you are in a hurry.

Whether to chop a tree high or low depends on what is most important to you. Certainly the lower you chop, the less wood you will leave in each stump. But there are good reasons for not cutting too low also. A very practical reason is to protect your ax from rocks or from the grit that is too often lodged in crevices of bark, even well above ground level. And with some trees, the lower trunk just as it emerges from the ground is considerably thicker through than it is a short distance higher up. Quite often the extra wood you might gain from cutting low might not be worth the additional effort required to chop through the larger diameter of the butt swell. Tangled grain is also common in the butt swell area. This can later prove to be an inconvenience in splitting. For purposes of cutting lumber, the butt swell wood is particularly undesirable because of cross-grain problems.

Have your ax ready before getting to the woods. For felling trees you need an ax that will sink into the wood easily at each stroke. The cutting edge must not be too fat as found on almost all new axes. Bring your ax sharp so you can spend your time cutting, not sharpening. Accidents do happen, though, and you should also carry a pocket stone for touching up the bit if that becomes necessary during the day.

Felling – Hinge and Kickback Stop

Having a tree drop into the desired lay is not an accident but a calculated accomplishment. It is affected by numerous variables that you cannot measure but only sense. That is why author Steve Conway said, "Cutting timber is an art, not a science."

The primary means of controlling where a tree will fall is to partially sever the tree trunk straight in from opposite sides until only a narrow strip of sound wood fibers remains inside the trunk between the two cuts. This strip is the "hinge." When no support for the tree is left on either side of the hinge, the pull of gravity on the tree will cause the hinge to "fold," guiding the fall of the tree perpendicularly to the hinge. Ordinarily, the tree cannot tumble sideway because the hinge cannot fold to the sides. As the tree falls, the hinge is quickly strained beyond its elastic limits and snaps, parting the tree from the stump. But by that time, the hinge has done its work and the direction of the fall is set.

A real hinge can fold either forward or back. When the hinge technique is the only artificial guidance for felling a tree, you form the hinge so that gravity ensures that the tree falls only "forward," the direction in which it already leans. So in that general direction, the straight hinge technique can provide deviation from what would be the natural lay, of about 45° on either side of the head lean. It will all depend on how you face the cuts at the front and rear of the tree to form the hinge. The pull of side lean must also be considered. To expand the arc of controlled fall beyond the 45° on either side of the lean you may have to use some other means to assist the simple hinge technique. Nevertheless, the hinge concept is so basic that it is normally used in conjunction with almost every other manual tree-felling method.

You start the hinge formation by making a "face cut" into the tree directly facing the desired lay. This notch is also known as the "under cut." The top side of it is chopped down into the trunk at about a 45° angle. The bottom side is chopped in levelly at a right angle to the trunk. Both top and bottom surfaces should converge in a straight and level line somewhat more than halfway through the trunk. You may find it helpful to mark the limits of the notch upon the bark of the trunk with your ax before you begin so that you will know just what has to be chopped out. On a large tree, the outer wood marked off may be too great to chop away in one tier. In this case, cut one or more intermediate notches within your marked-off zone so that the intervening kerfwood can be split out in shorter and more manageable chunks. In felling hardwood, a six-inch chip is usually long enough to attempt. Four-inch chips will be as great as most choppers will lift.

The face notch should ordinarily be cut to just past the middle of the trunk. Cutting this deep will expose heart rot,

---

Diagram 10

The Face Cut

Also known as the "Under Cut."

Notch of the face cut is chopped to face along the intended lay.

Chop the top edge of face cut in at about 45°. Begin with small notch at desired height and chop out more layers from top edge as necessary.

Lay

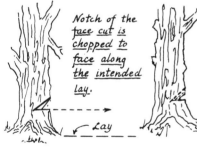

Bottom of face cut must be straight and level. Its height depends on how high you want the stump and other factors.

On a large tree, it may help to mark off the limits of the notch before beginning to chop. Normal depth of face cut is about 50(+) % of trunk diameter.

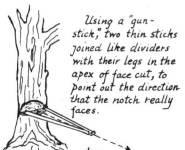

Using a "gun-stick," two thin sticks joined like dividers with their legs in the apex of face cut, to point out the direction that the notch really faces.

Double-bitted ax can also act as indicator.

Lay

Lay

Ordinarily, the tree will fall where the face cut faces. When the tree is large, or the exact lay is important, either of these means of reading the facing may be helpful. The gun-stick is more accurate.

if any is present. At the same time, adequate width will be maintained for formation of the hinge. It is also common practice to make the face cut somewhat less than halfway so the hinge will have maximum spread through the middle of the trunk. Desirable as this may be, if because of a more shallow face cut, you discover too late that substantial heart rot weakens the center of your hinge, you could have trouble. If the hinge failed, the tree could fall anywhere.

Remember that chopping is a series of succeeding strokes, each hitting behind the previous one along the same line of cut. The trick is accuracy. After cutting one line across the face of the tree, cut another line parallel to it about 4″ apart. The wedging impact of the ax will chip out the cut kerfwood between the lines. You can aid this process perhaps by using a little residual force to twist the ax immediately after each hit to help lift the large chips. As each row of chips flies off, it leaves a trough where further cutting in the same manner can penetrate even deeper.

Begin chopping the face cut at the middle of the bottom line that you marked off for the notch. Chopping the bottom of the notch is more difficult than the top because the bottom cuts into the tree at a right angle while the top slants down at an easy 45°. As you chop, let your strokes overlap just enough to ensure that your cut is continuous without gaps. Whether you chop forward or backward along this line makes small difference. Frequent change of footing is undesirable, so lean forward or back as necessary for accuracy. Just make sure that you have good footing, that your stance is not strained and that you strike on line.

When you finish, the rear line of the face cut, the fold where the top and bottom surfaces of the notch converge, should be clean, straight, level, and perpendicular to the desired lay of the tree. Because this line determines how the hinge will fold, which in turn determines the lay of the tree, you must know where the face cut really faces. As with sighting the lean of a tree, use of the unassisted eye can often deceive you. If a slight error will make no difference, "eyeballing" the face cut may be sufficient. But when the exact lay is a critical matter for some reason, perhaps a "gunstick" should be used. This is not one stick, but two longish, slender sticks fastened together at one end like a huge pair of draftsman's dividers. The sharpened legs should be of equal length and the joint should allow pivoting movement to adjust separation of the legs. When the legs of the gunstick are placed in opposite corners of the face notch, the apex of the gunstick will point perpendicularly out from the cut. If you have faced the cut accurately, the gunstick will also point along the lay you intended. If not, reshape the face cut.

A simple and rugged substitute for a gunstick is an ordinary piece of light plywood, accurately cut in a rectangle measuring about 18″ x 36″. With the 18″ base seated in the face cut, the approximate lay of the cut will extend out from the long edge of the plywood.

You can roughly perform the same function with a double-bitted ax. Place the top end of the ax against the rear of the cut as if it were a little T square. The handle will point perpendicularly outward, or approximately so. Single-bitted axes are not suitable for this purpose. Few single-bitted ax handles are perpendicular to the line across the top of the ax. Nor can the top corner of the single-bitted poll fit into the

rear line of the notch, so the difference in handle alignment created by this could cause significant error.

Another reason for knowing the exact face cut heading is the matter of side lean. The simple hinge technique will ordinarily permit selection of a lay within 45° to either side of the head lean. However, the "pull" of a side lean will deflect the actual lay by its own spread and to the same side. If the plumb bob shows that the top of the tree has about 10′ of side lean to the left, the top will come to earth 10′ to the left of the position it would have hit if there had been no side lean. The face heading must be cut to account for this, or along a heading that will amount to an additional 10′ to the right as measured where the top of the tree will impact.

Still another cause of felling deflection is uneven weight distribution in the top of the tree. The tree may fork unevenly, or have more, heavier, or markedly longer branches on one side than another. All these will tend to pull the tree toward that side in falling. Long branches that lodge in, or hit, other trees are still another cause of felling deflection that may make the tree twist, bounce, and rebound before finally coming to horizontal rest. All of these possible movements add to the danger of remaining anywhere in the vicinity of the stump during the fall.

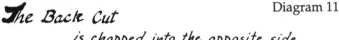

The Back Cut · Diagram 11

is chopped into the opposite side of the trunk from the face cut.

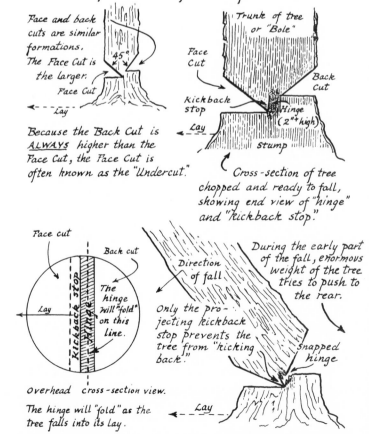

Face and back cuts are similar formations. The Face Cut is the larger.

Because the Back Cut is ALWAYS higher than the Face Cut, the Face Cut is often known as the "Undercut."

Cross-section of tree chopped and ready to fall, showing end view of "hinge" and "kickback stop."

Overhead cross-section view.

The hinge will "fold" as the tree falls into its lay.

During the early part of the fall, enormous weight of the tree tries to push to the rear.

Only the projecting kickback stop prevents the tree from "kicking back."

Additional Back Cut Techniques   Diagram 12
(Overhead Cross-section views through trunk of the tree.)

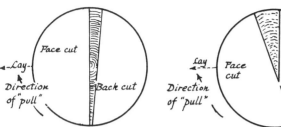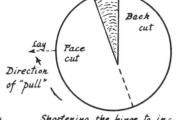

The thicker end of hinge resists falling better, and "pulls" the falling tree toward its end. Deliberately forming one end of the hinge thicker is a common method of influencing direction of fall to overcome adverse lean.

Shortening the hinge to increase "pull." This works, BUT... this is Dangerous. Shortening the hinge weakens its lateral ability to control direction of fall.

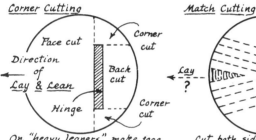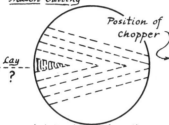

On "heavy leaners," make face cut much larger than the back cut. Then cut out corners to avoid splintering. Chop back cut last.

Cut both sides in from the rear in equal segments until tree falls. This is Dangerous. Use this technique only when the ground prohibits using any other chopping method.

To form the hinge, you must notch both sides of the tree. After finishing the face cut, chop out the back cut similarly, cutting the bottom levelly into the tree at a right angle and the top side in at 45°. Chop the back cut out in layers, working evenly back and forth so that the thickness of the uncut wood forming the hinge is reduced uniformly. When nothing else interferes, a hinge of uniform thickness will finally fold perpendicularly when it is no longer strong enough to hold the tree upright. To have one end of the hinge thick while the other end is thin will tend to pull the falling tree toward the thicker side.

As you reduce the remaining support by chopping out the back cut, the tree will finally begin to move. No matter how many trees you have cut, the moment has its drama. By watching the top, at long last you will learn the real direction of fall. In part, it can still be corrected. And of a certainty, it can still go wrong. If correction appears needed, you can still adjust the hinge in those hanging instants. Moreover, in each particle of time until the hinge breaks, every ax stroke will cut deeper. For as the gap widens, the ax will bind less and less. Simultaneously, the fibers of the hinge will cut more easily as they are stretched by the falling tree.

Toward the end just before the hinge snaps, an ax can sink into those strands of the hinge as if cutting butter. But you should also know that if you are there to see the hinge come apart like too-taut elastics, you may already be too late to save yourself if the tree should kick back.

Contrary to how it often seems, the duration of the fall is not long. It starts slowly, but it finishes fast. You may have time to give the hinge a correcting whack, or two, or three. It depends on you. And although the later strokes may seem more effective, the more the tree falls through its arc, the less the hinge can affect the lay. After about a third of the fall, perhaps more, the hinge will break anyway. What happens then at the stump can always be a matter of conjecture until it is done. It is not really sane to linger there to watch.

The period of the fall is a time of pure danger anywhere near the stump. The tree can twist and roll as well as kick back. It can split back and up, or conceivably, even fall directly on you. All of these have killed woodsmen in the past. The period of the fall is what you cleared your escape route for. At that time, that is where you should go.

The bottom of the back cut must always be higher than the bottom of the face cut. For this reason, the face cut is more often called the "under cut." About 2" difference in height is sufficient. If accuracy of cutting is a problem, aim at having the back cut 4" higher. The reason for this is not just tradition or woods fashion. If the back cut is not higher than the face cut across its entire width, the tree may roll or even kick back without warning, plunging backward off the stump as it falls. Cutting the back cut higher ensures that a spur from the butt will push against a ridge of stump as the tree falls. With this "kickback stop" properly formed, the tree will jump forward as it falls, not backward. For similar reasons, the bottoms of both face and back cuts should always be level, ensuring that the tree will not slide to either side as the hinge breaks. For even if the back cut were higher, if a tree slid or rolled off the stump while it was still falling, it might kick back as soon as it became free of the restraining stump.

Because the thicker end of the hinge "draws" or "pulls" a falling tree to that side, deliberately varying the thickness of the hinge is a common method of gaining additional directional control. Assuming that each bit of the hinge is of equal strength, the thicker area will be stronger and will still resist the tearing stresses of the fall even after the thinner end of the hinge strip has begun to fail. Gravitational pull on the tree will be most effective where the support is weakest, on the thin end of the hinge. Because the thicker side of the hinge resists falling better, a partial rotation will occur, the stronger end "pulling" the tree in its direction. So in this case, as the tree falls, it does not really drop perpendicularly to the face at all, but along a lateral deflection from the perpendicular favoring the thicker end of the hinge.

This aspect of felling also has many variables, and to attain a lay by chopping an uneven hinge you must have keen judgment as well as skill. The hinge of uniform thickness folds perpendicularly to an axis running through its middle. In general, this applies to a hinge of uneven thickness also. So you could effect only modest changes in lay as long as the hinge remained full length, as a substantial change of lay would require one corner of the hinge to be so thick that the tree might not fall.

It is another matter entirely when the hinge is so thin at

one end that it is really shortened. The hinge may also be deliberately shortened while chopping out the back cut. This is termed "corner-cutting." A shortened hinge is less able to resist rotation toward the stronger side during the fall, and considerably more deflection can be attained. However, shortening the hinge is a tricky business. It reduces the side-to-side control afforded by a full-length hinge and increases the risk of unpredictable fall.

The hinge is the residual wood unsevered between the face and back cuts. The kickback stop is the lowest tip of the tree trunk along the face side of the hinge. As the tree falls, the stop remains pushing against the remnants of the hinge and prevents kickback. Before the fall, it is vital to realize that both hinge and kickback stop are of one mass of wood. (See Diagram 11.) If you destroy one, you destroy both, as is partially done with corner-cutting. When you reduce this wood, be careful. You are proportionately reducing both control and safety.

Occasionally you may be unable to make either face or back cuts. This situation can be forced on you by trees you are unwilling to cut, other obstacles such as rock or ledge, or being next to water or cliffs, or on steep hillsides. You may still fell these trees by chopping in equally from both sides to sever the trunks. This is "match-cutting." Use it with caution, because it leaves directional control almost entirely lacking. Unless you use other felling aids also, do not attempt to drop a match-cut tree anywhere but in the lay that coincides with its natural lean.

A tree with a pronounced lean also presents a special problem. The wood fibers on the back side of the trunk will have resisted the pull of gravity for so long that they are apt to be brittle and fail sooner than would otherwise be expected. For such a tree, the face notch should be chopped deeper than usual to prevent the trunk from "splitting-up," or "barberchairing" as this splitting is called, before the back cut is completed. The same stresses may cause the sides of such trees to splinter during the fall. You can help prevent both by corner-cutting on both sides before making the back cut. All this will take a good eye, for if either operation leaves too little support, the tree will fall before it is back-cut enough. If this happens, the tree may either barberchair, drop out of lay, or both, anyway.

Felling – Other Means of Control

The technique of severing the tree from its stump is not the only means to control the direction of its fall. If a tree is small enough, you can push it into the lay with your bare hands. Only a minority of firewood trees will be that small, however. Whatever the size of the tree, make it a habit to watch the top for the first signs of movement. You will be able to detect movement against the sky or in relation to other trees long before you can notice the butt move. That early, you can still influence the fall by how you attack the hinge.

Another reason for sky-watching is to read the wind. Be aware of whether a breeze is moving the branches overhead. If so, how much? And in what direction? This can make a vast difference to you. Is the breeze constant? Depending upon its strength and direction, a wind can help you place a tree in exactly the lay you want or blow the whole business back over on top of you. You cannot ignore the wind safely. Because breezes are seldom constant, you may be able to deliver the final critical strokes to the hinge between gusts. An exception to this is when the tree is large or has a great amount of top to catch the wind. On such specimens, considerable force can be exerted by a light breeze. Also, the dangerous stage of completing the back cut on a large tree may take too long, making the tree repeatedly vulnerable to unpredictable gusts while having little stability. The best rule is not to fell trees when there is a wind. Its dangers will usually outweigh its advantages.

A surprisingly useful aid for making smaller trees drop where you want them is the "pick-pole," an extra long stick with a spike protruding from one end. The longer the pick-pole, the better, the upper limit to length being what you can conveniently handle and carry about. When you have a tree just about ready to fall, the hinge being suitable faced, put your pick-pole against the trunk and give the critical initial push to guide the tree into the lay you want.

The proper angle to jab the spiked end against the tree is about 45°, the spike preventing the upper end from slipping sideway off the trunk. The higher you place the pole, the greater leverage you can exert. Working unaided, you can push up and forward best by resting the bottom of the pick-pole on your thigh. If you are clever, you can work a lever arrangement against the bottom of the pick-pole and be able to command substantial advantage. Naturally, the pole must also be rugged enough to withstand this type of use.

Where modern timber operations are still done manually, the most common secondary aid for controlling felling direction is the wedge. Unfortunately, it is not easy to use wedges well on trees felled with an ax. The difference is that you can pound a wedge into the crack of a saw kerf. In the gaping

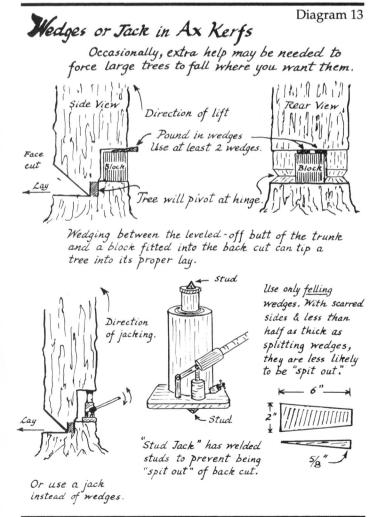

Diagram 13

Wedges or Jack in Ax Kerfs

Occasionally, extra help may be needed to force large trees to fall where you want them.

Side View

Rear View

Direction of lift

Pound in wedges
Use at least 2 wedges.

Face cut

Lay

Block

Block

Tree will pivot at hinge.

Wedging between the leveled-off butt of the trunk and a block fitted into the back cut can tip a tree into its proper lay.

Direction of jacking.

Lay

stud

Stud

Use only felling wedges. With scarred sides & less than half as thick as splitting wedges, they are less likely to be "spit out."

6"

2"

5/8"

"Stud Jack" has welded studs to prevent being "spit out" of back cut.

Or use a jack instead of wedges.

ax-cut notch, there is nothing to hold the wedge. Yet rigging this is possible. Where no other aid is suitable, you can use wedges in the back cut by chopping both top and bottom of the back-cut into the tree at right angles. Then by inserting in this space a rectangular block cut to fit nicely, a wedge driven into the crevice on top of the block will push up against the butt of the tree.

Chopping out the back cut to accommodate wedges on a block is not an ideal system, by any means. Under the best of conditions, wedges can suddenly jump out of a cut as you might pop a watermelon seed from your mouth. Using a block for the wedges to sit on only increases the chance of this occurring. Chopping a level top to the back cut is an extra chore and the block itself must be specially prepared. Nevertheless, you should know the tricks of felling, and this is one that requires no more exotic machinery than a wedge and a block you can make yourself.

With the back cut inletted as for a block, another directional tool worth having available can be a jack. Instead of inserting a block between the level floor and ceiling of the squared-off back cut, insert the jack. For its squat shape and ease of operation, the average hydraulic jack is ideal, but be certain that it is reliable and of adequate capacity for the tree you wish to use it on. A jack with the excess width of its base plate cut away is desirable so that the jack may fit into as small a space as possible. So the jack cannot be spit out sideway when under pressure in the back cut, weld a stubby pointed stud in the center of both the piston and the base-plate of the jack. With prudent formation of the hinge and proper placement of this "studjack," a tree that does not lean too much can be dropped into a lay even on the opposite side from its lean.

None of the foregoing applies to the "heavy leaner." When a tree is tilted far to one side, unless you have a skyhook to pick it up bodily, you had better let it fall in the direction that it grew. In general, the more lean you attempt to overcome, the more hazardous the job is.

Before using any hydraulic jack, check that it does not leak. Then after you have started to jack the tree, let the valve alone. When the ordinary hydraulic jack is under compression, it is not easy to release some hydraulic pressure without releasing too much. Should the top of the tree suddenly rock sharply rearward, it could plunge entirely backward. For this reason, a screw-type building jack may be preferable to the more compact hydraulic model even though the screw type of the same capacity will be larger, heavier, more awkward, and more difficult to work. Construction model screw jacks will usually be far more durable for the treatment they are likely to get in the woods than the relatively thin-skinned hydraulic jacks are apt to be.

Pulling a tree into its lay with a rope may not seem like proper Paul Bunyanism. Be that as it may, this technique has been extensively used for Pacific Coast timber operations on larger trees than old Paul ever hauled down or out of the woods. Setting up a huge dragline with its engines, pylons, and enormous cables is scarcely appropriate for home wood-lot firewood procurement, but again, you should know the general technique for adaptation to your own purposes.

The higher you tie a rope to a tree, the more leverage you gain, and the easier it will be to pull the tree to the lay you want. Cut the hinge normally to aid directional control as much as possible. In most cases, care should be taken to put no strain on the rope at all until hinge preparation is complete. Then a slight pull on the rope should drop the tree neatly into the proper lay. In some limited cases where both rope and the power source are equal to the task, the rope may be used to restrain the fall until all is ready, then pull the tree out of its leaning posture and into a lay on the opposite side. It should be obvious that this demands competence and good equipment, for poor judgment at any stage could bring disaster to either side of the tree, and maybe anywhere about it.

Merely roping the tree high enough is often a major trick for a firewood operation. If you have climbing irons and you can use them, you can climb any clear tree easily, but the average hardwood these days is not all clear trunk for a soaring 70' as many of its ancestors were. The intervening branches are obstacles to successively raising the safety belt. If you can climb high enough on the branches alone you are in luck, for woodlot trees do not always grow with branches so conveniently spaced. Attacking a dooryard tree, you may even be able to use a ladder to climb where you want. But however you get up there, the advantage of climbing there yourself is that you can carry the end of rope with you and tie it to the trunk just as you want it tied. Two half hitches is a simple and sufficient knot for this purpose. Be sure you carefully cinch it tight.

When climbing the tree is not practical or possible you can still use a rope if you can have means of getting a light line over a limb and then around the trunk at a point that is high enough to be useful. The descending end of the line should then be secured to your rope to haul that up and around the trunk. This will require a greater length of rope, because you must draw the end that circles the upper trunk back to yourself to tie in a loose loop around your end of the rope. You do not want a loop that will close on you. If you know how to tie them, tie a lariat loop, or even better, a bowline knot. Then draw all the slack out of the long noose until you have the upper trunk firmly secured in a tightened lasso.

The secret of the accomplished lasso is first getting the line up over the high branch. If you throw well, tie on a light, but strong, line a small solid weight, a rock perhaps. Throw this with sufficient force and the line will follow. Hold, or lay, the line in loose loops that will not tangle as they play out following the weight. If your accuracy is not up to throwing, try suspending the weight so it hangs down out of your hand a short distance and sling it underhanded. More force can be exerted by this cast than by the unaided arm.

Using a fishline secured to the top of an arrow, a bow can shoot the arrow and its trailing line through the tree crotch. A slingshot can also propel your fishline where you want it to go if the line is attached to a heavy buckshot or marble by masking tape. Either way, the fishline would be tied to an intermediate cord to haul the rope up.

Both of these shooting alternatives seem deceptively simple. But first you must have the items described and second, be able to use them. Third, keeping the fishline from tangling when you shoot is not easy. Any twig, long grass or tough leaf can tangle a light fishline loop in flight. The most reliable storage for ready fishline is on a fishpole spinning reel. Tape the reel to a light pole, a broomstick stuck into the ground will do. Unlock the reel so the line will play out

Diagram 14

Pickpole and Throwing Line

The higher on a tree you push or pull, the more leverage you gain to influence its lay.

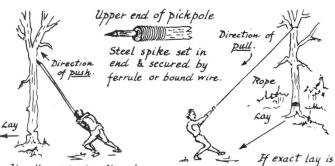

Upper end of pickpole

Steel spike set in end & secured by ferrule or bound wire.

Direction of push.

Direction of pull.

Rope

Lay

Lay

If exact lay is critical, roping your tree may make sense. Pull big ones with a vehicle or tools.

Use the pickpole after chopping both face & back cuts. Set pole against tree at about 45° for maximum push. Make pole as long as you can handle.

Iron weight for throwing line to lasso trees up high. Weight must be 1-2 lbs. to drag line through branches back to ground and be streamlined to prevent snagging in crotches when withdrawn from a poor throw. Strongest throw is an underhanded sling.

Tie line to rope with "sheet-bend." After pulling rope around high part of tree and back to you, tie the lasso with a "bowline."

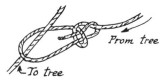

From tree

To tree

Then tighten lasso and pull tree into its lay.

freely when you shoot. Complicated? Maybe. But occasionally, landing a particular tree where you want it to fall may be worth the extra trouble.

The most forceful of these ground-based branch-lassoing methods is the underhand cast. Being the most forceful, it can propel the heaviest weight. Sufficient weight is needed on the line so the end will fall back to earth after passing over the branch. Too light a weight or too coarse a line can easily snag against rough bark, and instead of returning to you below, will remain suspended in midair like a fat spider. Sometimes you can free the weight by jerking or flipping the line and sometimes not. If it will not fall of its own weight, your only recourse is to withdraw it and try casting it again.

Ideally, the casting weight should be small, heavy enough to sling well, about one to two pounds, and have a smooth surface with no projections. The last is necessary so the weight can be pulled backward after an unsuccessful throw.

For attempting to withdraw the line with the weight caught in a sharp-angled and rough crotch can turn into a real project. For practical purposes, get another weight and line. Usable weights include a pear-shaped fishing sinker with a cast eye or a short iron bar with an inletted hole drilled in one end to receive the line.

Roping a tree is not only time-consuming for a firewood operation, but can give a false sense of security. You should always have a clear lay to pull into. For trees of any size, you will need more than your own strength to overcome natural lean. A block and tackle is cumbersome, but useful for providing limited pull over a short space. The block and tackle cannot give a swift pull or any pull over a long distance as would be needed during the initial fall of a tree. If there is room enough to permit, vehicle power is ideal. A four-wheel-drive pickup truck has many virtues.

Another marvelously effective way to guide a difficult tree into the lay you want includes use of the treetop swinger. (See Diagram 15.) The swinger itself consists of two overhead garage door springs hitched in tandem. Secured to the top section of your tree, when these are drawn out to maximum tension you have huge leverage pulling the tree toward your lay.

What distinguishes the swinger from other power sources is that when you finish normal cutting down at the stump, the treetop springs into its lay as the taut springs contract. No other normal power source is capable of such instantaneous response *plus* follow-through along the lay when it is most needed. For it is the initial pull that is decisive, not where gravity might pull it, but along the lay as decided by the contracting springs while the top is still essentially vertical. Then once the tree is in free-fall, there is no stopping it. It will drop in the lay because it was started on the lay.

For this result, preparation is needed. First, secure the rope as far up on the tree as possible. And because mechanical power will be involved, the rope must be sufficiently sturdy, preferably 140' of 1/2" braided nylon. Neither this nor other items listed below may be cheap, but they might be less expensive than hiring a crew to fell your tree. Too, depending upon circumstances, they might be less expensive than dropping your tree in the wrong lay yourself.

You will also need a "2-ton come-along" which is a small hand winch, three chains of 8', 10' and 30', all 5/16", with "grab" hooks on one end and "slip" hooks on the other, except the 8' chain should have grab hooks on both ends. Last, procure two overhead garage door springs of 90 lbs. or so capacity.

Fasten the springs in tandem with a 5/16" chain-connecting link. On the springs' opposite ends, fasten a 1/2" chain-connecting link to each. Cut off enough rope to securely connect these links and also match the maximum extended length of the two springs in tandem, probably about 20'. Complete your measuring and tying before cutting. This rope is both a maximum extension indicator and a safety connecter should the springs break. Finally, with 1/4" cable and clamps, connect each end hook of both springs to the chain connecting links. This prevents the end hooks themselves from becoming possible projectiles. Maximum stretch of the springs is a safety matter you should determine from your dealer.

The foregoing is the equipment. To use it, tie one end of

Diagram 15

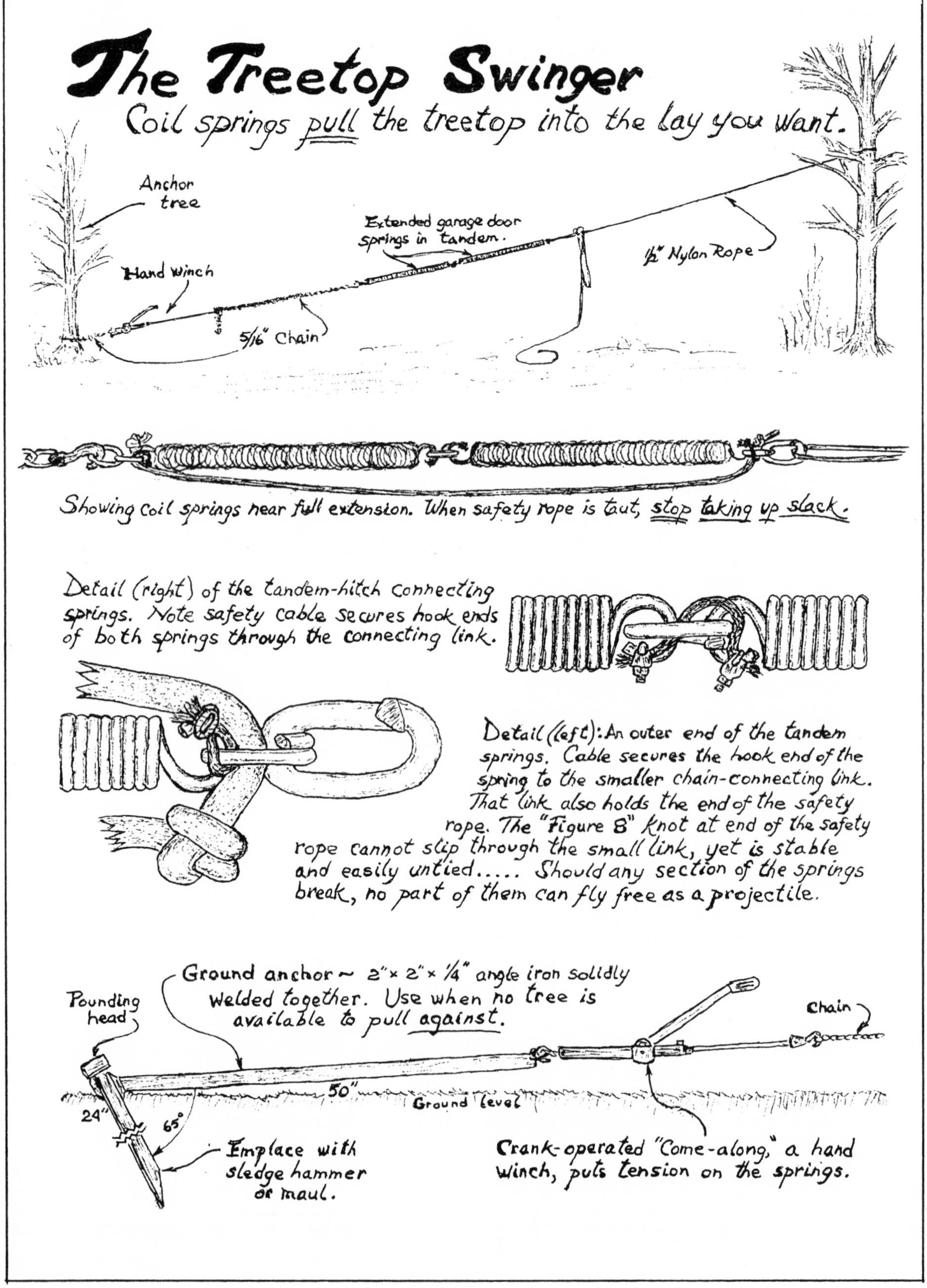

The Treetop Swinger
Coil springs pull the treetop into the lay you want.

Anchor tree

Hand winch

Extended garage door springs in tandem.

½" Nylon Rope

5/16" Chain

Showing coil springs near full extension. When safety rope is taut, stop taking up slack.

Detail (right) of the tandem-hitch connecting springs. Note safety cable secures hook ends of both springs through the connecting link.

Detail (left): An outer end of the tandem springs. Cable secures the hook end of the spring to the smaller chain-connecting link. That link also holds the end of the safety rope. The "Figure 8" knot at end of the safety rope cannot slip through the small link, yet is stable and easily untied..... Should any section of the springs break, no part of them can fly free as a projectile.

Ground anchor ~ 2" x 2" x ¼" angle iron solidly welded together. Use when no tree is available to pull against.

Pounding head

Chain

50"

Ground level

24"

65°

Emplace with sledge hammer or maul.

Crank-operated "Come-along," a hand winch, puts tension on the springs.

the tandem springs to the rope from the tree, passing the rope through one of the 1/2' chain-connecting links, using an easily released knot, such as a bowline. At the other end of the tandem springs, fix the slip-hook of the 30' chain to the chain-connecting link. Hook the other end of the chain to the pulley end of the come-along with the come-along pulley extended its full length. Have your 10' chain secured about the base of a strong tree in line with, but well beyond, the lay you want for your target tree. Hook the back end of the come-along to the 10' chain and you are ready to start pulling.

A come-along will only extend about 7'. The amount of slack you must take up is usually over 30', needing several cycles of drawing in slack, holding it, re-extending the come-along and rehitching it. To start, take up all slack you can by hand. When the entire line is under tension with the come-along fully wound up, hook one end of the 8' chain to the rear of the come-along. Hook the other end of the 8' chain on the 30' chain as far as you can get toward the tree to be cut. Then release slack on the come-along until the 8' chain is holding the tension. Now re-extend the come-along pulley, re-hooking it as far as it will reach on the 30' chain toward the tree to be cut. Resume taking in slack with the winch, and when the 8' chain becomes loose, remove it.

Repeat these cycles until the full length of the safety rope lies taut alongside the extended tandem springs. Do not exceed this limit. The spring assembly will be high in the air. If you use two 90 lb. springs, your tree will have 180 lbs. pulling it on the end of lever as high as your rope has las-soed it. At that stage, only at that stage, cut the tree off the stump in the normal manner.

The treetop swinger cannot work miracles, but for problem trees, the equipment is well worth the cost. A further item needed when there is no base tree to pull against is a ground anchor. A simple one that holds well, can be emplaced without difficulty and is easily removable is shown in Diagram 15.

A final method of controlling direction of fall is "lodge-driving." This is just what it says, felling one tree into another so that the driven tree is toppled over under the impact of the driver-tree. Even among experts, this method is used only when no other will work. At best, lodge-driving is hazardous, relatively unpredictable, and a mess to clean up. But when other methods of felling are impracticable, or if you want to earn a graduate degree in tree-felling by having the *driven* tree pound your stake into the ground along its lay, this is the procedure to use.

For lodge-driving, pick a day when there will be no wind until you are done. Inspect both trees, noting their balance and branches and how much twisting, if any, will result from impact. Decide whether the driver-tree should hit squarely or obliquely, and at what angle. Then prepare the tree to be driven, forming its hinge to facilitate falling into the lay you have selected. Leave just enough hinge uncut so the tree will stand until hit by the driver. Lastly, cut the driver, calculating its lay according to how you want the blow to fall. If you figured everything properly, the driven tree will drive your stake. Then be happy, go home, and never use lodge-driving again.

Felling Hazards

Even in a professional environment, tree felling is always dangerous. It is even more so for those who have not lived by it. The tremendous weight of wood suspended high in the air is an inherent hazard. How well is it suspended? Trees die and fall just as people do, except trees do that in pieces. But which pieces? When you enter the woods you should wear ordinary caution as you would a shirt. If another person is with you, or is in the vicinity, always cry, "Timber!" whenever a tree is about to fall. Another warning might serve the purpose perhaps, but the traditional one needs no explanation. It is universally understood.

The noise of chain saws and other machinery adds a complication. Often you cannot hear voice signals through the sound of machinery. Then a police whistle or similar is a virtual necessity. Its shrill blast can penetrate most other noise. The whistle must be instantly available. This will ordinarily mean tying it to a thong on your person so you cannot mislay it. You should tolerate a nuisance if it can mean saving a life.

Improper use or inattention to tools can create a hazard in any occupation and when the principal tool is an ax, carelessness can be costly. A thoughtless swing of your ax, especially a double-bitted ax, can wound you. It could brain or behead your partner. Each time you swing, be conscious of where you are, what you are doing, and where everything and everybody else is. It is also dismayingly easy to have an ax slip from your grip, its keen edge whirling many feet toward whatever target chance may present. Wet hands are the usual cause of that, hands wet from sweat, rain, snow-melt, ice—and I have seen it happen with blood. But in each case you will know the condition of your hands or your ax handle before the accident happens. Grip it accordingly or do not swing it at all. The handle that is slip-proof when dry can become a rocket launcher when wet. A third culpable negligence is leaving tools where you or anybody else can stumble or fall on them or into them. You are not safe in the woods unless you can keep a cool head. When a tree cracks, go for your escape path, but mind what you do with your ax. Think that out ahead of time also.

Another ax crime is letting the head fly off the handle. This too will never happen without warning you in advance. A loose ax head is an abomination. In almost all cases you can easily fix it in a few minutes with a couple of wedges, and there is no excuse for not doing that as soon as you notice

that the head is loose. The old farm solution of soaking the head in a bucket of water overnight is neither reliable nor likely to increase the life of the handle.

A tree lodged against another tree is invariably dangerous. Ordinary felling techniques will seldom suffice. Felling the supporting tree is one solution, but make sure you know how and where both trees will fall. If you have a power source, pull the lodged tree down if you can. Cutting a section off its butt may often be necessary first. In doing that, be careful of how the butt or top may twist or rebound when they drop. Clear an adequate escape route for just that cutting. You will save much time, effort, and perhaps grief, by doing everything reasonable to avoid getting a lodged tree in the first place. Be scrupulous about the accuracy of felling with every tree so that it cannot lodge.

Before cutting any tree, inspect it, and the adjacent trees as well, for dead or hanging tops or limbs that could be dislodged during felling. Traditionally known as "sailors" or "widow-makers," many of these great lengths of wood may be too rotten to remain suspended, but not too rotten to kill unfortunates they may happen to fall on. A published story of early Maine logging tells of a cutting crew encountering a great tree prime for cutting. High above their heads in the tree, a widow-maker lay poised, waiting for its time. One of the crew objected strenuously. Why, he argued, should they expose themselves to needless danger from the widow-maker? There were other trees to cut and the crew passed on, leaving the widow-maker to itself and the winds.

The next year the same crew returned, again confronting the handsome tree. It contained many feet of sound timber. The widow-maker was still there. On its precarious perch it had resisted all the storms of an entire year in the woods. The men looked up at its unnatural position carefully. To defy the ravages of weather there for a year, the widow-maker had to be well anchored, they decided. They knew trees. Felling trees was their livelihood and this one would not spook them again. And so it did not. But when the tree began to fall, it released the widow-maker. The plunging deadfall selected the man who had warned of the peril the year before. There was no social security then. His widow had four children.

The reason for clearing an escape route away from the stump area before beginning to cut is that hazards bloom with stupifying speed. You must be ready in advance. Nothing else preventing, a tree will always fall toward its lean.

Felling Hazards

Improperly felled, a tree can strike back at its chopper, even as it falls.

"KICKBACK," the tree plunging backwards off the stump as it falls.

KICKBACK CAN KILL

Direction of fall

Weight of tree pushes rearward.

For _this_ tree, the higher back cut forms a kickback stop, keeping butt in place on the stump.

Direction of fall

Weight pushes to rear.

On _this_ tree, back-cut on same level as face cut provides _No Kickback Stop_. Butt can skid rearward... _RUN FOR YOUR LIFE!_

Another kickback platform

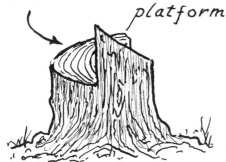

Chopping either face or back cut at an angle may permit the falling tree to slide off the stump side-ways and _then_ kick back. Always chop bottoms of _both_ face and backcuts _LEVEL_.

Lifted by a "Barberchair"

Usually caused by too _small a face cut_, or _No face cut_, a barberchair moves faster than a normal fall. Chop "Heavy Leaners" with _Caution!_

Diagram 17

Felling Hazards (cont.)

Often the secret of safety is not on the stump, but in the air.
Before chopping, Look Up!

Even the shock of chopping may break loose a rotten top weighing 200 lbs.†

Jarring either tree could dislodge this "widow-maker."

Lop-sided tree

Because of better light, less crowding, or other growing conditions, a tree may be heavier on one side. It will pull to that side in falling.

The Clump

Beware of interlocking branches. They make a tree twist as it falls. A falling butt that twists will often roll & bounce also. The distance it can strike may be considerable.

Therefore, keep out from under the natural lean of a tree. Practice until you can chop from any position so that you will not need to endanger yourself under a leaning tree. And while you chop, listen for breaking in the trunk. And watch. Particularly watch up. For the first movement will be visible in the top where its leaves move past those of other trees, or just against the sky. Being alert can keep you alive. The lurch of the beginning fall can often launch a widow-maker.

The weight of a standing tree is exerted directly downward, but as the tree falls, this force changes direction. When the angle of fall is 45°, the push against the stump is as much directly rearward as it is downward. Impelled by that force, if the tree has been improperly cut, it will kick back. "Kickback" is exactly that, the rearward thrust of the entire severed tree. When unleashed, it is swift and irresistible. It can kill, and it has. But keeping the back cut at least 2" higher than the face cut, making both cuts level, and forming the hinge properly will normally prevent kickback. This routine care is small price to pay for safety.

Trees having rot in the stump area present a special problem. Without sound wood in the center of a tree, it may be impossible to form the hinge or kickback stop of sufficient strength. If you realize this soon enough, the best solution may be to cut the tree higher, above the rotten-hearted area. Otherwise, you may have to extend the face cut entirely through a rotten core, requiring only a shallow back cut. This could make the hinge narrower than normal and perhaps unsuited for controlling direction of fall. With severe inner rot, you may have to chop the entire shell of the tree in from the face, working under the lean of the tree and remaining there until the tree cracks. The tree would fall into its natural lay, guided only by the backside which you would leave uncut. Obviously that violates safe practice. But with a severely rotted tree you may have no choice without the aid of other means of felling control. The huge face cut would at least lead to a reasonably predictable direction of fall. And it is the surprises you must avoid. Regarding that, avoid using wedges or a jack on trees with rot unless you are sure there is sound wood for them to work against. Any tree with rot is dangerous and you should treat it that way. And do not forget that rot can occur high overhead also.

A lethal cousin of kickback is "splitting-up" or, as it is called on the West Coast, "barberchair." The latter name is possible because a barberchair can lift any man within range. Splitting-up can occur without warning when making the back cut. The trunk will break too high, perhaps at head height or even higher. Breaking happens because the back slab of the trunk has been freed at its bottom end by the back cut. Then if the trunk has a weaker spot higher than the notch area, it may break there with released back slab lashing out at the chopper to the rear of the tree like a deadly seesaw working vertically. Splitting-up can kill or maim just as kickback can. The cause is usually insufficient face cut, or no face cut at all. Splitting-up may crack a considerable length of the butt log. For firewood, this may not matter, but for lumber, it can be real loss.

There is still another hazard in splitting-up. When the tree breaks and falls at its elevated rupture point, there will usually be enough sapwood splinters that will not pull apart and will retain the fallen trunk on its high perch. But that does not always happen. If the tree is dead, or particularly in colder weather when the wood fibers are stiffened with frost, the trunk may completely break apart at its pivot, especially when recoiling from the shock of the top hitting the ground. Then the entire tree may rebound to either side or even farther backward. Predicting its direction of bounce is virtually impossible, though the higher the stump the greater the lethal arc of the descending trunk and its unpitying back-slab extension. At the first crack of any splitting-up, get away from the fall and the entire stump area as fast as you can without stumbling.

Picking the lay of a tree, be sure to allow for the distribution of weight within its top. If the top is uneven, the tree may twist as it falls. Twist can also come from other causes. When felling trees immediately beside or interlocked with other trees, consider how adjacent tops may drag or deflect your tree as it falls. This requires close attention to cutting trees out of clumps, some of which almost resemble bunches of celery in how their tops are entangled.

One old woodsman cackled as he described a tree he had cut from a clump years before. Talking to me he had no teeth and tobacco juice overflowed on dirty stubble below his mouth. Demonstrating what he had done, he held his arms stiffly at his sides, his hands splayed frontward.

"Twixt those trees, it was like a cage! I couldn't go nowheres! Mucht I could, I flattened 'gainst the tree in my back while this other bugger rolled down crost the front of me. 'Twas supposed to go left, but it got hung up! So it twisted back quicklike and there I was! Took all three buttons off my coat!"

His eyes sparkled. Clearly, what he remembered best was not the terror of his peril, but the glee of his escape. To scrape the buttons from his coat without crushing him altogether would have been just one of those quirks of chance.

"All three buttons?" I marveled.

With a birdlike thrust, he cleaned his mouth with the back of his foresleeve. "There should of been four, but one was lost. Then there wa'nt none, so I tied a rope around me!" He grinned broadly, showing his bare gums at bay before turning to spit another quantity of the brown juice to the side. At eighty-four, he still earned tobacco money by knocking up firewood for his neighbors.

He had had a good life, and with his share of luck, too. The tree he had spoken of could just as easily have killed him as cleaned his coat. He knew it. He said that he had been alone at the time.

Everybody has to be alone sometimes. You may plan to do most of your cutting alone. Nevertheless, when heading for the woods, leave word with somebody as to where you will be and when you plan to be back. If something happened, you could save some searching and some time. Under some circumstances, you could also save yourself.

Tree Felling in the Marines

When I was a boy working for Lloyd Simpson, my skill increased far more than I had ever thought possible. But bodies are different. My muscles would never respond for me with the hairline accuracy with which Lloyd seemed to be able to guide his ax. But I remembered what he told me from time to time, much of which is repeated here. Several years later, during World War II, this paid off. Fresh from Stateside training, I had been put in charge of a group of battle-seasoned Marines on Guadalcanal. At that time, the island had long been secured and was used as a vast staging and training depot.

As far as the Marines I was assigned to were concerned, I was only nominally in charge. More realistically, I was there on trial. One time I remember in particular was when our immediate task was not fighting, or even training, but clearing the top edge of a wooded ravine so that it could be used for a trash and garbage dump. It is necessary to understand that EPA regulations were not in effect there and the garbage was dumped indiscriminately for the wild pigs to squall about after dark.

Blocking the top of the ridge where the trucks would have to back up to dump was a commanding giant of a tree. Beneath it was mostly grass, as was most of the ridge top. The trees grew up out of the ravine, and towering above them all was this magnificent specimen of beauty and girth. It was easily over two full feet in diameter. My platoon had axes, government-issue axes, great, long, club-handled things that would resist the inevitable abuse given them by users who scarcely knew an ax from a shovel.

Keeping my dignity as a leader of men, I detailed two of my more rugged people to chop down the tree. But just because Marines are superb fighters does not signify anything whatsoever about Marines' being superb workers. Both looked at me as if I did not know that there was a tradition against work. The more vocal of the two said, "It'll take the rest of the morning to chop that thing down. Why not just wrap it with some primacord?"

Primacord was a ropelike special-purpose explosive. There was none going to be made available to a working detail that was supposed to be using axes. I knew that well. And the tree had to come down. I also knew that. "It isn't that much of a job," I said. "I could do it myself in a half hour without anybody even spelling me!"

When not only the two men I had detailed, but others who were also listening began to laugh, I knew I had a job. Nor did it appear easy. But I had no choice. Remembering Lloyd, I figured that I could put on a decent show. That would be good enough. "Bring me the axes!" I said. There was a box of them and it was heavy.

Of the axes there, I made sure I picked the best, though they were all much alike. The one I picked had never been used. The heavy factory lip was thick, but at least the edge was not chipped. I cleared the weeds and a couple of bushes from the edge of the enormous trunk. The whole event had become a game with everybody stopping to watch. It had to be a good show.

Gauging the distance with that long handle, I started the face cut with a measured swing. To my amazement, the bit sunk in to almost halfway up on the cheek. Withdrawing it, I glimpsed a pasty white wood beneath a greenish inner bark. Even though sound, it was uncommonly soft. Afraid that the wood might change, I swung a second time, but hard. The ax sunk deeper than I had ever cut into any tree. That pasty-colored monument whose top soared at least 90' was truly soft, over twice as soft as basswood. And the ax did not bind! Jubilant, I did not even grunt. I gave care to each swing as I released it though, and as well as I could, followed each hit home.

From the corner of my eye, I noted a blankness creep over the grins on nearby faces. I had the advantage of having learned the backgrounds of each of them. All of them were town or city bred. Not a single one of them was able to recognize what was happening there almost under his nose. Most of them had used axes, but only since they had become Marines. After one lesson of trying to grind through the tough coconut logs with government-issue axes, they had a lasting aversion to the effort of chopping.

But they did not know wood, and specifically not the wood I was chopping. Nor did I, before my strokes had sunk so deeply into that majestic tower. To my delight, the whitish kerfwood split off crisply. Perhaps it was a variety of balsa. I never found out, nor did I ever try to.

I succeeded in making the top chips look like plates. It was small feat, but good show. Taking care not to get winded, I began on the next tier. My notch grew as no kerf ever expanded for me before or since. Yet the wood was sound and clean right to the core.

Halfway down the ravine the back of a coral outcropping

showed a blotchy cream flank through the green. Pointing to it as I turned for the back cut, I said, "I'm dropping it there. Throw the brush there too, so it will all be together!"

There was utterly no need to stow brush anywhere except to toss it over the lip of the ravine. But the demand anchored their attention to the target. What they also lacked the background to know for a certainty was that unless I sweated to redirect the tree, it could not avoid falling on the ledge. The ledge was dead under the tree's natural lay.

Starting the back cut high enough so there would be no kickback, I found the chopping in the rear just as easy as in the front. I paced myself evenly, quickening a little as the hinge shrank. It was not much over twelve minutes when the tree cracked.

The sound was unmistakable. It always has drama, but seldom the audience. As the top moved against the glaring sky, there were yells from the men. Almost as if the tree dragged them into motion, several of them began to dance about. The top moved faster, then downward. There became an audible hiss as its leaves raked the air during the long fall. Then it stumbled off the stump, head downward into the ravine. An instant later there was shock, and as if in an explosion, the whole mass seemed to rebound before settling back to die. Through the last leaves scaling earthward, the great stem of the tree curved in an unnatural bow, broken across the coral.

That tree had been the only one of its kind thereabouts. Nor were any of the remaining ones nearly its size. But there was still work to be done. Glancing noticeably at my watch, I thrust the ax at the man nearest me. Then I looked around at them all. "All right," I said, "you've had your break."

They returned to work untypically well. They did a lot of things better after that. I said nothing about the tree to anybody. Some stories are best lying dormant for a while. That tree seemed to be one of them.

Limbing and Bucking

When your tree crashes to the ground, in the lay or out of it, your tensions may relax, but don't you. Go clean the tree. Start at the butt and work up the trunk toward the top, taking off every limb, knob, and twig. If you come to a heavy limb or crotch, remember that the main stick should be kept relatively smooth and straight. Whatever bends too much should be cut off. Continue right to the top of the tree so that you have only a long log or logs left to "buck" (cut) into pieces.

If you have two axes, or maintain a thicker swamping edge on one side of a double-bitted ax, use the thicker bit to cut knots during limbing. Each branch grows from an enlarged base that is uncommonly dense and hard. This area is the knot. Similarly dense or tangled grain will be found wherever the growth of the tree has had to turn, reverse, or intersect. The shock of striking this compact material can chip a thin ax blade that may be otherwise suited for straight-grain chopping. The corners of the ax are especially vulnerable, so they should not be ground too fine, particularly for the thicker swamping blade.

The cutting angles and positions that face you during limbing can be both dangerous and inefficient. For much of the limbing, you will stand directly on the fallen tree. In the tangle of a downed top, it is easy to overreach, or to strike an intervening limb in front of your target. The penalty for either of these errors can be a cracked or broken handle. As an emergency measure, it is a good idea to always have a roll of black electrician's tape handy. A long, overlapped wrapping of this tape can do wonders for a cracked handle, and may even make it last indefinitely if you do not abuse it again.

Not infrequently, the fallen tree will be supported by one or more branches, and will not turn until the branches are cut off. Pointing downward, and perhaps partially or entirely masked, there may be limbs that are difficult to work on, but cut them somehow, even if in segments. By clearing all limbs that you can reach on the topmost side, you will not be struck by a flailing limb if the tree does drop or roll toward you. The larger the tree, the more dangerous such branches can be.

To turn logs, or even an entire tree, if it is small enough, use a peavey. This oldtime logger's tool is a heavy pike with a hinged and dogged arm (the cant hook) toward its bottom end. With the cant hook jammed into the side of a log or tree trunk, you can exert considerable turning leverage with the peavey. If you are still unable to turn a log, even with all its branches and stubs cleared away, you will probably have to cut the log into shorter, more manageable pieces.

The longer the handle of the peavey, the more leverage you can gain. As late as November 1948, Catalog #66 of Snow & Nealley of Bangor, Maine, listed peavey handles up

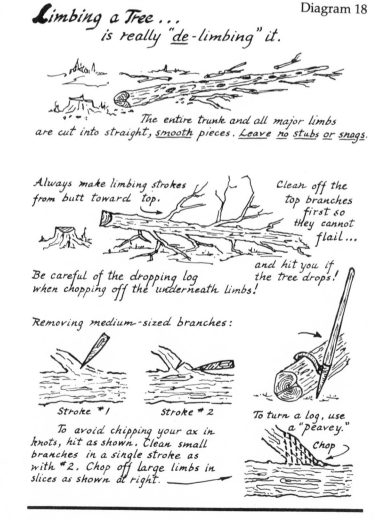

Diagram 18

Limbing a Tree... is really "de-limbing" it.

The entire trunk and all major limbs are cut into straight, smooth pieces. Leave no stubs or snags.

Always make limbing strokes from butt toward top.

Clean off the top branches first so they cannot flail...

Be careful of the dropping log when chopping off the underneath limbs!

and hit you if the tree drops!

Removing medium-sized branches:

Stroke #1   Stroke #2

To avoid chipping your ax in knots, hit as shown. Clean small branches in a single stroke as with #2. Chop off large limbs in slices as shown at right.

To turn a log, use a "peavey."

Chop

to five and a half feet. In spite of that, a peavey with a handle over three and a half feet is no longer common. In many areas today, locating any peavey is out of the question. So if you have a peavey, take care of it, for in home woodlot operations, a peavey is a handy tool. Cutting a long stick to use as a lever or pry may help, but it will not turn a log as well or as easily as a peavey.

Some knots or crotches are so large that the grain of their outer wood is as regular and even as the neighboring trunk, but inside, the grain will convolute and harden as with all knots. The reversible double-bitted ax is ideal for this purpose. Merely turn it over when the thicker swamping bit is needed. Do not let the term "softwood" fool you. Softwood knots can be vicious ax chippers, especially those of fir, spruce, hemlock, larch, and the harder pines.

In chopping off limbs, even large ones, concentrate on leaving the surface of the trunk or log as level as if the limb had never grown there. This is not just cosmetic. It is a practical means to shape logs that you can easily roll, drag, or stack compactly with no sharp protrusions to interfere with handling, truck bodies, safety, or storage. Somehow, every stub you neglect in the limbing process is almost bound to cause some kind of trouble later.

To cut a limb cleanly, always chop in the direction of the top of the tree, not toward the butt. You can clean a small branch off with a single swing, hitting the branch at its base and sending it flying. A swing that is about parallel to the log will tend to skip upward as it cuts through the branch, leaving a sharp stub that may require a second blow to remove. To compensate for this, swing on the base of the branch with just a slight downward angle. Too great a downward angle will cause your ax to dig in to no purpose.

With limbs too large to remove in one swing, aim the first blow a couple of inches higher, not parallel to the log at all, but sharply downward so the ax digs into the base of the knot at a slant, as if you were trying to cut into the log by first chopping through the knot itself. In most cases, this cut will almost sever the branch and leave little resistance within the base structure of the knot. Then a second blow that is parallel to the log surface can normally cleave off both branch and stub. The first slanted swing is also good insurance against chipping your ax in an especially hard knot.

Remove extra large limbs by chopping a notch, the bottom side of it even with the surface of the log. If necessary, expand the notch by cutting one or more higher tiers into the limb until it is all cut through. On this and any chopping of knots and crotches, chop only toward what was the top of the tree. Strokes chopped toward the butt end will tend to dig into the log rather than cut free even though you swing your ax parallel to the log. This is a common perversity of most woods. An occasion to take advantage of it is in splitting, when you should always split toward the butt, not to the top end.

Forest trees tend to have fewer and smaller limbs than trees that grow in the open. Yet a significant portion of every tree consists of limbs. Obviously, much limbwood can be used as fuel. This is another matter of priorities and what you judge most important. The old stories tell of European peasants gathering fagots for fuel. Fagots are bundles of tree branches so small that they include twigs. Such frugality seems unreal in an age and place when a cut-and-move-on

firewood contractor might leave so many whole tree tops tangled in the woods that you would scarcely be able to fight your way through the area years afterward. However, it is useful to remember that most of Europe was once forest and to guide our own affairs so that our children will not have to hunt for fagots some day.

How much limbwood you take or leave in the woodlot only you can decide. If the minimum diameter stick you intended to keep was 2″ you would clean all limbwood of any branch or segment under 2″ thick. With a sharp ax, this would take you surprisingly little time. The next step would be to cut all the limbwood into single, straight lengths, for bends and crotches are difficult to transport and worse to stack. Then cut the sticks to the lengths you need, placing them, or stacking them, where they will be available, together, out of your way, and not hiding other untrimmed pieces of suitable size.

The cutting of fallen trees and logs into transportable lengths is "bucking." Today, most commercial operations take the entire tree (after it is limbed) to a separate area or yard for bucking. The whole, delimbed tree may also be taken to a mill, with all cutting to size done there. Bucking firewood for yourself will ordinarily be on a smaller scale. The same principles apply though. You need your wood in usable lengths. The traditional length for firewood is 4′ long for stacking in a "cord." A cord is a volume measurement extending 4′ wide by 4′ high and 8′ long. As you will find out when you try accumulating one, a cord contains quite a bit of wood. Nevertheless, remember that in time past, an able axman working a good woodlot, could cut and stack two cords of wood daily. There is a measure for the modern axman to try himself against. The beginner will not find it easy to equal.

The cordwood stick subdivides well into the lesser lengths usually needed for firewood. Cut in half, a cordwood stick will give two 24″ pieces for fireplace, furnace, or the large heaters. Cut twice, the cordwood stick yields three 16″ pieces suitable for many medium and European heaters, and three cuts give four 12″ pieces for the smaller and cooking stoves. Bucking into 5′ lengths has some handling advantages and also cuts up well. A 5′ piece gives two 30″ furnace sticks. Other stick-length combinations are shown in Diagram 19.

It is not always possible to cut uniform and consecutive cordwood sticks out of a log. You may have to stop at a crotch, or take out a large knot for ease of later splitting. But other than such cases, cut your logs, beginning at the butt end, into sticks of uniform length that you can conveniently handle, stack, and transport. Cutting to ultimate use size in the woods is seldom practicable. Ground conditions often prohibit vehicular access to the woods, and time there should be conserved for what is essential, the felling, limbing, bucking, and transporting out. Also, green wood must be stacked for at least several months to dry it. A full year is better. A pile of wood will not dry as well in the woods as it will in the open, and transporting it cut into the smaller lengths means extra handling work that is needless. However, there are often other considerations also, as we shall see.

When the log is ready for bucking, measure it off, and cut a noticeable notch to mark where you will chop. Two of the more commonly used commercial measures are a belt-hung tape measure or a light stick of suitable unit length. The latter is useful because it can even be marked off into the various smaller lengths you may want as well. These marks will be more durable if they are grooved into the stick. Paint in the grooves aids easier reading, and a bright paint on the entire stick will make it harder to lose in the woods. Colored tape stapled to a marking stick at unit length points is also conspicuous, simple, durable and easily read. Length of a marking stick should fit the task. Cutting 16' logs, a 16' stick will save you time. Bucking a pile of cordwood, you need only a 4' stick.

One of the oldest and most available measures is simply the handle of your ax, the ordinary unit of measurement being two feet. Few handles are that short, so to identify where 2', or whatever other unit you wish, should be on your handle from the top of the axhead, requires some distinctive marking. The action of your hand would soon rub off the usual marking materials. A deep transverse marking groove can seriously weaken the handle as well as be an irritating roughness that can make blisters. The same applies to pounding a tack at this point to use its head as a marker. One easy solution is to inscribe sevaral longitudinal scratches or grooves on the side of the handle, ending exactly at the desired point. To some extent, paint or stain may adhere in these, but ordinary accumulation of dirt will be sufficient and will cover all else anyway.

Another common means of measuring with an ax is to know the normal distance between the top of your lower hand as it grips the handle and the top edge of the ax. Depending upon handle length, that distance may be two feet or another unit distance. If the gap is too great, elevating the first joint of your thumb will close the distance an inch or so, and extending the entire thumb will about double that. One of these combinations may give you the measuring unit you need in clear distance between your hand and the top of the ax. This may not be the most precise caliper, but no other one will ever be closer to hand.

When you are bucking on slopes, the cut-off piece or the log itself may roll. If you have a sharp ax in your hands, this can become an item of some concern, even beyond having to retrieve the runaway pieces. The hazard should have been eliminated earlier, perhaps by choosing a different lay, but side-hill bucking is not always avoidable. You can stop cut-off pieces from rolling on a slope if you chock them ahead of time, placing another chunk of wood beneath the downhill side to prevent rolling from getting started. Take advantage of natural roll obstacles such as stumps and other trees until you have the separate segments manageable.

For most bucking, you will need a felling bit, not the thicker edge you use for swamping, such as cutting knots, brush, or roots. Stand sideway on the log. Be sure that it is not going to roll, that you are well balanced, and that nothing can snag your ax. Because you will be more elevated, this means taking a fresh look for hanging branches within range after you are in position.

Cutting through a log of any size with the least waste will mean chopping to about the middle on one side, then facing about on the log and chopping into the other side until the two notches meet. To make a kerf as wide as the log is thick, chop in at 45°. Narrowing the kerf will be less wasteful but

Bucking...
Chopping the log into transport-sized pieces.

Diagram 19

Cut yourself a measuring stick of the length you will buck to. The length depends on the length of firewood you want. A bright-colored stick will not get lost.

Bucked length	Number of firewood sticks						
	12"	15"	16"	18"	20"	22"	24"
4'	4		3				2
5'	5	4			3		
5½'						3	
6'	6			4			3

Standing on the log and chopping below and between your feet, chop half into one side, then half into the other

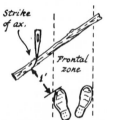

Overhead view

side until the log is cut apart. Angle of cut about 45°. Begin with a small notch and widen it in slices to deepen notch as needed.

How bucking notches are deepened.

If small, _unsupported_ sticks are not severed in one stroke, make the second stroke con-verge on the first as shown, NOT as below:

Strike of ax.

Frontal zone

1'

Position of chopper when bucking _unsupported_ small sticks on the ground.

more difficult to chop. For large logs, progressively widen the notch as you need to cut deeper, just as you would in felling. If you can turn the log as a unit, it may be helpful in some cases to finish the bottoms of these cuts away from the ground. Only about a quarter turn of the log is needed. Though these bucking cuts are made while you stand almost directly above them, your blows travel horizontally below the level of your feet at the moment of impact. You would ordinarily never hit the ground with your ax unless you overreach.

If you are cutting small sticks, do not stand on them. Never chop downward at them either, unless they are backed up against a stump, a log, or heavier stick. For if you cut through, there goes your sharp ax into the grit and maybe even into the top of a ledge. So unless you want to pick up every small stick and carry it to a stump, a backing log, or something similar—a time-consuming and onerous chore—you must find another technique to cut the smaller sticks to length. This is easily done by swinging at them sideway, just off the front of your feet. Being horizontal, such a blow will not dig into the ground if it strikes through or even misses. This is work for a sharp ax and a snappy swing, for the only thing that will back the small stick will be its own inertia. If you fail to cut through in a single swing, move to the other side of it and strike that side so the second cut converges with the first to sever the stick. Two converging cuts are more efficient than two cuts on the same line, even if the second cut is made from the opposite side. Obviously, chopping in this manner is no time to be absentminded. For each blow, have a care for how you are positioned, as explained in Chapter 8. Never strike at a target that is directly in front of you.

Chopping wood to usable lengths is bull work no matter how you view it. The thinner the piece, the more easily it is cut through. This obvious fact has practical application. Chopping through a large log takes a given amount of time and effort and wastes considerable wood in chips. Within limits, the same cutting would be more efficient with the log split into smaller sections first. The splitting time would not be lost, because the larger pieces must be split anyway, even if only so they will dry better.

But whether to split in the woods, at what lengths, and how fine the split pieces should be are all dependent upon your means of transport, time available, how long or heavy a stick you can handle, the ultimate-use length, place of stacking, and time of year. For wood chops far easier when green instead of dry, and splits best when frozen hard. Furthermore, splitting a short block of wood is disproportionately easy compared to the effort necessary to split longer lengths. Add the difficulties of performing nonfelling chores in the woods, and what you should do must depend upon your circumstances. Overall, it is usually best to get your wood home first and tend to all other problems later.

There is another wood-collecting trick that might possibly be useful sometime to you. If you fell your trees in the warm weather when the leaves are on, you can "season" the wood much quicker by omitting limbing and bucking for several weeks. The still intact leaves will draw much of the internal moisture out of the wood. The disadvantages are that after the leaves shrivel and fall off, you are faced with limbing and bucking drier wood which does not cut or handle as well. It will be somewhat lighter. Furthermore, trees lying on trees are always harder to clean up. Also, young growth can be killed underneath. However, if you need dryish wood in a hurry, this is one way to get it.

Splitting

Splitting is knocking wood apart along its grain. The heavy butts you chop down for firewood must be split at some stage and, usually, the sooner the better. The reasons for splitting are all practical. Split sections, being lighter and more manageable, are easier to transport if you are working alone. Split wood dries sooner, for as well as exposing new surfaces to the air, the bark is no longer a complete barrier to the escape of internal moisture. The latter is particularly important with birch firewood. Cutting firewood to stove or fireplace length with an ax is a far simpler task if the sticks are small enough to be cut with a minimum of strokes and minimum production of the wasted chips. The final reason for splitting is to reduce the girth of each stick to an appropriate size for its ultimate use, stovewood sticks being smaller than fireplace sticks or furnace fuel and so forth.

With renewed attention to using wood for heating purposes, a variety of new engine-driven marvels have appeared on the market to rescue home woodsmen from the drudgery of wood splitting. Most of these splitting machines feature a hydraulic ram mounting a wedge. Another type is a huge conical screw that you mount on a propped-up vehicle axle or other power source and thrust each stick against. Do not bet that these devices will split clear wood quicker than a good man swinging an ax, yet all of them are far more complex and expensive than an ax. Most of them accept only the shorter lengths of wood that are relatively easy to split anyway. There is much less need for mechanical splitters than for chain saws, but if you feel the need for a splitter, indulging yourself should do no harm. It would help, though, if you have plenty of money and storage space, are mechanically competent and inclined to cope with the inevitable frustrations of maintenance and breakdowns.

With but few exceptions, the ax you use for felling should not be used for splitting wood. The prime firewood-splitting tool is a heavy, long-handled, single-bitted ax with a relatively thick edge. Most ax manufacturers will be on your side in this instance, for the thick-lipped factory axes do make fine splitting axes just as they are sold, even if they do ordinarily need a lot of care before they are fit to use for felling. Since a sharp edge is an advantage for any ax, keep the bit of the splitting ax reasonably sharp, even though that is not nearly as critical for splitting as it is with felling. In splitting, a stroke may often plunge through your target into the ground, and keeping the bit in top condition is difficult. On the other hand, it is not really necessary.

Just as with a felling ax, both the weight and handle length of a splitting ax must be suitable for the man who does the work. However, the work is different. In splitting, you do not swing so frequently, but when you do, you want enough power to crash through your target in a single stroke. If you fail, you must repeat the stroke, and that can be tiresome.

A heavier axhead will materially add to the force you can deliver. If you had to swing that weight often, as in felling, fatigue would soon keep you from accelerating the downward plunge of the heavy ax, but the pace of splitting is normally slower, permitting your muscles to recover between strokes. Splitting is slower because the loose chunks of wood are not as stable targets as trees or logs are. In splitting, there is more frequent need to reposition yourself between strokes. Doing that slows the pace. For the average man, a four-pound ax is about right for splitting cut chunks of firewood. Procuring an ax heavier than four pounds will not be easy today, anyway. If you can get as good results splitting with an ax lighter than four pounds, by all means, use it.

The handle of the splitting ax should be long for the same reason that the head is heavy, to gain power, in this case by means of the greater speed that is realizable in the arc at the outer end of a longer handle. You sacrifice an important advantage if you do not have a handle at least 36". That is the longest handle you will find available today unless you locate a custom ax handle maker. 36" may seem awkward at first, but when you discover what you can accomplish with the greater length, you will be glad for every inch of it.

To split my modest stock of annual firewood, I use a 3½ lb. ax with 39" ash handle plus an 8 lb. maul on a 45" ash handle for use on cross-grained chunks. These combinations resulted from whatever rough handle blanks I had on hand in the past. Having used these longer handles, I would prefer a 4 lb. splitting ax on a 45" handle. More attention is required for accuracy, but this can be developed. The extra force generated by a longer handle is startling. As compared to an ordinary splitting ax, the over-heavy mauls in current vogue invite exhaustion at the end of the day. If you can make your own long handles, you will be able to split more wood faster with less effort.

Splitting Short Pieces

Diagram 20

For faster splitting, avoid handling the pieces.
Split as they lie in the pile.

When you can identify ends, split from top to butt. The splitting is easier.

Strike from outside to center of a chunk along the radii.

Splitting is easy...

along radii or directly across radii. Not so easy in between.

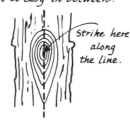

With elm and other hard-to-split woods, the easiest splitting is sometimes a series of slabs from the edges until all split.

Strike here along the line.

Knots are hard to split. When you must split them, be precise. Hit in center, aligned with major grain.

Leave the handle of the splitting ax just as thick as it was manufactured. The upper portion of the handle is frequently hit or squeezed during splitting and it will need all the strength it has. Wrapping the upper third of the handle with black electrician's tape is also good insurance against damage.

The longer handle has a longer reach to snag anything, so be sure your splitting area is clear. As distinguished from felling or chopping a log, when splitting shorter pieces of firewood, you must often move about between strokes to follow a block that escaped you, or to find the right angle to hit another chunk. You cannot be forever looking about for snags. So before splitting, clear the entire woodpile area of branches, twigs, or anything else at all. This is another reason for not doing the chore of the finer splitting in the woods.

The traditional picture of splitting firewood is one of carefully laying a stick on or against a chopping block, deliberately swinging on it, casting the split pieces aside, bending over to pick up another stick to relay it in the same spot and repeat. That is one method to split firewood, of course. But if

you want to get the job done, make up your mind not to touch a stick of wood with your hands unless absolutely necessary. And, for the vast majority of splits, forget the chopping block.

When you are ready to work on the pile of chunks to be split, take aim at the first chunk end available and swing on it. If your eye and swing do their jobs, your ax will cleave the chunk apart. Then without wasting time, aim at the end of another chunk and treat it similarly. The wood cannot move itself into position for you. You must position yourself for it. Vertical strokes are not necessary at all and the fewer you make the less often your ax will plunge through into the ground to get dull. On chunks lying sideward along the ground, and most of them will be, swing laterally as if you were playing golf. Aim, of course, but put force behind your stroke also.

Sticks will fly, sometimes 20' or more, but let them, as long as you take four precautions. Have the area clear. Be sure of your footing. Strike perpendicularly to every surface you hit at, or your ax may glance up, particularly if it is dull. Position yourself properly. Be sure that each successive target is to the left (or right) of your frontal zone, your "entire front", as explained in Chapter 8. Then if something goes wrong, the force of your swing will be directed past your feet and legs, rather than into them. Obey the rules and you will break splitting records. Disobey them and you will have trouble, probably soon.

Just keep swinging the ax, and the growing sprawl of the split pieces will surprise you. As a system for working off inhibitions, splitting wood like this is unbeatable. With short chunks of clear-grained wood, an active man can beat a machine splitter, the difference being the time the machine operator needs to load each stick into his machine. If a chunk needs turning, nudge it with your ax or kick it with your foot. If neither works, go on to a nearby chunk whose end lies right for splitting. Any pile will have dozens of proper targets facing you. Mindful of your footing and facing, climb up onto the pile. Climb all over it, splitting whatever is ready and facing you. All splitting targets are point targets. Unless you hit them vertically, keep them out of your frontal zone, hit them and keep going. When the split pieces hide the fresh chunks, then you can use your hands. Throw all the splits aside all at once and start splitting again. You will finish sooner than you have ever thought possible.

Unfortunately for ease of splitting, not all wood comes with clear, straight grain, and even some pieces without any knots at all may have a twisted, interlocked, or wavy grain that resists splitting with an ax. Strangely, some trees develop a spiral grain. The spiral may be uniform throughout the entire height of the tree, or it may straighten or even reverse its direction of twist. Certain varieties of wood are more prone to these faults than others are. But not infrequently, your ax may bind in a chunk instead of bursting it apart at a single blow.

What you should do then depends upon how heavy a piece you are stuck in. If the piece is too heavy to raise without great effort, or if your ax is only lightly embedded, work the ax loose and begin again. If you can, swing both ax and its clinging burden well into the air, reversing the heading so that the poll of the ax is underneath, and smash it down on an upended block as hard as you can. This will

"Chopping" Blocks

Diagram 21

are more commonly used for splitting pieces having knots & other hard-to-split chunks.

← 12" →

20"

Usual "chopping" block of elm or other hard-to-split wood. If too high, the block will be unstable. If too short, it will not be so easy to use and will also split sooner itself.

To split difficult pieces that your ax is stuck in, raise both piece and ax above your head and slam them back down forcefully on the block, *ax first*. This will use all the weight of the piece to split itself on upraised bit of the ax. It usually works!

Piece to be split ⟶

10"

15"

"Y" type of splitting block holds pieces securely while you split them. Make this type of block from a cut-off section of a large tree crotch.

---

drive the falling weight of the chunk down on the bit of the ax. As a splitting method, it is much more effective than as if the lodged ax were uppermost.

Such a stroke will usually split the chunk, but if several repetitions of this fail to split the piece, you may have to knock the ax free by pounding the top edge of the poll with another stick. Never use a steel hammer or another ax for this purpose as you can easily deform the soft steel of the poll. When the ax is free, then split the balky chunk by working along a different line of its grain.

. The need to split difficult chunks by upending a single-bitted ax when a chunk is lodged on its bit is why the double ax is not suited for splitting work. Under those circumstances, a double ax would be driven deep into the chopping block where retrieving it would be difficult. At the same time, the lower bit would help destroy the block that much sooner by splitting *it*. But as well as getting stuck and wrecking the block, a double ax used in this manner is also less efficient anyway. The energy of a descending chunk is cushioned as the lower bit is driven into the block. With the single-bitted ax, the smash of the flat-faced poll against the

unyielding block transmits virtually all energy of the falling chunk into splitting itself on the upraised bit.

There are two common types of so-called chopping blocks. More realistically, they should be termed "splitting blocks." Splitting the shorter firewood chunks as just described, you will not put primary reliance upon a chopping block and can really manage very well without one, most often by slamming upended blocks down upon the chunks that are still not split. Nevertheless, a chopping block is a convenience to have available.

The more common design of block is a sawed section of log large enough to stand on end without tipping and having a level top to strike against or to lay chunks on for splitting. To be stable, the block should be eleven inches or more in diameter. The height should be one or two feet. You can deliver a more powerful blow against a shorter block, but if it is too short, it is less durable. A section of tree crotch or a heavy chunk of wavy-grained log will make good chopping blocks. Where there is a choice, chopping blocks are often made of elm, which is a hard-splitting wood.

The other type of chopping block is usually used solely for splitting short pieces of wood. It is a Y section of a tree fork about 10" or more in diameter, laid sideway on the ground and with all ends cut off to about a foot long. The forked legs provide a convenient recess in which to lean sticks or chunks while you split them. With the bottom ends of the pieces to be split resting on the ground, the impact of splitting may often be more resilient than is desirable. The side grain of the forked block is also more resilient than the end grain of the log-chunk block, so it is also not as good for smashing upended chunks down on. But for somebody who does not feel safe splitting wood as if he were playing golf, the Y block offers a secure prop for splitting shorter pieces.

No stick of wood splits exactly as another does, for trees differ by individuals and species just as all living things do. But all types of woods also have a few similarities too. In splitting wood of any length or size, split down, not up. That is, a split will run more easily from what was the top of the tree to the butt rather than in the other direction. When a split is started, extend it downward and inward. Whether log, chunk, or smaller stick, first split it in half. Then subdivide the halves if they are still too large, and so on. Do not attempt to split a smaller section out from a log before splitting the entire log in half.

If you are splitting chunks and other short pieces, hit the flat of the top end to start the split, rather than the edge of the top end. But on logs, or any large pieces requiring the use of wedges, set the wedge on the edge of the top end and pointing diagonally down into the central axis of the log.

The general rule is to split any larger piece on or toward the central axis, or what was the center line of the tree, rather than from the inside toward the outside. Apply this principle even to subdivided lengths. However, there are exceptions. When a log has been split into quarters, or six or eight pieces, these lengths will have cross-sections like pieces of pie. These lengths usually split well directly across the piece-of-pie sections. So the rule is to split along a radius of the log or perpendicular to a radius. Splits that hit the radii at other angles will often be more difficult.

A special case using the perpendicular-split technique is with a chunk of wood that is difficult to split—elm, for

Splitting Logs

Diagram 22

Split logs from top to butt and from outside to center. First maul-hit, or first wedge, should be set on edge of the top end.

← Toward butt end

Cut connecting sections and splinters with maul or ax.

Some logs will take a wedge at first, then "spit" it out. To stop that, start two or more wedges on line and tap each gently in turn until the crack opens up.

A log may crack open the entire length of one side, yet still not fall apart. Turn it over with a peavey. Usually, hitting the blind crack with the maul will part the two halves.

CAUTION ... Did you leave wedges in the other side? If so, where?

instance. For a chunk that cannot be easily split in the usual fashion with an ax, you may be able to split off a succession of narrow slabs from the sides, proceeding around the chunk until it is completely split. Here, there are certainly many radii at the sides of each slab that are not split across perpendicularly. But the difference is small if the slabs are kept narrow, and this system often works.

Another special case concerns convoluted grain such as in large knots, or a fork area, which is really the same thing. If a chunk contains one of these areas, split off any straight-grain wood that you can, however you can. Let the convoluted grain alone. Removing one straight-grain slab will often expose another that can be removed by splitting across the radii. Surprisingly, you can often split away most of the straight-grained wood in small pieces until there is only a relatively small section left, with a grain as crooked as the lines of a jigsaw puzzle. Naturally, this is easier to do with shorter pieces of wood.

You can even split through large knots, though not necessarily with an ax. Strike the knot squarely along its lengthwise center line. If you hit accurately, the knot will

split almost as easily as if it were not a knot. But do not even bother to try to split a knot off-center. You can chop or saw a knot apart, but knots seldom split except precisely down the middle.

Good as an ax is for splitting, it just does not have enough heft to open up the heavier sticks or most logs. For them you may need a splitting maul, a tool resembling a sledge hammer having an ax-type bit on one end. In a return of popularity, steel splitting mauls have reappeared on the market in weights ranging from four to ten pounds. To supplement a four-pound splitting ax, an eight-pound maul is about right. The average man will be able to swing it for the limited number of successive strokes that splitting usually demands. A ten-pound maul might be even better, but to swing one efficiently, you had better be pretty rugged. Ten pounds is a lot to bring down snappily.

A patented and relatively expensive wood-splitting maul has just appeared on the market. It uses the force of the descending maul to thrust recessed levers out from each side of the maul bit on impact. If all goes well, this sideward thrust will split the log or chunk of wood. The claim is made

Steel Wood-Splitting Tools

Diagram 23

(Shown in approximate scale at useful weights.)

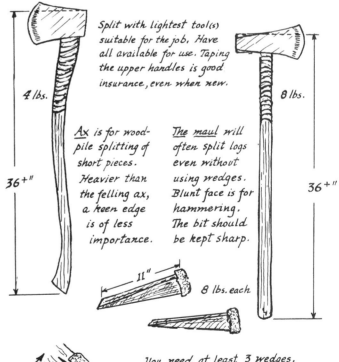

Split with lightest tool(s) suitable for the job. Have all available for use. Taping the upper handles is good insurance, even when new.

4 lbs. 36+"

Ax is for woodpile splitting of short pieces. Heavier than the felling ax, a keen edge is of less importance.

8 lbs. 36+"

The maul will often split logs even without using wedges. Blunt face is for hammering. The bit should be kept sharp.

11" 8 lbs. each

You need at least 3 wedges. Lighter ones are too short. To remove a wedge, pound against the crack, not with it. Guard your eyes against flying fragments of wedge.

that this device will not get stuck during use. That appears likely, because the patented levers permit the maul bit to penetrate wood only a little over an inch. Unfortunately, the same fact prohibits use in deeper cracks to cut stringy sections connecting two pieces, or to follow a crack that is open on one side. So the patented maul is of limited value in splitting logs. Used on short, easily split chunks, the patented maul gives excellent results. However, for such work, the much lighter splitting ax would be both faster and less tiring to use.

Even a maul is seldom enough to open the larger logs. Then you use the hammer end of the maul to drive a steel wedge into the log. How and where you place the wedge is important. Follow the same principles that apply to splitting with an ax. If your first wedge opens a substantial crack, you may be able to save some effort by finishing the job with the blade end of the maul. If the crack is stubborn in developing, or does not appear at all, start another wedge below it along the probable line of split and, if needed, another below that, and so on until the log falls apart. On large logs, take care that neither half rolls against you when the log falls apart.

Forcefully used, a steel maul is a potent splitting tool. With a little extra effort in starting a split, you can often split an occasional large log with the maul alone. But with most hardwood logs over 10″ in diameter, you are going to need wedges. And unless the wood is unusually clear and straight-grained, if you need one wedge, you had better have three, for one or two are often not enough. Small wedges are an abomination, for to open the wood wide enough, there is a tendency to drive small wedges too far in, hiding their tops. If they are thus masked, you cannot easily knock them out of position to help extend the crack farther down. Never drive a wedge in over three quarters of its length. With one quarter protruding, you can still retrieve it. To do that, hitting it side to side along the crack is next to useless. Hit the top of the wedge perpendicularly to the direction of the split. These hits help the stresses trying to close the crack to spit the wedge up and out. A few blows of the maul are usually enough.

Sometimes it can be quicker to open the same split down opposite sides of the log simultaneously rather than working a single split entirely down one side. If you do work both sides at once, be careful to avoid hitting the tips of wedges you have driven in from the opposite side of the log.

On hardwood logs or chunks, it is not uncommon for your maul or wedge to bounce back off the surface of the wood. A similar irritation is to have wedges be spit back out of the log, sometimes popping their own length into the air. This can be discouraging, but the same logs that will do this are apt to burst apart entirely if you force their elastic limits. Try to get two or more wedges started near each other in the same line of grain. Then tap each one alternately in turn, but not too hard. In most cases, that will open a crack along the entire piece. If it does not, you will have to try another, more vulnerable side and begin again. Strangely, splitting down the center of a knot may be the trick to start one of these difficult pieces.

Our forebears often used wooden wedges, carefully hardening them by heat. A "glut," as it was known, was of hardwood, and the better ones had rawhide wrapping, or even a ring of iron or steel around their tops to prevent splitting when struck. To seat the ring and permit passage for it in the crack, the top end of the glut was of smaller diameter than the upper part of the wedge section. No wooden wedge can equal a steel wedge in beginning a split, but it can do marvelous work in expanding a crack that has been started with steel. Cutting, shaping, and seasoning a few wooden wedges so as to have them on hand is a good way to save on steel wedges.

Such ideas of economy and "make-do" are a throwback to the past. The earlier Americans had little steel for any purpose, even hammers to pound gluts. The soft iron poll of the early American axes was not suited for customary use as a hammer, nor was the ax really heavy enough for pounding gluts. Furthermore, the pounding of an iron or steel hammer would soon destroy any wooden wedge, even if the top were bound. So it was only natural that wooden hammers were used to drive the wooden wedges. The type of hammer that resembled a great mallet was termed a "beetle," To make it last longer, the wooden head was also bound about its hammering faces, just as the gluts were, usually with a fitted iron ring.

Wooden Tools to Split Wood
Diagram 24

They used to split a lot of wood.

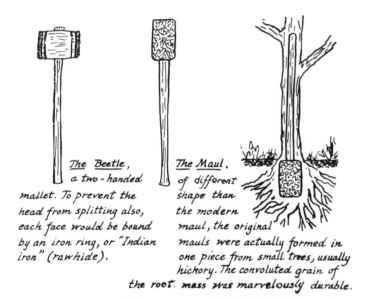

The Beetle, a two-handed mallet. To prevent the head from splitting also, each face would be bound by an iron ring, or "Indian iron" (rawhide).

The Maul. of different shape than the modern maul, the original mauls were actually formed in one piece from small trees, usually hickory. The convoluted grain of the root mass was marvelously durable.

The GLUT: a reinforced wedge, its top bound in rawhide or iron ring.

Ordinary hardwood wedges also.

Many wooden tools, and particularly these, were carefully heat-cured months ahead. But starting the split was too much to ask of wood. That was done with a precious iron "starter" wedge.

The pattern of early wooden hammer that was formerly termed a "maul" was the bottom section of a young tree, the best ones being of hickory. The tree was dug up, and its roots were cut off in the ground. The root stem area was smoothed to form a heavy, elongated mass that was the hammer head. The handle was the first three feet or so of the tree trunk, which was suitably reduced in diameter for easy grasping. The great advantage of the maul was that the gnarled grain of the root stem was not only dense and hard, but also so convoluted that it resisted splitting under repeated impact. Although strange-appearing to our eyes, the wooden maul was an efficient tool to drive gluts. Even today, both maul and glut are worth remembering if for no other reason than that they will do the job and cost you little or nothing besides your labor to make them.

How well different woods split differs greatly, both among varieties of trees and among individual trees of the same variety. And pieces of the same tree can have the greatest difference, as is easily compared when splitting both straight-grained sections and then knots, or merely an area of twisted grain. Unfortunately, some trees grow with a twisted or wavy grain, though some species are worse than others. For ease of splitting, look for a straight trunk without branches. This will be a forest tree, not one grown in a dooryard. The branches of trees grown in the open tend to be lower, larger, and more numerous. Accompanying them is the dense and twisted grain of knots that makes difficult splitting.

Remembering the foregoing and considering only some of the better and more common hardwoods, you will find that red oaks and white ash are among the best splitting firewoods. Maples and birches often split well also. Yet both of the latter not infrequently hide a wavy grain that would be beautiful on the surface of polished furniture but can be pure misery to split. Black ash, wild cherry, and most fruitwoods will all split decently in good straight sections. Hickories, beech, white oak, and hornbeam may not be the best splitting woods, but you can split them. They are prime firewoods, so neglecting them because they needed a little extra splitting effort would not make sense.

Elm has a reputation of being about the toughest common wood to split. Early hockey stick blades were once made of elm because of its resistance to splitting. Yet not all elm is that tough. As with many other items in life, not even all sticks are what they seem to be beforehand. You learn only when you hit one. If you have firewood of any size, you must split it to use. So just go do it. And remember, the shorter the piece, the easier to split.

The Right Wood

In selecting the right firewood trees you are pretty much limited by where you live. Different trees are native to different parts of the United States and Canada, some trees being widespread and others quite localized. Many fine firewoods are found only in the eastern regions. But everywhere except in cities, and often even there, firewood can be located somewhere.

Local dumps frequently have a plethora of good firewood discarded by contractors and municipal agencies. Highway construction projects often waste thousands of prime firewood trees. Many landowners may welcome your aid in thinning their woodlot so their better trees will grow more vigorously. You may even find an owner who wants a lot completely cleared and who will gladly give you the wood for the taking. By keeping alert for where wood is available and properly approaching the owners you may be able to corner all the wood you can handle. Real estate agents with lots for sale are also worth approaching. Present your proposition so that it is advantageous to the man who has wood he wants to get rid of. To properly thin stands destined for timber or other high-value uses is performing a needed service. You need only to present it in that light. If you are fortunate enough to have a woodlot of your own, you will not have to hunt for wood. But even if you do not own your own lot, do not give up, for even today there is still lots of wood. The amount that rots on the stump every year, or that is left in the woods to rot after some lumbering operations, is still startlingly large.

Diagram 25 shows what were the prevalent firewoods of the United States, and undoubtedly much of Canada also, up to the time that oil and natural gas became the primary fuels for home and industry. The northern regions listed adjoin Canada and the regional species of trees would have been common to both sides of the border. It is clear that each region burned what was available within it. Presumably the woods are listed in order of quantity used, showing that each of the listed varieties was not equally plentiful. Hickory, for instance, is not listed first in any region although it is probably the premier North American firewood. Perhaps there was never enough hickory to meet the demand. This is certainly true today.

Actual identification of various trees is beyond the scope of this book. If you are totally unfamiliar with the firewood varieties of your area, enlist the help of somebody who does know local trees. There are many fine books on the market that will make you expert enough to identify the more common firewoods native to your area.

In viewing the living trees, the most obvious differences from a distance are those of size, shape, and coloration. These characteristics vary by the kind of tree, of course, but may also differ because of the distinctive local soil, climate, weather, drainage, and even which side of a hill a tree may be growing on. As you come closer to a tree, you will be aware of differences in limb placement, quantity, size, and angle of growth. The bark of separate families of trees differs noticeably, the bark of the white or paper birch being just one dramatic example. The leaves and leaf buds of every variety of tree have identifiable differences, as do most of their flowers, seeds, and fruits.

A man who has worked extensively with trees and timber will be able to identify most woods merely by the appearance of the interior wood grain, whether transverse, radial, or tangential. The sapwood of a tree, the lighter colored wood growing next to the bark will usually have a different appearance from the central core of the darker heartwood. These can all become familiar with experience. Many trees even have a distinctive odor to the freshly cut wood. The scent of red cedar wood is probably known to most people even though they have never even seen a cedar tree, white or red, and would be unlikely to recognize one if they did see it.

There are many more American woods than it is feasible to list here. There are also many ways to classify them for identification purposes. One simple way is dividing "woody" plants into trees, shrubs, and lianas, or vines. Virtually all firewood is cut from trees, though some shrublike plants burn very well also. The principal difference between a shrub and a tree is really one of size. However, some trees remain shrublike in size where the climate, soil nutrients, and available moisture are not as plentiful, and the reverse situation is likewise true. Under some circumstances, even vines have been used as firewood.

Usable woods are commonly classified as either softwoods or hardwoods. The time-honored classifications must be recognized because they are generally used, but they are not altogether accurate. Some softwoods are relatively hard and some hardwoods are quite soft. The softwoods are the conifers, the cone-bearing trees, most of which are evergreens, pines, firs, and spruces, for example. But not all conifers are

Diagram 25

PRINCIPAL WOODS USED FOR FUEL,
UNITED STATES 1630 – 1930*
(from U.S. Department of Agriculture Circular #641)

Region	Species
New England*	oaks, maple, birch, pines, beech, hickory
Middle Atlantic States*	oaks, maple, birch, pines, beech, hickory
South Atlantic States	pines (yellow), oaks, hickory, gum, maple, ash
Lake States*	oaks, maple, tamarack (larch), aspen (poplar), birch, pines
Central Region	oaks, maple, pines (yellow), birch, hickory, beech
Eastern Gulf Region	pines (yellow), oaks, hickory, gum, ash, chestnut
Lower Mississippi Region	pines (yellow), oaks, gum, hickory, ash, maple
Prairie States*	oaks, cottonwood, hickory, maple, ponderosa pine, walnut
Northern Rocky Mountains*	ponderosa pine, Douglas fir, lodgepole pine, aspen (poplar), cottonwood, larch
Southern Rocky Mountains	juniper, pinon, aspen (poplar), ponderosa pine, oaks
Northern Pacific Region*	Douglas fir, ponderosa pine, larch, oaks, alder
Southern Pacific Region	oaks, ponderosa pine, Douglas fir, redwood, eucalyptus

*Trees do not recognize national boundaries. In regions marked with an asterisk, most of the listed trees are also common to the adjoining regions of Canada. Proceeding north into interior Canada where the climate is more severe, the predominating trees are conifers, especially black and white spruce. Useful broadleaf trees become limited to white birch, aspen (poplar), willow, and finally only a few white birch.

evergreens. Cypress and larch, both eastern and western larches, are conifers, yet completely shed their needles each autumn. Hardwoods are the broadleaf trees we are all familiar with—oaks, poplars, birches, maples, elms, cottonwoods, hickories, ashes, and many others. Most of the better firewoods are hardwoods. Generally, the harder and more dense a wood, the better firewood it makes. Some broadleaf trees produce wood that is relatively soft, but they are termed hardwoods nevertheless.

Softwoods are widely used for construction purposes. They are adequately strong and do not split as easily as most hardwoods. On average, softwoods, being generally less dense and lighter than hardwoods, do not contain as much fuel value per cord, the volume unit that firewood is usually sold in. Being resinous also, most softwoods do not burn as cleanly. This is a real disadvantage, for deposits from such burnt wood will rapidly accumulate in stovepipes and chimneys.

Diagram 26, showing "Characteristics of Firewoods," lists twenty-eight woods generally found in the eastern United States. The total number of varieties within this area is several times that of the list, but the ones given include those likely to be most available for fuel use today. The names listed are common, but not equally so for all areas. Larch is also known as both tamarack and hack. Poplar includes both popple and aspen. Many names are also generic and include numerous kindred varieties, as with alder, yellow pine, and

spruce. For such cases, the name listed seemed adequately representative of the included group.

It is best to remember that any arbitrary grouping of living things has an artificial quality. You will appreciate this better with increased experience when you will see for yourself that the characteristics of any particular wood may often vary more within its family than outside it. Yet to sort anything out, reasonable generalizations must be made. For firewood trees, these are listed in Diagram 26.

As concerns differences between Diagram 26 and other published lists, in 1979 the *Boston Sunday Globe* complained that firewoods were ranked differently in six published sources. For the record, Diagram 26 reflects the results of experience insofar as individual variation in particular trees permits.

Just a casual glance at the table shows that no single wood is best in all respects. For firewoods, naturally the most important matter is how good a fuel a wood is. A satisfactory fuel must not only give off heat, but must do so steadily while being relatively clean and long lasting. Woods that spit, crackle, and pop while burning may make a cheery sound, depending on how your ear is tuned, but would be an abomination to have loaded into an open fireplace or open-burning stove. Until the sticks were pretty much reduced to charcoal, glowing and blazing embers might shoot out onto your floor at any time. Any wood will occasionally spit as steam combustion products in some interior cells burst their walls, but many of the lighter woods often keep spitting until they are almost consumed.

Confined within a stove, ordinary spitting does no harm. But many woods that spit are also resinous and produce much soot while burning. The beautiful bark of the white birch has this fault. Deposited on the flue and in the chim-

ney, this soot combined with other distillates forms a stinking mess often termed creosote. From a smoldering fire, liquid creosotes can drip back, reverse fashion, down out of your stovepipe seams into your living quarters with an odor you will not soon get rid of. Heavy deposits of creosote in the chimney can ignite there with results that are potentially

CHARACTERISTICS OF FIREWOODS
Diagram 26

Type of Wood H = Hardwood S = Softwood	Fuel Quality (makes quiet, clean, long-lasting fire)	Will Burn Even When Green	Will Burn Only When Dry	Spits Often While Burning	Ease of Split-ting	Resists Rot
Alder (H)	Fair				V. good	Poor
Apple (H)	Outstanding				Good	Good
Ash, black (H)	Good		x		Good	Fair
Ash, white (H)	Excellent	x (–)			Excel.	Fair
Basswood (H)	Poor		x		Fair	Poor
Beech (H)	Excellent				Fair	Fair
Birch, gray (H)	Very good				Good	Poor
Birch, white (H)	Good				V. good	Poor
Birch, yellow (H)	Excellent				Good	Fair
Cedar (S)	Poor			x	Excel.	Outstdg.
Cherry, black (H)	Excellent				V. good	Excel.
Elm, white (H)	Good				Poor	Good
Fir, balsam (S)	Poor		x	x	Fair	Poor
Hemlock, East. (S)	Poor		x	xx	Fair	V. good
Hickory, shag. (H)	Outstanding				Fair	Fair
Larch, Amer. (S)	Good		x		Fair	V. good
Locust, black (H)	Outstanding				Fair	Outstdg.
Maple, red (H)	Very good				V. good	Fair
Maple, sugar (H)	Excellent				Good	Poor
Oak, red (H)	Excellent				Excel.	Good
Oak, white (H)	Outstanding				Fair	Excel.
Pine, red. (S)	Fair				Good	Fair
Pine, white (S)	Poor		x	x	Fair	Good
Pine, yellow (S)	Good				V. good	Good
Poplar (H)	Fair		x		Fair	Poor
Spruce (S)	Poor		x	x	Fair	Poor
Sycamore (H)	Good				Good	V. good
Willow, black (H)	Fair		x		Fair	Poor

disastrous. These are reasons enough for not adding the lighter softwoods to your woodpile unless you have nothing else to use.

There is great difference in the density and weight of different woods. A cubic foot of seasoned live oak, an evergreen oak native to southeastern and south central United States, weighs 62 pounds, or practically heavy enough to sink in water even though it is dry. A cubic foot of seasoned white pine weighs only 25 pounds. Yet pound for pound, any seasoned wood has about equal fuel value to that of any other variety of wood. Most hardwoods, however, are heavier than softwoods because the hardwoods grow more compactly and, being more dense in their cellular structure, have more fuel value per cord, a measure of volume, not of weight. So the heavier hardwoods are preferred for firewood since, for a given heat value, you handle less wood and can store it in a smaller space.

Starting a fire can be a fussy job, usually needing tinder and kindling. The less dense softwoods make better tinder because they are more easily heated to ignition temperature. The resinous quality of most softwoods also helps, for the resins also usually ignite at lower temperatures. The soot and creosotes generated from a small amount of tinder do little harm, but beyond that, keep the lighter, resinous softwoods marked "Poor" in Diagram 26 out of your woodpile. The only exception to burning any quantity of the less desirable softwoods should be when that is the only wood you have on hand and you have the means to clean your chimney out afterward.

The better firewoods fissure then break apart as they burn, dropping incandescent chunks from the burning sticks. These coals still have the capacity to generate heat, and as they give it up, their heat aids the combustion above. Then as the burning sticks become thinner, the pile of coals underneath mounts and much of the residual heat is contained in the coals themselves. This steadier, sustained heat is characteristic of the choice hardwood fuels. "Coaling" is conspicuously absent in both the lighter softwoods and the lighter hardwoods. Both of the latter tend to burn quickly with precious little heat left after the last flame. Alder sticks have been called biscuit wood for instance, because their quick blaze "lasts only for a batch of biscuits," though while it lasts, it is intense.

You can use only the wood you have available. That must be. But the better wood it is, the longer it will keep you warm and the less you will have to clean flues and chimneys.

Effects of Temperature and Weather

In the woods, extremes of summer heat are moderated. Because of this, there are no particular problems associated with working in the woods in the warmer months. It is just business as usual. But in the winter, the cold is always a hazard. Working in it requires care and extra thought.

One winter morning years ago, I was detailed to clean off a fence line, cutting down a ribbon of trees grown high during twenty years of neglect. Some of the trees were sizable. The clear sky was cloudless blue and the snow glittered. The temperature when I left the house had been near 0°F (−18°C). As I set to work with my ax, I progressively shed jacket, sweaters, and mittens until my upper body was clad only in my undershirt. Remembering the thermometer, I was surprised. For some reason, the pleasure I felt then at that method of conquering cold is a memory that has stayed.

In harvesting forest products, winter work is traditional. Swinging an ax, you are virtually guaranteed to remain warm as long as you continue working and are not wet. Under such circumstances, the cold is invigorating.

But to work continually in low temperatures, you must wear the right clothing. It must retain body warmth and also keep you dry. These two objectives can coincide. For example, if you wear long wool underwear under wool outer garments, you can wallow in snow and still keep dry and warm. The double-layered wool combination is so effective because little heat escapes to the outer surface to melt snow and wet you. If you could only keep dry, a single layer of cotton, consisting of only shirt and pants can keep you surprisingly warm if you do not stop moving. But if you wear only that, snow would melt wherever it rubbed against you. Then both you and your cotton clothing would be wet. On a cold day, that could mean trouble. Wet clothing steals body warmth rapidly, and outdoors in the winter you will have little to spare.

In selecting cold weather clothing, remember that two light garments are warmer than a single heavy one of equal combined weight. The advantage of the two worn together is the space between them. Slight as it may be, the space adds to the total insulation. Two garments are also better than one because you can shed half your insulation when you become too warm while working, yet still wear the other half. With a single heavy coat or jacket, there is always a tendency to keep it on while working until you have become overheated and perhaps wet with perspiration. And moisture, whether from the inside or outside, reduces a garment's ability to insulate.

If you can afford to pay for it, wool is still the king of outdoor garment materials for many reasons. It is not bulky for the insulation it offers, it is unexpectedly durable, and to some extent it can even give protection against rain. No other material (except other, exotic, and even more expensive, animal fibers) can beat the moisture-absorption capacity of wool. That permits the wool garment to take your perspiration and still keep you dry and, therefore, warm. Many of the modern garment materials are splendid, but when it comes to a cloth that will stand up to work and still protect you from cold, wool—good wool—is the first choice.

Modern cold weather footwear is far better than our ancestors had. But it follows the same protective principles that have always been used. You must have dry insulation between you and the cold. This can be attained with the "Mickey Mouse" boot featuring an actual air space contained within the boot walls or a variety of other impermeable layers and sealed foams. In such boots, your feet can be literally slopping in your own sweat, but warm because the sealed insulation keeps the heat in. But if the insulation barrier is ever breached, the insulation space will soon fill with moisture from the inside or out. Thereafter, unless repaired, those boots will be cold. Boots of this type, then, require more attention than other boots.

In boots of simpler design, you provide your own insulation, from either extra socks or felt liners. Either can become wet from perspiration and must be changed or dried after work if your feet are to keep warm. An outer boot that "breathes," letting your perspiration escape through its pores, is desirable unless an even greater amount of external moisture enters the boots via the same route. A combination that has stood the test of time is the rubber-bottomed boot with a high leather upper. Where there is opportunity to exchange dry socks to wear in them, these boots are practical.

For woods use, leather "choppers" are still deservedly popular as handwear. These roomy leather mittens are designed to accommodate knit woolen liners which can be removed as weather permits, or as you warm up. The better choppers are made of buckskin, which will usually last longer because it remains more flexible, even after being dried following use. Here again, the insulation-will-keep-you-dry principle also holds. When handling much wood with snow on it, keep the liners in the choppers or else work bare-handed. Used for handling much snow without the liners, the choppers will be warm enough to melt snow and shortly become soaked. You can partially prevent such wetting by regularly treating your choppers and boots with a leather dressing or grease. Doing this also lengthens the life of the leather.

Like other clothing, cold weather headgear has also had its styles. Knit stocking caps are traditional and have become popular again via the passion for skiing. The various models of visor and earflap caps are still practical because ear protection can be necessary in winter. In severe cold with wind, parka hoods make sense. One of the better items is a slip-on half-parka, protecting the entire shoulder area as well as the head and neck. Secured by straps under the arms, it offers exceptional working protection from storm or wind, yet easily slips off to fit in a pocket.

It is not only the body that is affected by cold. A 19th-century ax manufacturer published warning that axes should be warmed before using, lest they be too brittle. How a woodsman should manage that all day amid winter snows was not explained.

Even so, that manufacturer had a point. Cold can be a critical factor in the operation of machinery. Even commercial lumbering rigs are limited by winter rigors. Below -20°F, many materials begin to get brittle, including steel. And better steels, being harder to begin with, are no exception. At -50°F, few logging operations will attempt to continue work. Not only taut chains may snap like glass. It is too easy to crack massive castings given a sudden stress in deep cold. On large machines, one little crack in the wrong location could mean a loss of many thousand dollars.

Nor will personal and equipment worries be the only problems. In severe cold, trees are also more brittle. When felling, the hinge may give way earlier than expected. With a tree that topples prematurely, you will not have finished the back cut and the hinge may be crudely shaped. In this case, it would be less effective in controlling the direction of lay. That may be unavoidable. What you can do is chop the notch evenly rather than favoring first one end of the hinge and then the other. Even progress of the notch will give you whatever control is possible until the moment of fall. But be ready for anything. The gravity that is pulling your tree down will be working, cold or no cold.

Under ordinary cold conditions, winter is the best season to both cut and transport wood, but not unless you are equipped for it. If deep snow blocks access to and from your woodlot, forget about it until mid-spring at least. Early spring is mudtime.

Maybe you could just cut wood during the winter, stacking it for hauling when the roads are open. Snowmobiles make almost any woodlot accessible all winter. Snowmobiles can even draw wood, though that is really testing your machine. If you have a horse that you can work in the woods, snow need not be a barrier at all, and you can probably draw your wood out for pickup at roadside. Hauling logs in snow is not only easier, but usually much cleaner, there being no free mud and sand to coat logs with destructive grit.

When ice sheaths the ponds and streams, an entirely new scene beckons. Traveling on ice may seem to be the easiest route to where you want to go, but test it before you trust it. Two inches of clear ice will hold a man and four inches will support you with a horse. Ten inches of clear ice should hold anything you put on it unless you are a contractor with heavy equipment. The rub is that you will not often encounter clear ice. And if you do, will you know where springs or currents have kept a skimmed-over surface treacherously thin? Unless you are intimately familiar with a body of water and know how it freezes, you would be wise to avoid it. Not many people can climb out of a hole in thin ice without help.

Among the advantages of winter lumbering is being able to better see what trees you have and more easily identify the trees you should take. For cruising, you might have to use snowshoes. For chopping, you ordinarily would not. Snowshoes interfere with your feet while you chop and are too clumsy for safety purposes. A shovel can be useful for winter tree felling. It is not easy to kick the snow away from a tree so you can cut the stump at the same height you would cut it if there were no snow. But to avoid waste and to keep low stumps, dig down through the snow somehow. Remember to open up your escape route also.

When it comes to actual chopping, the colder the better. Chips clear from the frozen wood better in the cold. The ax will not bind in the cut as may happen in warm weather. Without leaves, each tree falls cleaner, with less likelihood of lodging in other trees. Even evergreens slide through other trees better in the cold. For the same reason, there is less damage done to young growth, even though twigs will snap off easier at low temperatures. The cold gives hardwood logs a resonant quality, and in sharp winter air the ring of chopping can carry a great distance. Not only is winter felling easier, but the wood will not dry as fast after being cut. This allows you more time to cut the wood to its ultimate lengths while it is still green, or partially green, and consequently with substantially less effort.

It is in the splitting of wood that the results of frost are most dramatic. Lloyd Simpson, who taught me so much when I was young, said that cold-soaked maple logs hit properly with a single stroke of the maul would burst apart with a report "like a gunshot." As I had learned to appreciate his uncanny reading of wood, I never doubted that statement, especially backed as it was by the precision of his awesome strength. Of my own experience, I know that when it is quite cold, heavy cordwood butts will sometimes fly apart at a blow. During warmer weather, the same genre of stick might require multiple hits and perhaps even wedging.

In speaking of working in cold, it is relevant to mention alcohol. A time-honored remedy for shivering is a wee nip or two, or three or four, or maybe more. But outdoor imbibers should know the mechanism involved. Alcohol downed in any mixture expands the capillaries in the skin. This is what imparts the warmth of the bar and cocktail floor. In those heated chambers, you may safely dissipate heat, and should, for the surroundings are often balmy when not torrid. Amid snow and ice, the conditions are shockingly different. The wasted heat you release to the skin by drinking may be the heat you need to keep a hand or cheek from being frostbitten later. Even sadder endings have been recorded. A good rule is to let the wee nip wait until you are back inside shelter with its blazing fire.

A specialty item for winter work in areas where you may have to return to where you worked previously are ice cleats for the feet. It is common for snow to turn to ice where it has been tramped down or rolled down in vehicle tracks. These tracks can make dangerous walking. Under ordinary circumstances an able man could maneuver such trails without taking a header, but ice may seriously slow him down, particularly if he is carrying a heavy load such as a 10″-thick length of cordwood. The old woodsmen wore cleated boots, but they are less common today. A compromise item for home use is a pair of cleats that strap to boots. Some hardware and sport stores still have them. In a pinch, you can make your own.

Winter does not last forever. One spring that was recent enough so that I should have known better, I drove down a woods road. I felt confident in a four-wheel-drive vehicle and the road was gravel-topped. Just beyond a well-used turnoff, a little pile of three rocks squatted beside the road. It was a warning signal I had seen before. To continue past it demanded caution. I stopped, left the vehicle and walked ahead fifty yards or more. The road was firm and unbroken except for tell-tale ruts beside the stone warning. To the side, a ditch paralleled the roadbed with a trickle of spring drainage flowing calmly downhill.

Even the ruts had dried out. There was plenty of room to pass around them anyway. The road looked good as far as I could see. I made up my mind. It was all systems go. Jumping back in the driver's seat, I restarted the engine and headed straight past the unblinking pile of three stones.

It was a short trip. In less than thirty feet the steering wheel snapped left. As the front of the vehicle responded, the entire left side also dropped and forward motion stopped with a lurch. I had lived through enough of that sort of thing before to know when to cut the engine. I clambered clumsily out, feeling stupid. The left front wheel hub was level with the road and the left rear almost as bad. The holes beside each wheel were filling with water. In the front hole, a piece of ice floated. There was no ice on top of the ground. I had broken through a rind of subsurface frost.

Fortunately, I had a shovel, a heavy knife, and loggers had left stubs of pulpwood lying about. Even so, it took me two hours of prying and filling to escape that trap. I was lucky to get out without being hauled out. The moral is, if you are entering the woods in early spring, stay on roads known to be safe. Otherwise, walk.

18

Handling Your Wood

Even a zealot about wood heat might admit that there are two sides to one central aspect of it, that of convenience. Heating with oil is simple. The oilman comes, sticks his hose in the filler pipe, and your thermostat does the rest. All you do is pay the bill. That the latter takes too big a bite out of your precious reserves is part of what this book is all about. But from the angle of convenience, you need only put your name to a small piece of paper, a check.

Heating with wood is different, quite different. Even its advocates will acknowledge that the process can give you a marvelously sharpened appreciation of how easy it is to use oil.

The table in Diagram 27 shows the number of operations performed on firewood. For each operation, the same wood is either cut or split, or physically lifted. Each lifting will usually be by hand. Even a casual glance at the table shows that if you intend to heat with wood, the simplest method is to buy the wood cut to length, split, and stacked in your storage area. Then you yourself would handle that wood only twice. Naturally, that is also the most expensive system. Columns 2 and 3 of the table show alternate ways to buy firewood that are usually less expensive but require your handling the wood more times. Column 4 shows minimum frequency of handling for harvesting your own wood. Success in keeping handling operations that low would not be common.

Column 5 shows normal frequency of handling. Of the total thirteen operations, eight require actual lifting of every piece of wood. In harvesting firewood with an ax, the other five operations (marked with an asterisk), viewed collectively, may be considered to require the same amount of energy expended as would five lifting operations. Therefore the two categories may be reasonably added together, not only for counting operations, but also for computing equivalent units of work done.

A cord of quality hardwood in half-dry condition might weigh, on the average, about 3,700 pounds. A cord of hickory in the same condition would weigh well over 4,400 pounds. Green wood that was just cut would weigh even more. A cord of green oak, for instance, could easily weigh over 4,900 pounds, or nearly 2½ tons. The weights stated at the bottom of the table are for wood that averages halfway between green and seasoned.

As figures go, the weights stated at the bottom of the table

may be thought-provoking for those who are not accustomed to doing much physical work. This will especially be true when these numbers are multiplied by the number of cords used annually. (See Diagram 36.) However, Rome was not built in a day and the operations listed do not have to be done in a day either. If you burn much wood, though, you will discover that you must do quite a bit on quite a few days.

Another point must be made. The figures in the table are entirely based on using an ax throughout. Using a chain saw would substantially reduce the labor of cutting the wood up to use-size. It would also help on bucking and, to a lesser extent, on felling. So if a chain saw is used, the work-equivalent of those operations should be proportionately reduced.

Because there is enough work connected with keeping warm with wood, it is only sensible to accept any help you can get and use all shortcuts you can devise. As shown in Diagram 27, by far the best work saver is to buy your wood all stacked and ready to burn. No other aid can beat that. This is so obvious, and such wood so reasonable a purchase even in the current market, that the only wood-burners who will not go that route are: (1)those who are too poor; (2) those hardheads who, damn the torpedoes and full speed ahead, are going to cut their own wood anyway. It is for the succor of both these species that this book is written.

So if you own a tree harvester that will cut, limb, and load a whole tree in one gulp, you are lucky and had better use it. The same applies to log skidders that can drag a half-dozen trees at a time, overhead drag lines, tree-length log trucks, all-weather crawlers, hydraulic loader trucks, dump trucks, or even fine teams of pulling horses that look as if they were borrowed from the Budweiser barns. Use them if you have them. If you do, you need little help here. But if you have only a pickup truck, or even just curiosity and an ax, maybe we are ready to talk. If you do not even have those, yet you want to keep warm in spite of the price of oil, you had certainly better gather around.

Prime firewood trees have a way of growing where there are no vehicular roads. It might be possible to build a road to each tree you cut, but you could sacrifice much young growth doing it. Time would also be a factor in a small firewood operation. It may often be easier to retrieve the wood without a road than to take the effort to make one. If so, you must work out another system to collect the wood for

Diagram 27

FREQUENCY OF HANDLING FIREWOOD

OPERATION PERFORMED	1. Buy Wood Cut, Split- & Stacked.	2. Buy Wood Cut, Split- But Not Stacked.	3. Buy Wood in 4-Ft. Lengths.	4. Fell Own Wood. Cut, Split in Woodlot.	5. Fell Own Wood. Normal Handling.
*Felling				x	x
*Limbing				x	x
*Bucking				x	x
Area collecting					x
Loading for home				x	x
Unloading at home					x
*Cutting to size			x	x	x
*Splitting			x	x	x
Loading for storage					x
Stacking in storage		x	x	x	x
Loading hand-carrier					x
Filling woodbox	x	x	x	x	x
Feeding fire	x	x	x	x	x
Total operations	2	3	5	9	13
†*Tons lifted per cord* (equivalent)	3.7	5.5	9.2	16.6	24.0

* These operations are performed only with the ax. Considered together, the work to perform them approximates at least an equal number of lifting operations.

† Assuming quality hardwood, half-seasoned, at 3,700 pounds per cord.

pickup by truck or however else you may transport it home. I once saw a man load a firewood log big around as a barrel by cutting it into slices right where it lay. His truck was downhill and he rolled the slices down there like huge hockey pucks, then up a plank into the truck body. Each slice was fully as much as he could handle, but he loaded them.

What collection and loading methods you use will depend upon your location and the nature of the ground, of course, but also upon the size of your wood, both in length and in girth. Light sticks can be thrown a few feet. Even in quantity, throwing sticks may be the quickest way to move them a short distance. Because it is difficult to move heavy pieces, thin them down by splitting until you can move them from where you bucked them.

For handling purposes, length is important. Unless you are immediately beside a vehicle, extra short pieces are awkward to move in quantity. The 4' cordwood stick is traditional and convenient in many ways, but not for carrying if heavy. A heavy 4' stick must be picked up by main strength and carried crosswise at about waist height. For any distance, this is excessively tiring. Carrying a stick balanced on your shoulder is much less tiring, but lifting a heavy four-footer up there is not easy and can be dangerous.

Naturally, there is a limit to the weight that anybody can reasonably carry. But whatever that limit is, within it, sticks longer than 4' are much easier to raise to a shoulder-carry. Stand the longer stick upright in front of you. Then bending toward it, lean your shoulder into its balance point. Putting a tentative lifting strain on the stick will tell whether you are too high or too low. As you straighten, lift the stick with your arms also so it cannot slip, and as you come erect the stick will swing to a balanced position on your shoulder, parallel to the ground and steadied by your hands. With a stick balanced, you can carry a respectable weight a considerable

Lifting Loads

Diagram 28

Half the secret of moving a heavy weight is how you do it.

Lift with back straight and heels together...

If heavy, a 4' stick is difficult to lift. Longer sticks of the same weight lift much easier.

With the stick upright, put your shoulder into the balance point. Lift so that stick flops on your shoulder. Then straighten up and carry it away.

If it's too heavy to lift that way, stay away from it!

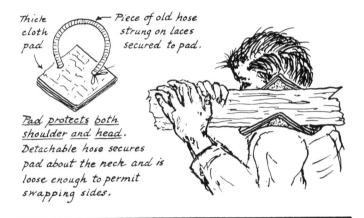

Thick cloth pad — Piece of old hose strung on laces secured to pad.

Pad protects both shoulder and head. Detachable hose secures pad about the neck and is loose enough to permit swapping sides.

distance. When you get rid of it, throw it off to the side, eliminating one more time that you must bend under weight. The average man cannot raise an equally heavy 4' stick to his shoulder as well in that fashion because the balance point would be too low unless he assumed a dangerously bent position for lifting so great a load. Back injuries are too simple to incur and, afterwards, too difficult to forget.

With longer sticks permitting a greater load or less effort, you save not only strength, but also time. Fewer trips will be necessary to carry the same amount of wood. However, one man can carry only just so much weight no matter how he juggles it. So the longer sticks cannot be too thick or they will be too heavy. For the larger pieces, this will mean splitting them where bucked. Regrettably, the longer the piece, the harder to split. But even so, splitting on-site will often permit collecting bucked wood for pickup easier than any other method.

Unless you are really tough or well-padded, carrying many heavy sticks will soon make your shoulders sore even though you alternate the side you carry on. A pad to protect

your shoulders is well worth having. It should be at least ½" thick of burlap, cloth, or other soft material sewed or tied together.

Tie a boot lace somewhat in from the middle of each of two adjacent edges of the pad. These are to secure the pad to your neck so the wood will not scrape it off. Your neck also needs protection from a taut lace, though, so cover one lace with enough old garden hose to loosely surround your neck. Thread some folded material through the lace above the hose to act as a washer and knot the lace above the washer. This will keep the hose on the lacing. With the hose around your neck, tie the lace from the hose tightly to the other lace at the surface of the pad. The upper corner of the pad will ride high, protecting the side of your neck and head. What this pad will add to your efficiency is surprising. You can concentrate on weight and footing instead of abrasion and splinters. Just balance each stick on your pad, lift it, and walk away with it.

For winter transportation, a sled is a good item. When conditions are right, it can even be used over dry grass or fallen leaves. A rugged, workable sled can be cut from the straightened side of a 55-gallon oil drum. This is sort of a reinforced toboggan. It will not look impressive, but drawing it over level snow, one man can easily move a load of 300 pounds or more. To draw even half that load uphill is another matter entirely, but if you want something enough you will find a way to do it. One solution is to unload or reload as necessary to suit the ground. An ordinary toboggan makes an excellent freight sled as long as it lasts, but few of them are strong enough to haul wood for many trips.

With a sled, and occasionally without one, working a crude dragline may be possible with your automobile or pickup truck as the motive power. Besides the pickup and the sled, you need sufficient rope, perhaps a pulley or two, and a straightaway piece of road to drive the truck for the hauling distance. Because your straightaway will seldom line up exactly with the direction you haul your wood from, you need the pulley tied to a tree or stump facing the straightaway to allow for change of direction toward the loaded sled.

With this arrangement, your problem will no longer be motive power, but finding a sufficiently level, obstacle-free path to draw the sled on. More than one change of direction could require use of an additional pulley. In that case, you could haul the sled only to the first pulley, stop, go transfer the sled past that pulley, and return to your vehicle for the second stage haul to the straightaway. For one man, that much running back and forth would probably be justified only if the wood were being hauled up a steep slope. The same system could be used to drag logs without a sled, though the friction would be far greater, perhaps even so much that your pickup would be insufficient for the job after all.

River driving was the old-time way of moving logs. Formerly the only practical means of transporting great numbers of logs over long distances, the annual drives depended on melting of winter snows. Normally the tributary streams contained sufficient water only during the spring runoff. While the weather was still cold, oxen or teams of horses hauled logs out on the ice to wait for the thaw or, more commonly, enormous piles of logs along the shores of streams would be rolled into the newly opened freshets as there was room for them to fit.

There was a schedule that had to be met. The inexorable pattern of the weather could be neither hurried nor slowed. Every stick that had been cut all winter had to be floated downstream in a few swift days of spring runoff or else wait another year in the woods with borers and rot. The woodsmen turned rivermen, armed with pickpoles and peaveys instead of axes. The drives downstream were as exhausting as they were dangerous. With flood waters boiling under them, logs would lunge, roll, twist, dive, leap, and smash. Logs would catch on obstructions and on each other. Often they could be freed only by the perilous extrication of the key logs from the maw of a straining pile that would all vomit downstream as soon as the logs no longer held each other. They who turned those keys were men.

On the worst jams, explosives were used, but even they had to be cunningly placed, so huge were the forces involved between the relentless push of the waters and the mounting crush of the logs. One such jam at Carratunk Falls on Maine's Kennebec River in the spring of 1881 became a mile long and rose over 100' at its face. It took weeks to untangle. Now the river drives are gone. On that same Kennebec River, though, the shorter pulpwood sticks still flowed downstream through 1976.

On your operations, if you haul logs to your pickup yard, stack them on skids, logs laid crosswise on the bottom of the pile. This will keep the stack up out of moisture from the ground. By log-cabin-type construction of the skids, you can elevate them to facilitate loading on your truck. Lay two skids on the side of the truck and roll each log up into the truck.

Loading heavy logs by yourself can be tricky. You can almost double the weight of log you can roll up skids by using the parbuckle shown in Diagram 29. This consists of two secured ropes passed under and around your log. By pulling their free ends from the truck, you roll the log up into the body. To make a parbuckle, tie two 25', 5/8"-diameter ropes to secured stakes or to a heavy log already within your truck body, one rope near the front and one toward the rear. Then pass the free end of each rope down over the skids, straight under and around the corresponding end of the waiting log and back to you in the truck body. Your log will be enclosed in two loops. Now just pull evenly on the free end of each rope and the log will roll easily up the skids and into the truck. The secret of the parbuckle is that the log rolls, giving you a mechanical advantage of almost two to one.

When you finally have all your wood home, it must be cut to size and split, or vice versa. These are major tasks, but even after you have done them, there still remains more handling and lifting. If where you cut and split your wood is where you intend to stack it for seasoning or permanent storage, you need only stack it on the spot. If not, you have another relocation chore.

Again, for a change of location of only a few feet, throw the wood there. If the distance is greater and circumstances permit, use the truck. If the distance is too great to make throwing the sticks practical, or is around corners, or the truck cannot enter where you need the wood stored, what you need is either a wheelbarrow or two-wheeled garden cart or both.

Unless you live on a postage stamp lot in suburbia, or in a condominium or apartment or barracks, one of the most useful outdoor tools you can own is a heavy, contractor's wheelbarrow of the type used to manhandle fresh-mixed concrete. One of these would be too much for your grandmother perhaps, but with careful loading, you can haul away a cord of stovewood in a dozen trips. For that kind of loading, your path had better be fairly smooth and not too steep, but for reasonably level ground, an able man can do it, including maneuvering a fully loaded wheelbarrow through an average exterior doorway.

A light wheelbarrow is strong enough only for light loads. If you load a light wheelbarrow heavily, it can break if it lurches to the side and you try to save the load. Regarding stability, the wheelbarrow's single wheel is a marked advantage where ground slopes sideways, for the load can be stabilized by the operator. The ordinary cement wheelbarrow also has a pneumatic tire that absorbs small obstacles without the jolting shocks that can throw a load.

If you do not have to cross steep side slopes, a large, two-wheeled garden cart is an efficient wood hauler. Though wider than a wheelbarrow, it can carry a greater load, is

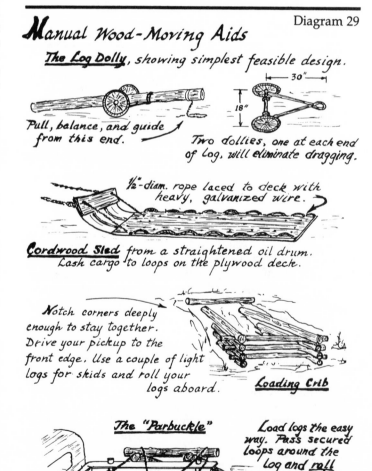

Diagram 29

Manual Wood-Moving Aids

The Log Dolly, showing simplest feasible design.

Pull, balance, and guide from this end.

30"
18"

Two dollies, one at each end of log, will eliminate dragging.

½"-diam. rope laced to deck with heavy, galvanized wire.

Cordwood Sled from a straightened oil drum. Lash cargo to loops on the plywood deck.

Notch corners deeply enough to stay together. Drive your pickup to the front edge. Use a couple of light logs for skids and roll your logs aboard.

Loading Crib

The "Parbuckle"

Load logs the easy way. Pass secured loops around the log and roll it up.

2 to 1 Advantage.

more stable and can traverse rougher ground. Like a wheel-barrow, the two-wheeled cart can also tip forward to dump its load. When needed, this is an advantage. But have a care to load the cart evenly. If the forward portion becomes over-loaded, the cart will abruptly dump, the load plunging downward, the cart and handle pivoting on the axle to flail upright. You would be lucky to be out of range.

Where you stack the wood for seasoning need not be the final bulk storage site, though you will save one more han-dling if it is. But in either case, there are two more lifting operations, even if you buy your wood already stacked and ready to burn. Unless your bulk storage is within hand reach of your stove or fireplace, an unimaginable location for most households, you must periodically fill your stove woodbox or fireside wood basket. From that last station, you stoke the fire as it requires or, as you desire, piece by precious piece.

The simplest way to fill the woodbox or basket is merely to pick up an armload from the woodpile and carry it in. It is not always the cleanest method, or even the quickest if you need more than a half dozen sticks. A wide variety of firewood carriers is available commercially, some quite useful and others impractical. Ideally, these carriers should permit car-rying a maximum load with minimum effort, while protect-ing the bearer's clothing from contact with the splinters and wood debris. One of the least expensive and most durable devices for this purpose is a five-gallon paint pail. Using such pails in pairs, you can easily carry more of the shorter stovewood than you would care to load in your arms.

Many more industrial products are packed in five-gallon pails than just paints. The empty pails should not be too difficult to procure as they are customarily a throwaway item. Some are better constructed than others. Loaded with wood up to 16″, they carry in the normal position. With 24″ wood, the balance becomes so high that the pail will dump if you lift it. To avoid this, use the pail-carrying sticks shown in Diagram 33. These are nothing more than hardwood sticks a little longer than the pail is high, with the stub of a sturdy branch protruding near the bottom end for a handle. Insert one of these sticks upside down in a pail with the wire handle of the pail resting on the stub. Then fill the pail with wood and pick the whole business up by the stub. The pail will tip but not dump. With longer hardwood, two of those pailfuls will be all you want to carry.

Of all wood-handling operations, the most difficult for the small operator may be bringing his wood to a collection point for transport. There is real need of smaller wood-hauling devices that are not yet on the market. The growing need of many homeowners to view trees as fuel provides some foresighted manufacturer with rare opportunity to be there "fustest with the mostest."

The most obvious void is a small-engine prime mover that is both small and stable enough to use off-road among trees, yet powerful enough to draw a respectable-sized log or equivalent load. It would probably be two-wheeled. As for power, modern rototiller engines and power-trains would seem adequate. A log-hauler adaptation must be feasible. From all signs, the market is there. Considering other modern wonders from the small-engine people, this should not be asking too much of them.

Two auxiliary items for use with or without the prime mover are a durable log sled and a log dolly. The latter, a stout pair of wheels with a rudimentary chassis for attach-ment to a log would perform the same function in warm weather that the sled would for winter. Both items should be simple to design. The way things are going, they should be equally simple to sell.

Woods roads are seldom smooth. Any load of firewood that protrudes above the sides of a vehicle or sled used in the woods must be tied down. Yet tying a load tightly is more than a man can do without additional aid. Large loads should be secured with chain. A load binder for use with chain is described in Chapter 25.

On a smaller load secured by rope, tie the load loosely so that you can form a small loop in the principal rope over the load. Thrust a strong 3′ to 4′ stick through the loop. Now turn the stick about the loop, twisting the rope. The slack will disappear into the hard twists about the stick. The stick is a lever and if you turn it too far you might even snap your rope. To prevent the stick from untwisting when you release it, work the longer end into a crevice between the logs of the load. If you cannot do that, tie the stick fast to the load with a free end of the rope or a piece of twine. Tied in this manner, you need not worry about your load falling off. You can even cinch chain up tightly by the same method if your stick is rugged enough and the slack is sufficient to begin a loop.

Big Ones into Little Ones

When you have finally trucked, hauled, or carried all your wood home, pile it on sticks running crosswise so the good firewood is well separated from the dampness of the ground. If there are trees, posts, stakes, or other woodpiles to keep the ends of the new pile vertical, fine, but that is not essential. With straight-ended piles you can fit more wood into a smaller area, because you can stack it higher. However, unless you have already split and cut every stick to size in the woodlot, the pile you make now is not the final stack and niceties can be omitted. For the ordinary case, this stack is just the size-reduction depot.

If you work entirely without saws, an important order of work is reversed at this point. You must split the wood to use-*thickness before* you chop it up into use-*length*. The reason for this is that each piece must be split into thinner lengths that will permit subsequent chopping to length without excessive effort, time or waste. Chopping thinner sticks is vastly more efficient than chopping heavier pieces because the thinner ones can often be severed with a stroke or two.

Many of the long lengths will have been split sufficiently already so that you could carry them in the woodlot. Much limb wood may not need splitting at all. Separating the sticks that still need splitting should start while you are unloading from the truck or other transport. The heavy pieces that are still too thick can be thrown on one pile and those ready for chopping to length piled elsewhere.

In splitting the long lengths, use the splitting ax as long as it does the job. Once a log is split in half, reducing the halves to thinner lengths is usually not too difficult. But when a piece balks, or even looks balky, take the maul to it. As you split, re-pile the splits into the finished stack or you will shortly have such an unmanageable jungle underfoot that you can no longer work.

With the splitting done, you are ready to chop the split sticks into the lengths you need with a minimum of blows and chips. Often, one stroke of the ax on opposite sides of a stick will sever it. Do this whenever possible. To ensure the depth of your cuts, a woodpile chopping ax may be somewhat heavier than a felling ax, for you will not swing it so often.

Chopping wood to its ultimate size must be done as soon as you can after felling the trees. For all wood chops easiest when green. Chopping dry wood is dismayingly more difficult. Interim stages will vary in proportion to how much the wood has seasoned. So if you fell and bring back wood in warmer weather when it will rapidly season in a stack, chop it to size right away. Drying being slower in the winter months, delaying the cutting to size may be less critical, but it should not be neglected long.

When splitting, if you drive the splitting ax completely through a stick into the ground, it does not make a great deal of difference, unless you are unlucky enough to hit a large rock head on. The splitting ax does not require an extra keen edge. The ax you use for cutting to length does. It must be sharp. When you chop through a knot, you should use the thicker limbing bit. To eliminate actually reaching for a second ax, the double-bitted ax is the obvious answer. The double's keen and stout bits are both available at a turn of your hand.

With a whole woodpile of sticks ahead of you, many of them finely split and most of them needing to be chopped apart twice or more, the chances of repeatedly driving your honed bit into grit and stones are too big to fight unless you make special arrangements. A relatively simple solution is the chopping platform shown in Diagram 30, two short hardwood logs fastened side by side. Sticks to be chopped are placed in the trough formed by the upper sides of the logs. The logs should be 10" to 12" in diameter and 5' to 7' long, the length depending on the length of stick that will normally be chopped.

The chopping platform is not just a device to keep your ax from eating grit. Important as that is, even more important is the fact that the platform lets you routinely use "vertical backed-up" chopping strokes as described in Chapter 8. These are the most powerful strokes of chopping. The platform provides the back-up. So being both vertical and backed-up, your strokes will cut deeper every time you hit. If you sink in far enough on sticks of an appropriate size, you will sever them without notching them first. In chopping a winter's supply of wood to size, the saving in time and effort will be substantial.

When you are chopping at the platform, any horizontal swing (such as hitting toward the blocked end, for instance) will strike in your frontal zone as described in Chapter 8. Doing that, you will one day maim yourself. So consider the chopping platform a "vertical-chopping platform." Keep every stroke there vertical. Sticks that require substantial notching to cut apart should not be chopped there, but

Diagram 30

The Chopping Platform
To chop firewood to size _faster_ & _easier_.

Face platform at 45°. Strike vertically at sticks in trough. Turn half-cut sticks to cut the other side.

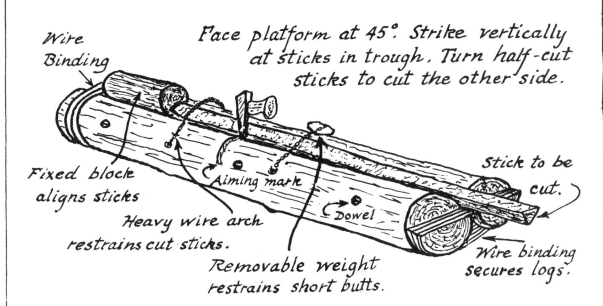

Wire Binding

Fixed block aligns sticks

Aiming mark

Heavy wire arch restrains cut sticks.

Removable weight restrains short butts.

Dowel

Stick to be cut.

Wire binding secures logs.

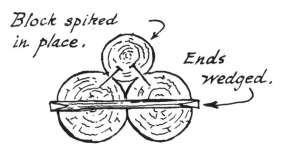

Block spiked in place.

Ends wedged.

Cross section: Have at least 3 one-inch dowels. 3/4" bolts could replace both wire and dowels.

Wire binding: Pull tight. Twist ends together...

Use a spike or screwdriver to twist both strands until taut.

Make platform of 10"-diam. hardwood logs. Length from 5½' – 7', depending on wood you chop. Wood should be well split and greener the better.

beneath the feet, as in bucking.

Another point needs emphasis. Sticks cut better if cut at an angle. About 45° is suitable. Therefore, the chopper should face the platform at about 45° as he hits each stick vertically at the aiming point. The goal is to sink halfway or more into each stick at each stroke. For sticks that need it, turn them over to hit the other side at the same point. The second stroke should part the stick without your having to notch it.

The success of the system is measured in how few chips you make as you chop the long lengths into short firewood sticks. Obviously, you will succeed better with wood that is still green and soft and that is also well split. Difficult as meeting these demands may be, meeting them will be far easier than *chopping* a woodpile of seasoned logs into use-size chunks that will still have to be split before burning.

To construct the platform, block one end of the trough between logs with a flat-faced chunk. The sticks to be chopped will be laid in the trough up against the face of this block. Mark the platform logs at an appropriate distance from the face of the block to provide an aiming point for chopping pieces of uniform length. As you chop each piece, remove it and slide the long length up to the block again.

When you are chopping small sticks apart, one end will often fly upward. To stop that, fasten a loop of heavy wire arching over the trough and about 6" from the face of the block. The sticks to be cut will slide through and beneath the loop, but cannot leap free when severed. Alternate means of accomplishing the same purpose would be nailing a sheet-metal hood to the block or selecting a large enough block so that it could be recessed to receive sticks in the trough.

The butt ends of sticks being chopped can also catapult upward when cut short enough. Preventing this requires a different guard to keep the trough clear for feeding. A work-able guard is a weight of about four pounds secured by chain just long enough to cross over the platform. A lump of lead or an old sledgehammer head would be ideal. Screw or bolt the chain to the platform a half-firewood-stick length down from the aiming point. When you have a short stick to chop, flop the weight over the stick so that the chain rides on the stick. Then when you chop the stick, it may jump, but it will not go anywhere. Afterward, throw the weight aside until you use it next time.

The entire chopping platform must be able to resist the continual impact of chopping. The logs can be pegged to-gether with at least three "through and through" dowels at least 1" thick. Their ends should be wedged just as with an axhead. Following that, the ends of the logs should be bound together with wire, as shown in Diagram 30. If available, long bolts joining these logs would be a preferable method because of the ease of further tightening as required. Bolts could replace both dowels and wire.

The efficiency of the platform is enhanced if the logs are of good hardwood, not so much for durability as for the greater weight and rigidity backing each stroke. The more solid the backing, the better your ax will cut each stick. In time, the chopping point will become gouged. Do not let it become too deep as this is the launching pad of the flying sticks. One way to cure it is to shift the aiming point and adjust the block to fit. It is another reason for beginning with an adequately long platform.

Now you may never have heard of a "chopping *platform*"

before. And perhaps assuming that none existed in colonial and post-Revolutionary days, you may wonder how our ax-wielding ancestors managed so well without one. The answer is that a different situation existed then. True, there were no chopping platforms. At least we have no record that there were. But what were also lacking in those times were stoves of the modern variety that take not only more but smaller pieces of wood. Most early American heating, and virtually all cooking, was done in gaping fireplaces that took great chunks of log. Our American forebears had less split-ting to do and less cutting to size.

Unblushingly, this is a book of the ax. Of the five steps listed in Diagram 27 that convert a tree into firewood, cutting the wood to use-size is without question the most difficult for the ax. But using the methods of the chopping platform, the ax can compete with honor. No, it cannot beat the chain saw, but it performs very creditably nevertheless. And the ax needs no babying. Nor does it need gasoline, special oils, special maintenance, replacement parts that may or may not be replaceable, or substantial bankroll to purchase and re-peatedly repurchase any of these. For any of these reasons, chain saws may not always be as available as they have been. Just from the viewpoints of cost, convenience, and simple prudence, if you want to be certain of keeping warm with wood, you should master the techniques of the ax.

With that said, turn the picture over, for there is another side. Cutting your annual wood supply to size with a chain saw instead of an ax is an entirely different proposition. Using the chain saw, you would not split the long lengths first, nor would it be so critical a matter to cut the long lengths while they were still green. In no other firewood operation is the advantage of the chain saw so clear, provided that you use the chain saw as you would use a cheese knife, cutting straight down into your woodpile.

Clear as that may be, it is not at all unusual to find a cautious chain-saw operator cutting his firewood one piece at a time, each piece carefully placed first in a sawhorse. That system is satisfactory if you have unlimited time and do not mind picking up each stick in the pile, and the saw also, at least two times more than would ordinarily be necessary. But that system by no means exploits the capabilities of the chain saw.

To accomplish that, work a few minutes on the pile first. Take a maul, hammer, or medium-sized stick and tap in all protruding sticks from one side through to the other until you have one side of the pile as nearly a vertical wall as you can reasonably get it. Then with your chain saw, trim the rough side of the pile, cutting off any pieces that protrude farther than they should. After the trimming, the pile should be the proper width to divide into a whole number of vertical slices.

Next, on several of the outer sticks of the pile, mark the line to saw along. Do this with your ax, chalk, or anything that marks. On snow-dusted piles, draw furrows with your finger or a stick. Even though you intend to make two or more cuts into the pile, draw only one line at a time. If the outer sticks shift position after cutting, you may have to mark again for the next cut. Guided by a good eye, you can omit the marking, though the marks permit better concen-tration on where you are sawing. For somehow, sawing a woodpile into slices of uniform thickness (that is, into sticks

Woodpile Cutting — With the Chain saw...

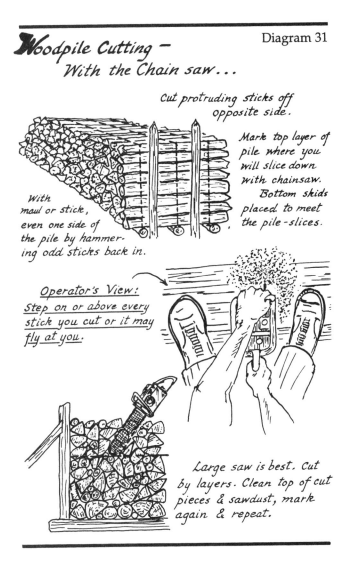

Diagram 31

Cut protruding sticks off opposite side.

Mark top layer of pile where you will slice down with chainsaw. Bottom skids placed to meet the pile-slices.

With maul or stick, even one side of the pile by hammering odd sticks back in.

Operator's View: Step on or above every stick you cut or it may fly at you.

Large saw is best. Cut by layers. Clean top of cut pieces & sawdust, mark again & repeat.

slice a loaf of bread. While cutting deep inside the pile, you need not fear that sticks will jump at you from the top.

A flat-topped and square-ended pile is best for this cutting so that you can stand on a level surface, though the very act of cutting will make the sticks you stand on less stable. Remember also that a chain saw snagged on the upper edge of the chain bar tends to buck upward. So you will have four items to keep alert about: your stability atop a high pile of wood that settles beneath your feet as you cut it, flying sticks that can maim you, a bucking saw that could open your brainpan, and cutting an accurate slice from a pile that moves. These are good reasons for the cautious man to cut his wood on a sawhorse even though he possesses a chain saw. Even so, if you keep your wits about you, it is possible to cut your wood in but a fraction of the time and energy that the overcautious man will have to expend. Using your head plus caution, you can emerge unscathed.

You can slice into a pile only as deep as your cutter-bar is long. Then throw off the layer of cut sticks before sawing another layer downward. It is usually easier to keep the cuts aligned by clearing an entire layer before sawing any portion

Sawhorses (or Sawbucks)

Diagram 32

If you saw your woodpile stick by stick, a sawhorse holds the wood.

A common design, although many sawhorses have less reinforcement. There are commercial models that even fold up for storage.

Saw beyond the end of a sawhorse, not in the middle.

Two designs from the woods need no nails or lumber, if you find the trees with the right branches.

A compact, rugged design that can even double as a fireside seat. Having bottom section of the legs oversize prevents them from pushing through.

of uniform length) is not as simple as it appears to be.

As the chain saw revolves, it re-enters the body of the saw at the bottom, tending to fling light sticks back at the operator. A heavy log will resist this pull and remain in place, but lighter sticks will not unless otherwise restrained. Even though you may seem to cut a lighter stick without noticeable drag, when it is almost severed, it will lose its rigidity at that point and, if not adequately backed, will begin to pinch the blade. Although this drag on the chain could stall the saw, a more common result is for a severed stick to catapult rearward. A large chain saw can probably throw a stick with enough force to crack a man's leg, and any stick shot toward the head carries grievous potential.

You should not underestimate the danger of slicing down through a woodpile with a chain saw. It is a reasonable risk only if you prevent its sticks from becoming projectiles. Fortunately, that is not difficult. You must stand on both ends of every small stick you cut, or be entirely certain that your target stick is restrained by other sticks which will not also fly up. Usually, you merely climb on top of the pile, straddling the marks you made, and cut vertically down between your feet, sawing a slice off the pile as you would deeper. Where a slice has veered out of alignment, lay out a new set of marks to saw by. The farther you cut into the pile, the more of a problem sawdust is. To see what you are doing, sweep the sawdust aside.

At the bottom of the pile, if you had previously laid sticks crosswise to raise the sound fuelwood from the ground moisture, you can reap another dividend. The skids will provide a space to keep your saw from hitting the ground in cutting the final layer. Even greater protection can be gained when first laying the pile by having the skids lie in vertical alignment with the cuts to be sliced down through the pile later. Then in the final layer, even if the saw bursts through too forcefully, it still will have protection from the ground. For grit and stones do not agree with chain saws, either.

Sawing cordwood or other long sticks to shorter lengths with a cordwood saw rig is cleaner and more accurate than slicing a pile with a chain saw. The circular cordwood saw is usually powered from a tractor takeoff or independent engine. A crew of three men with a cordwood rig can cut more wood to size better and faster than a single man with a chain saw can slice off down through a pile. But the dif-ference would not be that great. For a man cutting firewood to size by himself, slicing the pile with a chain saw is mighty difficult to beat.

Except for using an ax, the oldest method of cutting firewood to size is with a hand saw. As with all other cut-to-size systems with saws, you saw the wood before you split it. Exceptions to that rule would be logs that would be too heavy to handle before they were split. In the early days of cordwood sawing, the woodpile saw would have been a wooden-framed buck saw or a one-man straight saw. If two men were working together, they would probably have used a two-man straight saw. The hand saw of choice today would probably be a steel bow saw.

In hand-sawing, you pick up a length, plunk it down on a sawhorse, cut off a piece, then readjust the length in the sawhorse as many times as it needs to be cut. If you keep hand saws sharp, they will cut well. They are not as fast as chain saws. Not by a good bit. But much firewood has been cut on sawhorses with manual saws. This is another miscellaneous fact that I can personally vouch for.

Storing Your Wood

As with the ant in Aesop's Fables, if you want the necessities of life during the cold winter, you will have to fill your storeroom ahead of time. This is doubly true for firewood. To burn well, it must be dry. The drying, or "seasoning," period luckily meshes with the fact that cold weather is ideal for felling and collecting firewood. The wood you bring back one winter will warm you the next.

Where you locate the bulk storage pile of cut and split firewood will hinge on availability and shelter. Availability comes first, for you will make many trips to the woodpile during the winter, and the nearer it is to the fire, the better. Advantages of having the woodpile under the same roof that shelters you will be obvious on any stormy winter night, but whether you have enough interior room may be another matter. In wood country, all old-time houses had woodsheds, but times have changed. With limited space, you could end up having two piles, a small inside pile that you would replenish every week or two and the outside pile you would draw from.

The quantity of wood you burn in a year will dictate the space you need for storage. Though that will be different for every household and even every year, some quite general estimates of quantities are listed in Diagram 36. For figuring the space you have available, a cord of wood, the usual measure of firewood, is a stack 8' long, 4' wide, and 4' high, having a volume of 128 cubic feet. However, this usual definition is based on 4'-long "cordwood sticks," the cut pieces of log and limb just as bucked from the tree. Usually these sticks would not be split. The exact definition makes a considerable difference, for the standard cord of wood, cut, split, and stacked in stovewood lengths will shrink almost 20%, having an average volume of only about 103 cubic feet. Even so, in a modern house, this is still an impressive amount of space. If you multiply that by the cords you intend to store, it may use most of your extra room and still not be enough. This is the case for building a woodshed.

Incidentally, if you buy firewood, be sure you and the vendor have the same definition of cord, for the term is much abused. Many buyers have learned to their sorrow that a pile appearing to be 8' long and 4' high was not really stacked 4' wide. This is the notorious "face cord." And because most wood buyers must depend upon the vendor for delivery, it is useful to know the interior dimensions of his truck body to compute whether you are actually receiving the quantity agreed upon. But there, too, you must observe how the wood is fitted in. As opposed to being stacked in a cord pile, loose-thrown stovewood might fill a space as large as 150 cubic feet. If you accepted a 128-cubic-feet volume, you would be receiving only 85% of a cord, if that were the agreed measure for the purchase. Know your vendor.

In finding storage space for your wood, other factors may even increase the space you must allot. There may be valid reasons for leaving passageways between tiers of piled wood. One such reason could be that the wood you stacked first, having seasoned the longest, is the wood you wish to burn first. It would be only sensible to leave an access path to that stock.

Wood begins to season as soon as the tree is cut. Freshly cut wood is spoken of as "green," though the term has little to do with the color of the wood itself. Green wood is heavy with the natural internal moisture of all living things. After being severed from its roots, wood can also absorb moisture from external sources, such as precipitation, ground moisture, or even from immersion in water. Such wood is called "wet," or water-soaked. Wood that is either green or wet may take months to dry, even under favorable conditions. The rule of thumb is to allow a year between felling and burning.

Firewood dries best in single tiers where both sides of the stack are ventilated. In the open, single tier stacks broadside to prevailing winds may even dry in a summer. Direct sunlight is a huge help but can also bring complications. A high single-tier stack of green stovewood may shrink so much on the sunny side that it sags. If it is not prodded or pounded back to the vertical pretty quick, the whole pile may fall over. Reconstituting it can be a lot of work.

In the sun or out of it, all firewood shrinks a bit as it dries. Within woodpiles, this causes erratic settling. Single-tier woodpiles are desirable to facilitate drying, but being unsupported on either side, high ones also require more care than multiple-tier piles for at least three months. When building a single-tier pile, leave enough working space alongside to permit knocking a sagging section into an upright position again. During this tap, tap, tap chore, never forget the crushing weight the wall of sticks would release if it sagged out of control.

Ventilation is vital for any drying process, and is of particular importance for wood stored in cellars or basements that have a tendency to be damp. Leaving ventilation aisles between tiers may be desirable, though these also increase the amount of space required. Basement storage areas should have cross ventilation of some nature in the summer months, and the piles of wood must always be kept off the floor (if damp) by rows of sticks beneath each pile. The same principle applies to woodpiles anywhere. Any measures necessary to eliminate the usual dampness of a basement will be even more essential when a large amount of green wood has been stacked there releasing moisture of its own.

A basement may seem to offer the only practical choice for woodpile storage in many homes. But if the basement gets wet, or merely holds dampness, any other reasonable storage place should be seriously considered. Some perfectly sound firewoods can turn punky in a cellar that is only seasonally damp if the wood is stacked there green while the cellar is damp. In such a location, I once grasped a single stovewood stick from the pile and lifted four. The other three sticks were bound to the first by a tangled lacework, the white fungus strands of "dry" rot. Each stick had been sound when it was stacked there a year before.

An open shed with wide overhang to the roof will provide excellent wood storage. A closed shed could be better if it is not too tight. Either one is better than the average basement. Temperature of the storage area is of less importance than ventilation. Not that the broiling temperature inside a closed woodshed in the summer would not induce rapid drying, for it would. But wood exposed to all ambient temperature extremes, cold as well as hot, will be about as dry after a year as it is going to get. Ventilation is what counts. Exposure to relatively dry air is what takes moisture from the surface of wood.

For this reason, outdoor storage of wood is satisfactory for seasoning purposes. If the piles have no cover, the top sticks will get wet from snow and rain, but no more than several layers deep. Then when the sun shines again, its direct rays fall on the top sticks, drying them quickly, and the entire pile has the constant caress of circulating air. You occasionally see outdoor woodpiles covered with tarpaulins or plastic, but these covers probably do as much harm in stopping ventilation as they help by shedding rain and snow. Wood should not be left in the open indefinitely, but for the first year you need not worry about it. After that, use it up.

Wood stored outdoors under less than optimum conditions as in shade, under trees, under roof drainage, porches or decks, can greatly benefit by being covered with woodpile shingles. (See Diagram 34) These sheets of plywood shield the woodpile from overhead moisture, do not stop cross ventilation, interlock to block leakage from shingle to shingle, will not shift in ordinary winds, overlap the sides of the pile and are easily positioned and removed. Woodpile shingles cannot protect the lower sides of the pile from splash or driving precipitation, yet overall, their use substantially extends the time firewood can be stored in the open without deterioration.

What should rank as rural works of art are the conical woodpiles that some connoisseurs build with each piece slanted upward into the center. They require loving care to build and, to my eye, they are beautiful. But from a practical viewpoint, they are probably inefficient. Though rain may slide down the sides of the sticks, the ends rear upward like

so many blotters. Wood absorbs water some dozen times better through its end grain than it does laterally. But the worst mischief is that the overlapping sticks stop ventilation to the interior of the stack. In the ordinary pile, the ends of the sticks and the voids between them are open to the horizontal movement of air currents. Nor would the usual pile be as wide. So with more air able to penetrate inside the stack, the wood in the ordinary flat-laid pile will dry better.

Square-ended woodpiles are desirable for more than appearance. Not only can you cram more wood into a smaller ground or floor area by building upward, but for outdoor piles, building higher results in less exposure to weather for a given amount of wood. So though building a vertical end to a woodpile may be a nuisance, it will often be worth the extra effort.

The easy way to square the end of the pile is to stack against a post, tree, wall, or another pile. If stacking inside a shed whose walls have only exterior siding, either stack only against the studs or add some protective boards on your side of the studs to avoid punching the siding of the shed off from within. Stacking against the outside of a building is simple, but may not be wise for either firewood or building. Unless

---

Stacking and Storage

Diagram 33

Ventilation is the greatest need for seasoning wood.

Up to a year, wood may even be piled outdoors without damage, if skids elevate piles off the wet ground. Avoid prolonged storage in damp cellars.

Pile more wood on top to hold the sticks.

The Criss-Cross method of ending a woodpile is the best one. Building it takes care. Use no load-bearing sticks that roll or wobble. Keep layers level.

5-Gal. Paint Pail Wood Carrier Stick. Carry 26" wood in a pail with one of these sticks. Use in pairs to balance all you can lug.

Diagram 34

Woodpile Shingles

protect firewood from rain & snow without blocking side ventilation.

Galvanized sheet-rock screws for tight sealing.

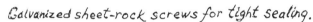

4'

2'

Woodpile Shingle
(Top side)

Size is optional. However, the size shown fits 16" stovewood. Four "shingles" of this size can be cut from one sheet of 4'× 8'× ½" exterior plywood.

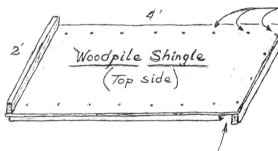

Top cleat

Gap

Side cleat

Lengthwise edge view showing interlocking cleats cut from split 2"x 4"s. Top cleat fits in gap behind bottom cleat on next shingle, locking shingles together and blocking water from running under.

Top cleat

Side cleats

Edge views from top cleat end. In use on the woodpile, firewood sticks fit between the side cleats, stopping the shingles from shifting side to side.

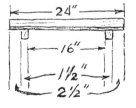

24"

16"

1½"

2½"

Total overlap of shingles beyond the woodpile face on either side is 4", preventing dripping water from hitting the pile.

the building has gutters, the wood will be deluged by drainage from the roof. As for the building, it will be kept damper than usual by the presence of the wood.

For a small woodpile, you can keep the end vertical by stacking against a stake driven into the ground. A junior-sized stake will not be sufficient as the pile grows higher unless you brace it with a diagonal strut as shown in Diagram 33. To fit that method to a high pile would take strong stakes and braces. The diagram also shows how to support the end-stakes with hook-sticks secured inside the pile. Unfortunately, this method is more suited to cordwood than it is to firewood piles. The hook-sticks can also loosen, letting the pile spread. If you really want to secure the end-stakes to the pile, tie the end-stakes to each other through the stack. Though this arrangement takes a lot of rope, it will not loosen, not unless mice cut the rope for nests. Stacking wood against trees is fine if your dooryard trees are in the proper locations and are large enough. Trees less than 6" in diameter tend to sway during high winds, gradually dislodging the end of a woodpile. Stacking against permanent posts dug into the ground may be acceptable if you care to have the posts there all year, every year, whether used or not.

Sooner or later though, after weighing other methods of squaring a woodpile end, you will turn to criss-crossed layers of sticks. This method is stable, can be done anywhere, and requires no extra materials. It does require care in building, and using split sticks, not round ones. Split sticks are needed because they cannot roll. The end of the stack becomes a little tower of split sticks laid in alternating layers, the first across the stack, the second parallel to it, the third across, and so on.

In placing the layers, build each one level and keep the two end corners of the pile rising vertically without leaning. Usually there will be about four sticks to a layer. Of these, the two outer sticks are most important to provide a firm base for the succeeding layer. If a middle stick were highest, for instance, the next layer could seesaw, endangering everything above it. Sticks thicker at one end than the other are less suitable for criss-cross construction. If used, they must be compensated for by irregularities in other sticks so as to keep successive layers level. For 24" sticks the criss-cross pile end will still be stable 6' high. Shorter sticks criss-crossed that high will stand well enough if not disturbed, or if stacked abutting other tiers.

In a basement or room with exposed joists overhead, a long plank can provide an easy way to end a pile without sprawl. For each tier of sticks, get a plank several inches longer than the distance from ceiling to floor. Providing the woodpile runs at right angles to the ceiling joists, block off each tier of sticks by standing the plank on end in front of it, the top end of the plank resting against a ceiling joist, the bottom end slanted to the pile. Then stack the wood against the plank as high as you care to. The bottom of the plank cannot push away because its top will be caught in the angle of ceiling joist and ceiling. If you do not have the planks for this trick, two poles will do for each plank.

Safety is not usually associated with woodpiles, but if you have combined high piles with standing single tiers for better ventilation, or have narrow accessways, the woodpile area is no place for children to play. When withdrawing wood for use, keep the slant of the diminishing tier gentle, so that pieces will not cascade at a touch. With heavier pieces, not even all cats are always quick enough to escape injury.

The last stop in the storage chain is the woodbox or basket, usually placed a hand reach from the fire or stove for both convenience and cleanliness. Whatever the container, it should hold enough to obviate too frequent trips to the woodpile. It is fashionable today to combine wood carrier and wood basket. There is no harm in this, though what you can carry in one load with the common wood basket will not last too long. In former times, some most useful fireside benches and settles served a dual purpose as containers or covers of a plentiful supply of wood. It is still possible to marry utility and beauty. The homely woodbox can be designed as a striking piece of furniture.

When the interior arrangement permits, a through-the-wall woodbox having a port for exterior loading can offer some advantages. If the exterior is exposed to outside weather, though, protection against heat loss must also be one of its integral features.

The fireside wood container can also serve another purpose. Firewood sticks must fit within the chamber of stove or fireplace. If sticks are too long, they cannot be used. A futile struggle to jam an overlength stick into a blazing fire can be dangerous, sometimes resolved only by a room full of smoke and perhaps worse. That real-life scenario would not happen if the overlength stick had been previously rejected by the woodbox. The box itself can be a caliper.

Having oversize pieces slip through the supply process is all too easy. A common source is cutting the woodpile slices inaccurately with a chain saw. Other than sawing more skillfully, the only other alternative is to deliberately saw the woodpile slice undersize. But the profusion of really runty sticks generated by that solution is irritating. Even more irritating, though, is attempting to thrust an oversize stick into a stove or fireplace that cannot accept it.

Several different stick calipers are simple to construct. An easy one is a long board with a section cut from the middle of one edge to fit the longest stick you can use. Stand this board beside the woodpile to test each stick before carrying it to the woodbox. Throw oversize sticks on the fireplace or re-cut piles.

It is reasonable to wonder why overlength pieces could not be identified before stacking. The only answer is that they should be. Yet stacking is just another of those massive handling operations integral to wood harvesting. The only way to face them is to plunge in and work. In the flurry, it is easy to overlook an occasional stick that is slightly too long. When you have only a few sticks to lug to the woodbox, you have more time to look at each one. Somehow, this fact is related to the old adage that if you want to get a job done, give it to the busy man because he is the one that *will* get the job done. Perhaps the moral is that there is room in the world for both kinds of people.

21

Burning Your Wood

To burn, a wood fire must have fuel, air, and a high enough temperature. You cannot set a log blazing with a match because the tiny flame is not enough to heat the massive surface of the log to 523°F (273°C), the temperature at which wood ignites. So you start a little fire to get the bigger one going. For practical purposes, consider this done in three layers. The bottom layer is tinder, the next is the kindling, and on the top are the heavy sticks or logs.

Unless you are rather isolated, you probably have plenty of tinder on hand. For igniting with a match, newspaper is excellent tinder. Just save your newspapers, for if you light a fire every day, you could use several pages daily. Even without newspaper, there are numerous natural tinders—dry twigs, cedar or paper birch peelings, for instance. You can manufacture tinder by whittling dry wood into fine chips or splinters. Softwoods and other light woods are best.

For the usual fire starter, crumble two double sheets of newspaper in a loose-twisted roll. Do not roll the papers too tightly. Lay three of these rolls side by side in the bottom of the fireplace or stove. It is best if the ends of the rolls face out in the direction of the draft. On top of the rolled newspaper lay the kindling, and on top of the kindling the stovewood sticks or logs. You light the paper with your match and the rising heat and flames do the rest. If all components are dry, if you have enough of each, and if the draft is adequate, the fire will catch and grow.

If the fire does not catch, or goes out later, it will leave blackened sticks without tinder and perhaps without kindling. To start over you may need only drop in a bit of lighted paper but if you want to make sure, stuff both paper and kindling underneath the larger sticks. Once you have begun rebuilding, keep at it, for coals may ignite the paper before you are ready. Then unless you have the kindling and top sticks arranged properly, you may have to wait for a third try.

Kindling can also be dry twigs, but for ordinary household use, finely split wood handles more easily. Softwood is better than hardwood because it ignites more easily, but having kindling dry and well split is the principal requirement. Splitting creates fine splinters and thin-walled sections that ignite well. If the kindling sticks average little-finger thickness with some heavier and some lighter, they will do the job well enough.

Length of the kindling depends on where you have to use it. For many stoves, one or two handfuls of short kindling pieces about 3″ to 4″ long and thrown in a heap on top of the newspaper rolls will be sufficient. Kindling of that length is versatile, and a lot of it will fit in a pail for ready use. Fireplace kindling should be longer to span the space between the andirons.

Diagram 35

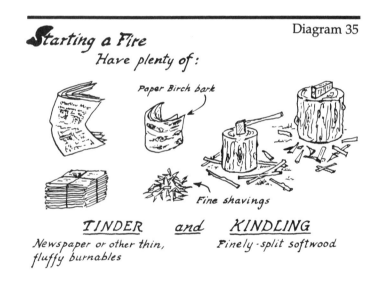

Starting a Fire

Have plenty of:

Paper Birch bark

Fine shavings

TINDER and _KINDLING_

Newspaper or other thin, fluffy burnables

Finely-split softwood

Light

In fireplace, lay tinder below andirons & criss-cross kindling.

Cover crumpled newspaper rolls with kindling sticks. Lay wood on top.

75

To start a fireplace fire without fail, place the rolled newspapers between the andiron cross members and below their level. Over the papers and on top of the cross members place a layer of long kindling, with sticks about 1″ apart. Over them, place a second layer of similarly spaced shorter pieces at right angles to the first layer. In the same manner, add two more kindling layers before placing the heavy sticks. That takes a lot of kindling, but consider it fire-starter insurance. Many times, you might need only the first layer, but the four-layer method will start a fire without fail if the other components are right.

Splitting kindling is a picky job. Keep plenty on hand so it will be available when you need it. You will need a chopping block to work on. Placing that high will save a lot of bending. Using an ax in one hand, split short blocks or short pieces of old board into fine pieces. A little bit of wood will make a lot of kindling, but it is not a speed job. Use clear-grained wood that splits easily. Converting wavy-grained, stringy, or punky wood into kindling is just not worth the effort.

Many of the woods that are ranked low as firewoods in Diagram 26 make excellent kindling. This is particularly true of resinous softwoods. Even among the softwoods, however, there is considerable difference in how well they split. This quality is also assessed in Diagram 26.

White ash is listed in the diagram as capable of being burned even when green. This is a relative quality, for every wood, white ash included, burns best when dry. Though no wood will burn when wet, with enough heat you can dry out almost anything, including wet or green wood. Some that are particularly difficult to burn until they have been thoroughly seasoned are listed as "Will not burn when green."

The only really dependable fire-starter is dry wood. After a fire has burned long enough to generate a good bed of coals, the better-burning green woods can be added, though they will not burn as well. For this reason green woods are sometimes used to hold a fire for longer periods, such as in a stove overnight. This often works, but the increased smoldering will also add markedly to the creosotes and soot deposits in the flue and chimney. So burning green wood is not a sound practice unless you are willing to clean the flue and chimney frequently. For minimum maintenance, use dry wood all the time. Even that requires attention. Dry wood will also generate quantities of creosote if a stove is closed so tightly that the wood smolders.

Wood with considerable moisture still in it will hiss softly while burning as its water is converted into steam. Frequently you can see moisture driven bubbling from the end of a stick, then boiling as it hits the external heat. Converting this moisture to steam absorbs a great deal of heat, so that a fire of green or wet wood tends to be a cool one. It is also wasteful. You must feed a larger amount of green or wet wood into a fire to gain the same heat that you could normally coax from a much smaller amount of dry wood.

When starting the fire in a stove, heater, or furnace, give it plenty of air. All draft ports and chimney dampers should be wide open. As the blaze catches, the air supply can be reduced to give you a steady, controlled fire of the size you want. Keeping the air intakes fully open will give you a climbing fire and intense heat, perhaps more than you need all at once, and the fuel will soon burn out.

In the wide-open fire, flames and heat in the flue become so intense that the creosotes deposited there are liable to ignite. In a heavily coated chimney, there may then be a chimney fire as the soaring flames touch off the deposits. The issue of fearful, roaring flames can make the outdoor view of the chimney look like a wrong-way rocket. If the chimney is sound, perhaps no harm will be done. Certainly a chimney fire is the best chimney cleaning obtainable.

On that theory, periodically operating the stove wide open can eliminate all creosotes before they become too heavy and dangerous. Prior to trying that, though, you should know how sound your chimney actually is. For inside the walls, one little chink crumbled through the bricks and mortar could start a fire in the inner woodwork that would leave nothing of your house but your naked chimney.

Stovepipes should also be inspected regularly and should be screwed together with sheet metal screws joining every section. A rotten stovepipe can actually fall apart in use, particularly during a chimney fire when the failure of the pipe could be most dangerous. When you install new pipe, knock it with your knuckles so you can remember its tinny resonance. When knocking a used stovepipe gives only a dull and muffled sound, the pipe needs cleaning.

The thinner material a stove is made of, the quicker it heats up after the fire is lighted. But sheet metal stoves are not too durable. Cast iron stoves heat more slowly but, because of their mass, give even, long-lasting heat. For a rule of thumb, the more cast iron the better and, often, the more durable the stove.

By far the most efficient use of wood fuel is to burn it in as hot a fire as possible. Then more of the volatile extracts are also burned and produce heat rather than being deposited in the chimney or spewed off into the atmosphere. Heat would escape up the chimney in this fashion, but much would also remain in the stove itself and even in the room about the stove. To conserve this heat is why better stoves are constructed so massively. The same thick walls of iron also make the stove stronger and longer lasting.

Reawakened interest in wood fuel burners has been dramatic. Not only have older models been refurbished and recopied, but entirely new ones have appeared, some imported, and many differing from any that have ever been in use hitherto. These include stoves, heaters, fireplaces, furnaces, combinations of these, and complete heating systems of novel and promising design. The variety in size, cost, and operation of these items deserves more attention than a book devoted to use of the ax should spend on them. The same old caution applies for potential users and purchasers of any wood burners: Look before you leap. The variation of purpose and quality of the items now on the market is considerable. All of them burn wood. Some of them accept other fuels as well. Many of them will become increasingly familiar in the years ahead.

What is said here pertains merely to wood stoves, heaters, and fireplaces in general. As between a stove and a fireplace, a stove is hard to beat. It does not have the splendor of an open fire, but there is also something splendid about just being warm. For a given amount of wood, the stove yields far more heat than a fireplace. Some idea of the proportions involved can be gained from Diagram 36 which gives a general guide of annual firewood consumption. Specific figures for any particular installation could show wide variation from those listed.

Most fireplaces have no draft control in the sense that they operate wide open all the time. The fire is controlled by the amount and type of fuel. In the average fireplace, the blaze should be kept to the rear. If it creeps too near the front, smoke may enter the room rather than go up the chimney.

Sometimes a fireplace will smoke anyway. Temporary wind conditions or chimney obstructions can cause this. Or a repair may be needed, such as lowering the front face of the fireplace, altering the chimney shelf or flue, extending the height of the chimney, or eliminating nearby trees that have grown tall enough to interfere with air currents over the house. Such faults can affect stove operation also, but a fireplace is much more susceptible to smoking backward.

On days when the difference between inside and outside temperatures is not too great, a chimney may develop so strong a downdraft that to light a fire at that moment would be disastrous, driving both smoke and flame into the room. Should that happen, immediately smother the new fire with ashes, stamp it out, or drown it with water.

To avoid that sort of mess, before starting any fireplace fire hold your hand or a lighted match in the top of the fireplace at the entrance to the flue. If you perceive air descending down into the room, wait before touching the fire off. Get a few crumpled newspapers, twisting their bottoms together like a newspaper bouquet. Grasping the twisted bottom, ignite the flared top and thrust it into the flue opening. Except under the most adverse conditions, the flames from this torch will reverse themselves and go up the chimney. What you will have done is heat the column of air in the chimney so that it rises, not falls. Then immediately light the tinder rolls below. Keep the torch in the chimney until the fire is surely started, after which there will be no trouble.

Fireplaces have another nasty characteristic that is anti-heating. In the midst of radiating bright warmth into the room, a fireplace also sucks a huge quantity of house-temperature air back up the chimney and discharges it outdoors. This process goes on whenever the fireplace is operating. When the outside temperature is lower than that inside, and this will usually be the case, your delightful fireplace fire may cause your house to suffer a net heat loss. If you do not feel it, it may be because your old faithful oil burner is pumping away to make up the difference. The critical outside temperature at which net heat loss occurs has been stated as high as 37°F (2°C), though the exact point would undoubtedly vary with the efficiency of the fireplace and the insulation of the room.

As with stoves and heaters, fireplaces also have vast differences in how they burn wood. The optimum fireplace principles laid down by the American, Count Rumford, in 1795 have never been discredited, yet are seldom faithfully followed. Many modern devices featuring air-heating passages and chambers decrease the heat loss of fireplace systems. Heaters such as the so-called Franklin stove also rescue much usable heat that would otherwise escape up the chimney. Most modern Franklin stoves can also be closed, making them fit the concept of a true stove. A number of imported, free-standing fireplaces of somewhat different design become efficient closed heaters merely by shutting their doors. Those who enjoy the dance and crackling cheer of an open fire will find all these items worth looking at.

ANNUAL FIREWOOD CONSUMPTION (CORDS)

USE	Small Stove	Stove/ Medium Heater	Large Heater	Average Fireplace	Furnace
Occasional	0.2 to 0.5	0.3 to 0.8	0.4 to 1.3	0.5 to 1.5	—
2–4 Hours Daily	0.8 to 1.5	1.2 to 2.5	2.0 to 4.0	2.5 to 5.0	—
Continual	3.0	5.0	8.0	——	10.0 up

Diagram 36

Every fireplace should have a screen. If you choose your wood carefully, there will be minimum need for it, but no wood can be guaranteed against throwing sparks. A wide hearth in front of a fireplace will also prove its worth. With a screen that fits securely, you can leave a fire unattended. Without such a screen, you probably should tend your fire until it is out. This can be hastened by burying the remnants of a fire in ashes. That is also a trick for keeping live coals for nearly a day.

Fireplace accessories traditionally include andirons and five tools: poker, shovel, tongs, bellows, and brush. You can pay a lot of money for sets of these and still not possess much, unless you happen to believe that you can buy tradition.

If you like watching an open fire, the upright stems of the traditional andirons interfere with the view and serve no purpose except to look scruffy after being ravaged by fire. Cleaning andirons is a truly authentic chore. Two lines of firebricks set on edge can serve the same purpose as andirons and be much longer-lasting. A fireplace should always have a bed of ashes, and with ashes about them, the bricks would scarcely be noticeable. That solves the view problem, and rather economically, too.

Of the fireplace tools, a 30″ hardwood paddle as shown in Diagram 36 can perform the functions of poker, shovel, and tongs. You can poke and lift a log a few inches inside the fireplace with the paddle. It will perform this function better than tongs. The paddle is sufficient to shovel anything that needs to be shoveled while the fire is burning. Removing the excess ashes can be done later with the stove shovel. If after several years, the paddle gets charred out of shape, making a new one will cost you about ten minutes and another hardwood stick.

For rousing a sleepy fire, a blowpipe of old rubber machinery tubing lashed lengthwise to a stick as shown in Diagram 37 will do a far better job than any bellows whose puffs are ineffectually intermittent. The blowpipe will also keep you from getting singed as you blow the flames to life.

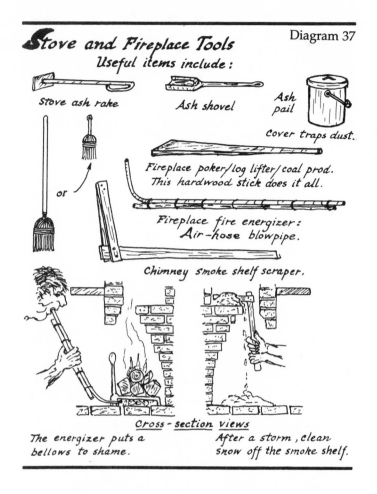

Stove and Fireplace Tools   Diagram 37

Useful items include:

Stove ash rake

Ash shovel

Ash pail

Cover traps dust.

or

Fireplace poker/log lifter/coal prod.
This hardwood stick does it all.

Fireplace fire energizer:
Air-hose blowpipe.

Chimney smoke shelf scraper.

Cross-section views

The energizer puts a
bellows to shame.

After a storm, clean
snow off the smoke shelf.

In colder areas, there is another tool needed for fireplaces, the shelf scraper (Diagram 37). The scraper cleans accumulated snow off the fireplace smoke shelf after a heavy storm. This can save you much mess. If you begin a fire when the shelf is loaded with snow, the fire may smoke up the room. Even if you escape that, the chances of having your new fire quenched by a sudden avalanche of snow are too great to play with. Clean the shelf before you lay the fire.

For stoves, a small ash shovel and an ash rake (Diagram 37) are needed. The ash rake is a great convenience in bringing live coals forward when loading an airtight stove. It has other uses also, but there it is a virtual necessity. The ash shovel can also serve the fireplace for removing excess ashes.

In burning wood, you can never afford to forget the chimney factor. The nearer to the fire, the more deposits there will be in the stovepipe and the chimney. Sooner or later, these must be removed somehow. To delay too long means trouble, even if only because of a reduced draft. If you do the cleaning yourself, you will need proper tools for the job. For lengths of stovepipe, just a long stick may be enough. Chimney brushes are now made in sizes to fit most flues. Other methods can be used such as lengths or bags of chain, weighted bundles of brush, or a long bushy sapling. For inspecting chimneys from a flue, a mirror on a stick can be useful. In many cases, the chimney will need cleaning only a short distance above the flue opening and can be cleaned from there.

However it is done, just as tradition has it, cleaning chimneys is a dirty job. But it has to be done. It is just one more cost of keeping warm with wood. And everything considered, it is worth it.

22

Sharpening Axes

The bit of an ax it must be sharp. If it is not, instead of cutting wood fibers, it will try to tear them apart, and good firewood does not tear easily at all.

Sharpening an ax is seldom a job that you can do in fifteen seconds by zipping a stone a couple of swipes across each ax cheek. If you expect an ax to cut well, you usually will have to spend some time readying it. Almost customarily, a new ax will have a bit that is too thick. You must reduce it to have a bit that cuts well. Slimming down a tempered steel edge requires caution. If you overdo the job you can irretrievably spoil an ax. Slow as hand tools may be, it is safer to use them for sharpening unless you have a lot of experience in grinding fine tools.

To put an ax into usable shape, get a file. A 10″ or a 12″ mill bastard file will do the job. The file will be easier to use if you put a handle on it. In filing, bear down against the axhead as you push the file away from yourself. Use firm, even strokes. Lift the file off the work on the return stroke and keep both work and file free of filings.

If you have a vise or other means of holding the ax securely while you file it, you will be able to do the job far quicker and probably better. Otherwise, you must hold the ax with one hand and file with the other. Then your efficiency will be but a fraction of what it should be, for filing is a two-handed job. With your second hand on the tip of the file you can direct it better and also exert four or five times as much downward pressure as you can with one hand alone.

Examine the cheek area of the bit. If it is too thick, file it down. The edge thickness must also be reduced if that is too heavy. Do not let the file reach the actual cutting edge. It is difficult to prescribe exact dimensions for proper thickness, for they vary according to both the design and the weight of an ax. However, Diagram 39 lists cross-section angles of representative ax bits, the angles formed by the two sides of the bit at the points indicated. Note the difference between the heavier swamping bit and the felling bit. These angles are only an approximate guide. They are conservative as concerns extra slim bits. But remember that steels differ. A too-slim bit slammed into a hard knot may leave the knot intact and wearing a little half-circle of ax bit to prove it.

To check your ax against Diagram 39 you will need an ordinary protractor and some device similar to large dividers to reproduce angles from your ax bit. Two old hacksaw blades screwed together at one end so they can just pivot will

be excellent for copying the angles of the cutting edge and the cheek area. These two angles are the more important ones. For the two deeper angles, you may need something longer than hacksaw blades—two straight pieces of thin wood, for instance, or even strips of stiff cardboard. To measure the angle of thickness, close the inner legs of your

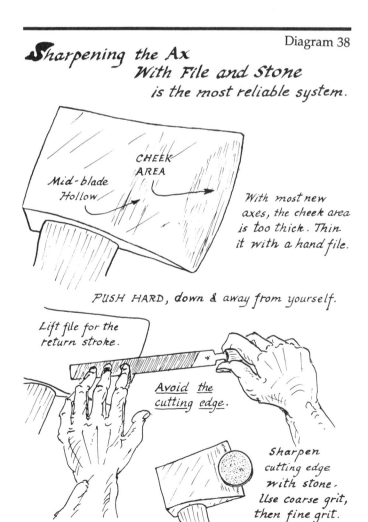

Diagram 38

Sharpening the Ax With File and Stone is the most reliable system.

CHEEK AREA

Mid-blade Hollow

With most new axes, the cheek area is too thick. Thin it with a hand file.

PUSH HARD, down & away from yourself.

Lift file for the return stroke.

Avoid the cutting edge.

Sharpen cutting edge with stone. Use coarse grit, then fine grit.

Relative Thickness of Ax Bits
Diagram 39

*An ax is not a straight wedge. Its
angle of thickness varies with position.*

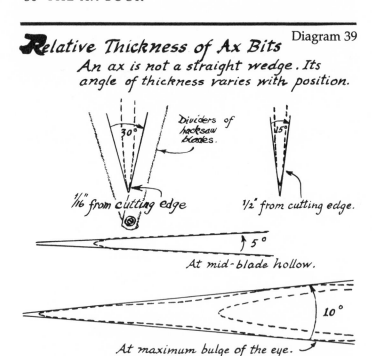

Dividers of hacksaw blades.

30° 45°

1/16" from cutting edge 1/2" from cutting edge.

5°

At mid-blade hollow.

10°

At maximum bulge of the eye.

RELATIVE THICKNESS OF AX BITS

BIT	Average angle between sides (cross-section)			
	At Maximum Bulge of Eye	At Mid-blade Hollow	Cheek 1/2" from Cutting Edge	1/16" from Cutting Edge
Felling Ax	10°-13°	5°-8°	15°	30°
Swamping Ax	10°-13°	5°-8°	19°	35°
Average New Ax	9°-12°	4°-7°	18°-21°	35°-45°

dividers against the sides of the ax bit at the point you are measuring. The apex of the dividers should be as close as possible to the cutting edge as the legs contact the bit at the point of measurement. Then without letting the dividers pivot, check the angle they form on your protractor.

The angles listed on Diagram 39 are difficult to measure because the sides of an ax bit are not, or should not be, straight anywhere. The cutting edge and the cheek of an ax are both gently convex surfaces whose angle of curvature decreases as the distance from the cutting edge increases. In filing the bit, be careful to maintain this curvature and don't create flat surfaces that will make the ax bind while chopping. A bit with convex surfaces may be somewhat harder to drive into wood, but it is far easier to withdraw. For the cut wood is straight-sided. Because the sides of the ax are curved, there is less surface-to-surface contact and the pressing wood cannot grip the ax as well. Beyond the cheeks, the sides of an ax become straighter, but an ax is seldom sunk that far into sound wood.

An even more cogent reason for the convex bit is for strength. An ax is not a razor, even though you may be able to shave with a sharp ax. The leading edge must be heavy enough to resist deformation and breakage. The average

cross-section thickness of the entire blade is about 11°. But if this angle were continued down to the cutting edge, the ax would be too fragile for the repeated impacts of chopping. So an inch or more back from the edge the angle of thickness becomes noticeably heavier. This is the cheek area. Then just back from the cutting edge itself, the angle of thickness may be as much as three to four times heavier than the average for the entire blade. (See Diagram 39.)

In shaping the bit of the ax, favor the corners. These lack the two-sided support that the midsection of the bit enjoys. So because the corners are inherently less strong, they should be left just slightly thicker. Certainly never let a corner be thinner than any portion of the bit's midsection.

Ax thickness is a compromise of several needs. The cutting edge is relatively blunt to resist breakage. In the cheek area, the angle of cross-section is reduced to permit better entry into the wood, yet remains thick enough for strength and keeping the cut wood from gripping the deeper portion of the blade. Beyond the cheek the mid-blade depression also helps keep the bit from binding. And past the depression, the ax again widens to enclose the eye. Remember each of these needs when shaping the bit. Because dull and slow as filing may be, it is easy to file off too much.

With the bit properly shaped, put the file away. For unless you chip the blade someday and must dress it all down to even it off, the filing process is over. What remains to be done is the finishing with the hand stone. This may take as long or longer. Your object is a keen edge and a silky surface to both sides of the bit, with neither bumps nor depressions.

To give a keen edge to an ax, one of the best and most essential tools is also one of the cheapest. This is a round, pocket-size, ax-sharpening stone with two different grits, coarse on one side and fine on the other. If you could have only one tool to sharpen the ax, that should be the choice. You use the stone with a circular motion, the coarse side first, scouring the surfaces that you reduced with the file. Rotate the stone in your hand from time to time so that it will wear evenly.

The round stone is a "dry" stone, so do not put oil on it. The used grit and steel particles both fall off as dust. You can help that by tapping the stone gently against the bit every few strokes. If the stone should become clogged with oil, grease, or wax, wash the stone with strong soap and a bristle brush and allow to dry before using again.

In using the stone, the greater your pressure, the faster it will cut. Keep your circular motions deliberate. It is easy to overshoot the bit and grate the stone directly against the edge you are trying to sharpen. For the same reason, grip the rim of the stone with just your fingertips so that overshooting the cutting edge will not gash a dangling finger before you can halt your return stroke.

Even though progress may seem slow, keep in mind the blade angles you are trying to attain. Use the coarse side of the stone until all file marks are scoured off, with no sharp variations of surface contour left on the bit. You can spot surface differences by how light reflects from the steel. At any point, there should be only an even dullness without sudden irregularities.

When the bit is even on both sides, turn over the stone. Then with the fine grit and the same circular motion, cover the same area and rub out the heavier marks of the coarse grit. Be patient and you will gradually gain an overall satin finish. Extend this from the cutting edge to include the entire cheek on both sides. It is that business end of the ax that pries the wood fibers apart. The smoother the bit, the less friction there will be and the deeper the ax will cut.

It is erroneous to believe that the fine grit only smooths. To smooth the steel, it must cut steel away and it cuts more rapidly than you might think. The final shape of the cutting edge itself is made with the fine side of the stone. As you complete giving a fine sheen to the entire forward part of the bit, your circular movements will likely have left the outer rim of the cutting edge too fine. Before putting the stone aside, run the fine grit directly along the outer rim of the cutting edge. Alternate several times on both sides. The stone should be held at a slight angle to the edge. These few strokes will make the tiny beginning angle of the cutting edge heavier and therefore strong enough to resist the repeated impacts of chopping. Do not overdo it. A few strokes of the stone on each side will be enough.

For most people, this is where the sharpening process stops. Many might have stopped earlier, after the rough shaping perhaps, then cursed the ax as a useless tool that would not perform. But you, having invested good sweat in your ax already, would be foolish not to complete the final step. The ax should be stropped.

The word "strop" is a corruption of "strap" and means to make a cutting edge more keen by stroking it against a length of leather. The direction of each stroke runs away from the cutting edge, of course, not into it. The reason the term is associated only with razors is that, outside of industry, a keen edge is seldom put on any cutting tool except a straight razor. Today, these are only rarely used. In a world of machine-cutters and throwaway blades, this makes small difference, but if you want a keen ax, strop it.

After you finish with the fine grit stone, your ax would typically be left with a feather-edge, a wispy border of steel up to about .04" wide. This is attached to the length of the solid cutting edge, but extending out from it like a tiny fence. It is a stubborn rind of the steel you have sharpened away. It is flexible, and because it will bend to either side of the bit it is not easily parted from the bit. To chop with an ax having a feather-edge intact is not wise. You will damage the honed bit because the feather-edge will tear off and crumple back, steel-on-steel against your keen edge.

If you are careful, light strokes of the fine stone can eliminate a feather-edge. However, impatient and too vigorous use of the stone can also perpetuate a feather-edge. As some sloughs off, more grows under the stone. Furthermore, as your bit was just about in its proper contour when you finished with the stone, you can easily blunt it too much in merely attempting to rub off a maddeningly clinging feather-edge.

The answer is the strop. Mine is an old length of machinery belting. A professional razor strop would cost you a penny or two if you could find one and it would likely be too small for stropping an ax. Perhaps one of your old clothing belts would work if you have one of real leather instead of glue-bound leather dust or plastic. A clothing belt would be narrow, but you could compensate for that by extra strokes. Hang the buckle on a nail or other strong hanger about eye-level. Now get a stick of fine polishing compound at the hardware. This stick contains a buffing abrasive in a wax. Rub the entire surface of the strop with this stick and you will have made a flexible buffing strip.

Grip the ax just below the head and pulling the strop taut with the other hand drag the bit backward toward yourself along the surface of the strop. The stroke must be forceful so there is pressure between bit and strop. At the end of the downward stroke, reverse the ax so the edge faces you and push it back up along the strop. The angle of the bit to the strop should be about 35° to 40°. After a dozen or so strokes in either direction, rub the bit clean and examine it. The feather-edge should be gone. If not, continue stropping until it entirely disappears. You will also notice the new shine to the cutting edge. It will be keen, so treat it accordingly. An easy test is to try shaving with it. Unless you are experienced at it, you might better begin with the back of your hand instead of your throat.

Stay away from a bench grinder to sharpen an ax. However, if you own one, it is less than realistic to suppose that you will not try it, so some explanation is in order. If you could drastically slow the speed of the average grinder, it would be a better, though slower, ax sharpener. The high speed creates heat at the point being ground. Unless you have a light touch and move the bit continually, enough heat can accumulate to draw the temper from the area you are grinding. Then unless you are skilled at smithing and have the equipment and tools to go with it, your best solution is to buy another ax. Or maybe you could keep that one for swamping.

How to avoid burning an ax with a power grinder is best learned by sad experience. There are many variables. The critical temperature is influenced by the type and size of grinding wheel, its speed, your action in moving the ax against the wheel, and most of all, the thickness of steel at the point being ground. Held firmly against an average grinder wheel of medium grit, the outer cutting edge of an ax can become red hot about as fast as you can blink.

To reduce the thick factory dimensions of the average new ax, there is no arguing that a grinder is the fastest means to do the job. If you keep well back from the cutting edge you may avoid burning problems, but making uneven depressions and gouges is also easy to do with a grinder. If you must try your grinder, practice on an old ax first.

There are still a few of the old-time grindstones around with a foot pedal, or perhaps the handle by which the hired boy turns the wheel for you when he is not watching television. Some old grindstones have even been fitted with electric motors to take the work out of using them. If the speed is not over about 40 to 60 revolutions per minute, depending on its size, you will have a usable and reliable grinder. These natural stone wheels must be used wet or the surface will glaze. A suspended can with a tiny hole in the bottom is the traditional way to provide water. Usually, the natural grindstone will not cut nearly as fast as a bench grinder, and because grindstones are used wet, there is little danger of burning an ax bit. On the other hand, if you shape a new ax with a new file, you would probably beat the time you might spend doing the same job on one of the old grindstones. They are faster than a hand stone, of course. If you have a grindstone, hang on to it. It is valuable for more than just being antique.

Ax-Sharpening Tools

Diagram 40

Old Faithful

Caution: A power grinder
can easily spoil a good
ax by "burning" the edge.

Always fill drip can with water.

FINISHING

For a keen edge,
strop your ax. Work
buffing compound
into the strop.

As a rule, oilstones are not used to sharpen axes. They cut well, but are not as adaptable to carrying about, being both messier and not made in the round shape that is particularly useful on the beveled bit of an ax. In recent years, other devices have come on the market featuring abrasive particles bonded to steel shanks. These cut well when new, but do not have the continued exposure of fresh grit that is characteristic of a stone. Nor are any of these sharpeners that I know of manufactured with two different grits. And for maintaining a keen edge under all conditions, you will need both the cutting and polishing that only two grits can do.

How long your ax will stay sharp depends more on how you use it than on anything else. Avoid grit, stones, and metals as you would the plague. Knots are another matter. You will have to chop your share of knots, but if you have two bits available, keep the felling bit away from knots and also away from ground-level cuts that may have grit on them. Have the felling bit easily identifiable. This does not necessarily mean you must use a double-bitted ax, though that is the easiest way to solve the problem. It is not impossible to carry two single-bitted axes. If you are a hardhead, prefer the single bit and will carry but one ax, then always carry the hand stone also. Sharpen the edge whenever it needs it, and never let the bit become too thin.

The keenest of blades can get bruised in transport and even in storage. An ax sheath is easily made. It can save much sharpening and may even save injuries. A sheathed bit is also infinitely easier to move with because you have no need to guard yourself or to baby it. (See Diagram 53.)

Lending your ax is asking for trouble unless you also trust the borrower to sharpen it as well as you would. For accidents do happen. It is no trick at all to dull or chip a bit, but quite a trick to restore its keen edge. If a man wants to borrow your ax, tell him "No." If you will not do that, then you do his chopping for him, or buy him an ax, or even give him your wood. But whatever you do, Keep your own ax for your own use.

23

Handles

Without a handle, an ax is only an awkward chunk of steel. An ax handle must be a good handle. It must be clear-grained, limber, and tough. When most people think "ax handle," the shape that will come to their minds is the gently curving S of the single-bitted ax. Somehow, the straight line of the double-bitted ax handle is overlooked. That was not always so. The straight handle has a much longer history than the curved model.

During the colonial period and the settling of the nation, all axes had straight handles. Then sometime in the middle of the last century, perhaps as early as 1840, the double-curved handle for the single-bitted ax began to gain acceptance. Details of this change seem to have escaped the historians. Among available references and histories nothing is recorded about why the straight handle was phased out in favor of the curved design that has been accepted for the single-bitted ax ever since.

That handle design changed from straight to curved is solid historical fact. For whatever reason, the change was made more than a century ago, it is impractical today to change back. This is simply because all modern handles manufactured to fit the eye of the single-bitted axes are curved ones. A double-bitted ax handle cannot be properly hung in a single-bitted axhead. The straight double-bitted handle has insufficient wood in its upper end. The eyes of the single and double ax are shaped differently, making their factory-turned handles noninterchangeable. Today, if a man wants a straight handle in a single-bit ax, he will have to make the handle himself. For a good craftsman, that might not be too much to ask, but he would also have to have the right wood. Preferably, ax handle stock should be quarter-sawed sapwood, be of hickory or a similar wood, and be of adequate seasoning, size, and quality. With these specifications, most lumber yards will strike out.

Perhaps the curved handle came into favor because it seemed to promise greater springiness and whip. Its shape gives this illusion. Whether actual usage would bear this out is something that could only be determined by test. But as just noted, there are practical difficulties to making such a test unless you have time on your hands plus the resources and the skill in making handles.

In the mid-19th century, a number of things were happening. At about the same period that the straight-handled single-bit ax was fading away, an entirely new ax (for that era) was emerging, the double-bit. And then in surprisingly few years, the double-bitted ax virtually supplanted the single among men who depended upon axes for their livelihood. The double ax had to have a straight handle. That was a necessity to enable chopping in both directions. The coincidence of events made it quite improbable that the curved

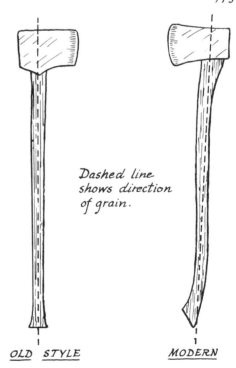

Single-Bitted Ax Handles

Diagram 41

Sometime in the mid-19ᵗʰ century, all the older straight handles on single-bitted axes became curved. Results have not been happy.

Dashed line shows direction of grain.

OLD STYLE   MODERN

The run-off grain of the curved handle breaks too easily when hit.

handle ever enjoyed sustained use among professionals. At first this would have been because of the residual use of the straight-handled single-bit axes. Then following that came the nearly universal adoption of the more efficient double-bit, also with a straight handle.

Professional woodsmen who swung their axes all day would not have tolerated clublike ax handles if there had been any alternative. The incessant pounding of a stiff handle would have been too great. Among the comments left from the 19th century on the double-bitted ax, no criticism seems to have been recorded alleging that the straight handle lacked the springiness of the curved handle. This is understandable, because the straight handle could safely be made more limber. Where the wood grain could not run continuously throughout the full length of the curved handle, to attain equal average strength, the curved handle would need to be kept heavier—and stiffer. It was a built-in disadvantage.

The case for the straight handle is at least related to what B. S. Mason said as quoted before: "[The double-bitted ax] is easier to handle and use than any other. Once accustomed to it, the single-bit seems awkward and clumsy. The weight of the double-bitted head is in line with the cutting edge—it swings truer and bites deeper." Presumably this quotation would not have been quite so lyrical had Mason believed that the straight double-bit handle was a stiff, bone-bruising club.

Mason undoubtedly sensed an even worse deficiency that has never been given the attention that it deserves. The curved handle is intrinsically less accurate than the straight handle. This is a serious charge, for accuracy is what chopping is all about. If a chopper cannot be accurate, he might lose a tree-felling contest with a beaver.

The most baneful defect of the modern single-bitted ax handle is its short bottom curve. The lower end is the grip where the chopper guides the ax. The grip portion bends from the adjoining shaft of the handle by about 10°. Unfortunately, this pretty little curve magnifies the effect of wrist pivoting.

If the chopper involuntarily allows his wrists to pivot as little as 5°, barring compensatory counteraction, the consequent deviation from the line-of-cut would be .39" for the straight-handled ax. But for the ax with the curved handle, the deviation would be .78", or *twice as much.* We have already viewed the sad results of "slight" deviations of the line-of-cut impact in Chapter 6. Even larger angles of pivot would increase both figures proportionately without changing their relative difference.

Computation of these startling figures is based on several common average dimensions using 30" single-bitted ax handles of both straight and curved types. The curved handle has the usual 10° bend just above the grip. The grip portion is 5" long, leaving the upper length of the curved handle 25" long. A fore-section distance of 4½" is assumed for each axhead forward of its respective axis of lateral pivot. (See Diagram 42 and also Diagram 5.)

When the straight-handled ax is pivoted 5° about its axis of pivot, the bit will move laterally .39", the distance that subtends an angle of 5° with sides (of the bit) being 4½" long. Note that the straight handle has no movement except the turning movement about its axis. But with the curved han-

dle, *when the handgrip is rotated, the upper 25" not only rotates, it also swings sideways,* a result of its 10° offset from the handgrip.

This reveals a fact that was not investigated in Chapter 6. The method used there for locating the axis of lateral pivot in an axhead is fine for comparisons of single-bitted axes hung on handles of similar curvature. But the string suspension method cannot validly compare an ax hung on a straight handle to an ax hung on a curved handle. The axis of pivot for a straight-handled ax lies in the center of the handle throughout its entire length, from end knob to top side of the eye.

But with the curved handle, any rotation is controlled by the chopper's hands grasping the lower curve *at the grip.* Therefore, the real axis of pivot does not pass through the axhead at all because the 10° bend of the lower handgrip is not pointed in that direction. The effective and real axis lies in an extension of the grip and passes somewhere to the rear of the entire axhead.

The trouble-making grip with its 10° bend subtends an arc of 4½" at the handle's residual length of 25". That means that the curved-handle ax already has a constructive "fore-section" of 4½" *behind* what we have hitherto termed the "axis of pivot." But there is also an additional 4½" waiting at that point. Remember, we stated that each ax has a fore-section distance of 4½" *forward* of the axis of pivot (by the string-suspension method). For a curved-handle ax, then, the constructive fore-section length between the real axis of pivot and the bit is: 2 x 4½", or 9".

So the ax with a curved handle will act as if it had an imposing bit 9" long. For a rotation of 5°, its bit will swing .78", exactly twice what that same ax would deviate if hung on a straight handle. Greater rotation would bring greater deviation in the same proportion. This is the most damning case against the curved handle. It is substantially less accurate than a straight handle.

However, the human body is a marvelous machine. It can adapt to nearly anything. If the handle of a golf club were shaped like a pretzel, some people would still play golf. A chopper soon adapts himself to a curved ax handle even though that handle is designed to frustrate accuracy. The chopper acts as if there were a straight axis throughout the entire length of the handle, even though there is not.

But this unconscious adaptation has a price. Use of the curved handle requires more practice to cut well. And even with practice, the chopper cannot attain the results possible with a straight handle. In our history, this is at least partially confirmed by the woods professionals of the era when trees were felled with axes. These men graduated from single-bitted axes on straight handles to double-bitted axes, also on straight handles. Curved ax handles do not seem to have ever attained widespread professional acceptance.

But if all this is so, there remains a mystery around single-bit ax handles. In the decade or more before the American Civil War, what made the curved handle so attractive that it drove its straight ancestor out of existence? Until the advent of shape-cutting lathes that could produce curved handles automatically, the curved model would have been more difficult to make by hand. However, such lathes were in operation by the mid-19th century. A fault of all curved handles of ordinary size is that they cannot be mass-

Diagram 42

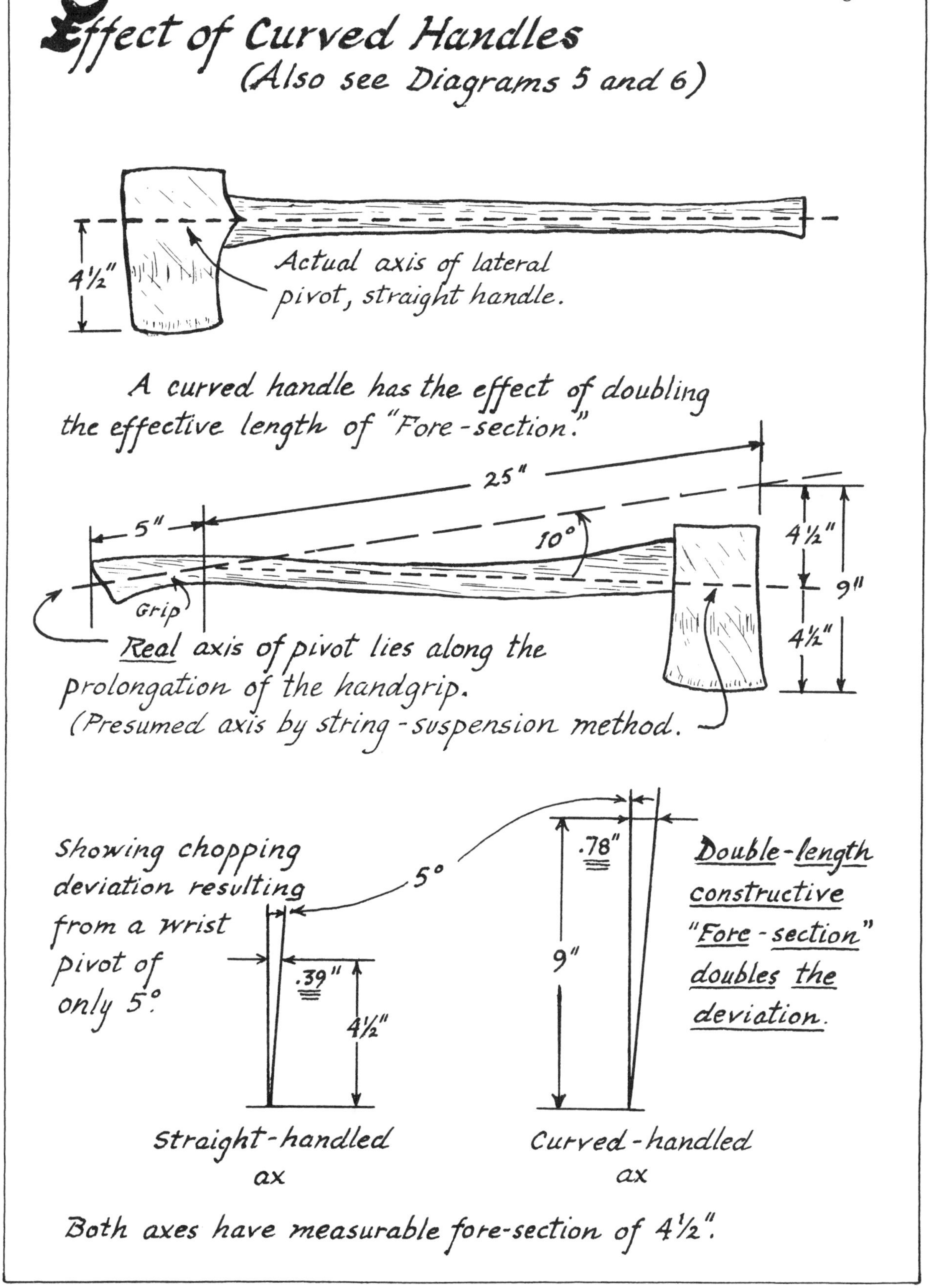

Effect of Curved Handles
(Also see Diagrams 5 and 6)

4½"

Actual axis of lateral pivot, straight handle.

A curved handle has the effect of doubling the effective length of "Fore-section."

25"

5"

10°

Grip

4½"

9"

4½"

Real axis of pivot lies along the prolongation of the handgrip.
(Presumed axis by string-suspension method.

Showing chopping deviation resulting from a wrist pivot of only 5°.

5°

.78"

9"

.39"

4½"

Double-length constructive "Fore-section" doubles the deviation.

Straight-handled
ax

Curved-handled
ax

Both axes have measurable fore-section of 4½".

produced to coincide with the grain of the wood along their entire length. As we have noted, this makes the curved handle more damage-prone than a straight handle of the same lateral dimensions. You might expect that curved handles would require more frequent replacement. If so, it is easy to see why manufacturers would have enjoyed marketing curved handles. Yet the same fact gives even more reason to be curious as to why the curved handle has lasted so long. Were there no consumer revolts?

The initial introduction and establishment of the curved handle is not difficult to imagine. Its graceful curves would have evoked the image of a leaping whip. In an ax handle, a whiplike quality would enable the chopper to strike harder and simultaneously protect him from the resultant shock. Even though accustomed to the old straight handles, any axman would have welcomed the prospect of improved performance. It takes time for ideas to rattle in the mind between action and reaction, then finally to settle in some equilibrium. Probably, by the time that the pre-Civil War chopping population came to realize that curved handles were more fragile than straight handles, that a man could not easily make a curved handle himself, and that the whiplike image could not deliver greater resiliency after all, many curved handles would have been in use.

Transitory popularity of an idea or item is not at all limited to women's clothes. The history of axes abounds in examples. Or take automobiles. What happened to the running board, free wheeling, rumble seat, vent window or convertible top? These were not casualties of technological improvement. Each was immensely popular in its time. Manufacturers stopped producing them on finding that the public popularity had diminished. In each case, the fashion had expired.

A particularly depressing example of the power of fashion has been the two-generation reign over educators of the pictorial method for teaching children to read. When general acceptance of the method finally proved that children were no longer reading well at all, the pictorial reading fashion finally lapsed back into the phonics method of teaching reading. This instance is remarkable because the principal movers were the cream of the intellectual set. So to suggest that a sudden preference for curved ax handles over a century ago was born of popular impulse rather than the real merit of curved handles should not strain belief.

But when the bloom had faded from the curved handle's promise of improvement, then why did it not disappear? Again there is a void in ax handle history, but it seems reasonable to assume that desire of the handle manufacturers to sell a faster-moving item cannot be the entire answer.

A more important clue probably lies in a sad fact that is still unchanged as you read this. Only the curved model of handle will fit the eye of the single-bitted ax. At the first flush of the pre-Civil War curved ax handle fad, ax manufacturers would certainly have furnished axes compatible with the new handle design. And to produce axes with the new handles, or fitting only the new handles, would have been but one more logical step. That would not be conspiracy of the sort that consumer advocates find in every corner today. It would simply have been commercial evolution.

But the result was unfortunately the same. An inferior handle was kept on the market without any reasonable substitute available to replace it. The old straight-handled single-bit axes had gone the way of the stone ax. On all the newer single-bit axes the eyes would fit only the diagonal-grained curved handles.

At a period when, as Eric Sloane said, the ax was "the most important implement in America," the curved-handle mistake would have been short-lived had not the needs of industry found satisfaction in another direction. During the same years that we have just been speaking of, the startling innovation of the double-bitted ax swept down through the woods from Maine. In a remarkably short time, in every region of the county where timber was felled, the double ax became the standard for professional woodsmen.

It was the occasional user of the ax, the host of farmers, small woodlot owners, householders, and others who fell heir to the single-bitted ax and its curved handle. Unwilling to accustom themselves to the greater hazards of using the double-bit and not burdened by the production goals of professionals, the part-time axmen were perfectly content with the single-bit. Limited use broke a limited number of handles and the virtues of the double ax were sacrificed for the security of the single. As the years passed, fewer persons even remembered that a straight handle could be hung in a single-bit ax, and that, in the past, the straight handle had been the only handle known.

Then a generation ago, the roar of the chain saw sounded the funeral dirge of the double-bitted ax as a professional tool. As of that moment, the straight ax handle joined the buggy whip. The double had done its task, but its time had gone. Save barroom decorations and rusting residuals in country barns this is the situation that prevails today.

The story of the straight ax handle is relevant because that design deserves to be resurrected for the single-bitted ax. Replacing an ax handle properly, or making a new handle, is painstaking labor that nobody should have to do more than necessary. The curved handle is more easily broken. Its curves cut across the grain, increasing the likelihood of splitting when stressed, as when overreaching in limbing. And worse, it is less accurate. The only sensible solution is a straight handle. For a double ax, you can buy one. For the single-bit, you must make one yourself. If you want some fun, try it.

Not many varieties of wood are suitable for ax handles. Hickory is the usual wood of choice for tool handles requiring flexing strength. Virtually all commercial ax handles are hickory. It is dense, hard, tough and strong. If hickory is not available, several other woods will do. Among the better ones are black locust, hop-hornbeam, white ash, white oak, and sugar maple. None of these is extra plentiful.

For making an ax handle, whatever variety of wood you select, use only the outer, lighter-colored sapwood of the tree. The inner heartwood tends to be more brittle. Saw a log without knots or defects to the length you need, leaving a few inches at each end to allow for seasoning checks, the small cracks that often open on the end-grain of wood as it dries.

Then cut or split the chunk into sections thick enough for handles. Quarter-sawed stock as in Diagram 43 will remain straight without warping. Cut the heartwood from these handle blanks and store them in a dry location to season. Painting their ends with oil paint or linseed oil will help prevent checking during seasoning. Each piece should be laid on two or more evenly spaced cross-sticks beneath it to allow circulation of air. If stacking is needed, the spacer sticks separating each layer must be exactly one above another. That ensures that the weight of the stack is supported on the spacer sticks rather than on an unsupported portion of the blanks. Stresses during the drying process tend to permanently distort lumber. Length of seasoning will depend on conditions. For ax handles, usually allow a year.

The proper length for an ax handle depends on what chopping you will be doing. Two general principles of handle length used to be recognized. The larger the trees, the longer the ax handle, and a felling ax needs a longer handle than a swamping ax. Today, if you chop your own firewood with just one ax, a 30″ handle should prove about right.

The handle is measured by its entire length, including the portion enclosed by the eye. Assuming that any length below 20″ is a hatchet handle as distinguished from a handle for an ax, known ax handles have ranged from 20″ to 42″ at least. In the past century, handles over 36″ were distinctively western and 42″ was a common handle length for working on the enormous trees of the Pacific Northwest. For swamping work there, 42″ was too awkward and a representative swamping ax handle was 36″. Among the smaller trees of the Northeast, ax handles were shorter. In the Maine woods of about 1900, the average handle length was 32″. For the same period, the average for the rest of the county was 36″.

The relationship between size of trees and length of ax handles mirrored events. Second- and third-growth trees seldom equaled virgin timber. Cutting had been in progress in Maine for generations when a 1948 woodsmen's supply catalog there listed no felling ax handle longer than 30″. Apparently, the size of Maine timber had shrunk.

The matter of handle whip is not minor. A limber handle permits hitting harder, yet cushions each blow. Dividends in lessened fatigue can be substantial. You can make a handle springier by reducing its lateral dimensions. But when using it, make sure that you can give it the protection it deserves, for a too-slender handle is particularly susceptible to damage. The other major factor of handle fragility is the noncontinuous grain of the curved handles. For their protection, curved handles are often made heavier. Too often, the result is a rigid club that transmits every shock of chopping because it has next to no spring.

A reasonable solution for the owner of an ax lies in slimming down the commercial handle, provided that this is not overdone. It is best to be conservative at first, for in spite of any handle defects, the most common cause of breakage is user abuse such as slamming the handle into a limb.

Diagram 44 gives representative lateral dimensions at the midsection of 30″ hickory ax handles. The larger the dimensions, the stiffer the handle. You might be able to drop a cow with the last handle listed. It is that heavy. The first handle listed is a craftsman's tool. Chopping with it would be a pleasure, but it would not stand abuse. For handles either shorter or longer than 30″, the lateral dimensions of the table would vary in direct proportion to length.

In making a handle or reshaping one that is too heavy, be careful to form or retain an elliptical cross section. The shaft of an ax handle should never be round. For any given thickness, the round shape would be insufficiently strong. It also

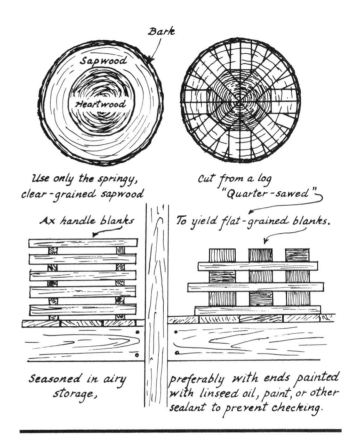

Diagram 43

Handle Stock Selection and Storage
Use hickory or other tough wood.

Bark
Sapwood
Heartwood

Use only the springy, clear-grained sapwood

Cut from a log "Quarter-sawed"

Ax handle blanks

To yield flat-grained blanks.

Seasoned in airy storage,

preferably with ends painted with linseed oil, paint, or other sealant to prevent checking.

would pivot too freely in the hands. In the usual midsection proportions, handle width (front to rear dimension) is just a shade less than one and three-quarters times handle thickness.

Cross-section proportions along the rest of the handle are also important. For both models of handle, the maximum lateral dimensions just below the head should gradually lessen in a long taper covering the upper two-fifths of the exposed portion of the handle. This upper section is subjected to most abuse and needs the greater dimensions the taper provides for strength. Let the next two-fifths of the handle, or slightly more, be regularly dimensioned in whatever weight range is chosen from Diagram 44. The final fifth, or slightly less, should again swell evenly in both lateral dimensions to make a comfortable grip. The end has a pronounced flair, a knob that keeps the whole handle from slipping out of the hands while chopping.

On straight handles, the end knob is cut straight across. Commercial curved handles customarily finish the end knob with a cut slanted at about 40° to 50°. (See Diagram 44.) This is the "fawn foot," so-named because of its likeness to the upraised hoof of a young deer. Picturesque and traditional as

Diagram 44

Ax Handle Dimensions

Length of handle should fit the chopper and the work. A 30" handle is good for felling & bucking trees up to 12" in diameter.

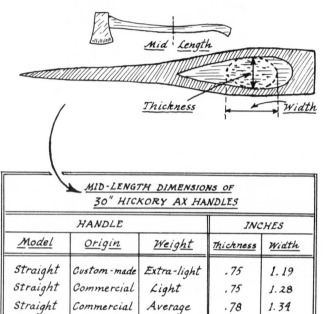

Mid Length

Thickness   *Width*

MID-LENGTH DIMENSIONS OF 30" HICKORY AX HANDLES

HANDLE			INCHES	
Model	Origin	Weight	Thickness	Width
Straight	Custom-made	Extra-light	.75	1.19
Straight	Commercial	Light	.75	1.28
Straight	Commercial	Average	.78	1.34
Straight	Commercial	Heavy	.81	1.41
Curved	Commercial	Light	.78	1.38
Curved	Commercial	Average	.81 - .84	1.44
Curved	Commercial	Heavy	.88	1.50

the fawn foot may be, get rid of it. Its sharp toe will gouge out your ribs when working in close quarters, as in a limbing tangle.

It is common to cut the tip of the fawn foot off at right angles to the handle. Another method is to shear the entire lower half off at about 70°. The remainder of the end knob will still be of maximum width and thickness and will still keep the hands from slipping off. In addition, on the end of both models of handle, there will be a flat surface to hit when hanging the axhead. Before pounding this surface, bevel its rim so that its edges will not chip, crack, or spread.

If you decide to take the plunge and make an ax handle, copy a pattern from a handle of your choice, or make up your own and trace this on the handle blank. If available, a bandsaw is excellent for cutting out the blank. If not, a sharp handsaw can perform wonders. In the curved portions that a handsaw cannot follow, saw a series of close parallel cuts down to the line and then split or chisel out the waste wood. Holding the blank in a vise is almost essential. As the handle

nears completion, shield it from the vise jaws with cloth, paper, cardboard, or leather to prevent scarring.

For intermediate shaping, a drawknife is a good tool if used carefully. A spokeshave is one of the best tools, and a curved spokeshave the best of all. Lacking these, a block plane is surprisingly helpful, though it cannot reach some concave surfaces. A sharp rasp is capable of doing the entire job but the final touches through it will not be as sharp when you finish. If possible, save the woodrasp for where you must use it, such as the concave sections. To measure the emerging handle, use calipers. If you do not have them, improvise them. A slot sawed into the edge of a board can serve as a caliper for the job. Have one for width and another for thickness.

Finishing can be done with files, sanding, or even sharp pieces of glass. Steel wool is good for final touches. Make the finish smooth and you will save future blisters. Lastly, rub in raw linseed oil daily until the wood will take no more. From time to time, and especially after a wetting, work in more linseed oil to maintain a protective finish. The handle is worth it.

Ax handles are no longer made exclusively of wood. In the past several years a number of innovative ax, maul, and sledge hammer handles have appeared using fiberglass or fiberglass-reinforced shafts. Some designs secure the fiberglass handle to the axhead with epoxies or other cements. In a more conventional technique, other models use special aluminum or plastic wedges to fix the slotted top end of the handle within the eye of the axhead. The fiberglass shafts are usually slender and, most typically, of uniform dimensions from end to end. Therefore the exterior grip of these handles is furnished as either a cement-on or pre-attached boot of traditional contour for either a single- or double-bitted handle design. The boots are of vinyl, rubber, polypropylene, etc. Consequently, some of these handles have a total weight greater than a similar wooden handle.

The new handles have been presented as being superior to wooden ones. One label even boasted, "lasts 80 x longer . . ." Such extravagance is not easy to prove either way, but some comparisons can be made. The first is price, with the newer fiberglass handles costing two to three times as much as wooden handles.

Although weight for weight, fiberglass is stronger than wood, a fiberglass handle is nevertheless susceptible to the severe impacts of overreaching in chopping, just as a wooden handle is. And like wood, fiberglass has grain. Behind a bruised area that has been hit, some of the new handles can split internally. Not uncommonly, such splits continue to grow with use far more than would be normal with wood. If these cracks creep up within the eye, they can loosen the head, particularly with handles secured by wedges. If it is a cemented-on handle that must be changed, the difficulties of cleaning out the eye are multiplied by cement clinging to the interior of the eye itself.

The end boot that gives the grip area of the fiberglass handle its contour and hand-filling bulk is often ribbed to provide a "better grip." The upper cuff of this boot presents a ridge that the upper chopping hand must slide forcibly over at every stroke. If you do much bare-handed chopping, both of these features will soon give you blisters. For all except casual use, a working ax handle must be smooth.

Handle flexibility can be critically important for chopping much wood. How limber a fiberglass handle is will depend upon the dimensions of its shaft. These dimensions seem to vary considerably with different makes of the new handles. You can shape a wooden handle by cutting some of the stock away. Fiberglass handle design does not always permit doing that. If you have a handle-reducing problem, or an unusual fitting problem for either the eye or the grip of a handle, the best solution could be to use a handle of wood.

Considering the potential of fiberglass, further development of fiberglass handles bears watching. But to date, watching these handles seems a more practical course than using them.

24

Hanging an Ax

"Hanging" an ax is not displaying it over your fireplace. It is fitting the ax with a handle that works. Not all handles do. But even if you start with a good handle, it will be of little help if after a couple of swings the axhead flies independently through the windshield of your pickup. To depend on the ax, it must be hung right.

A properly hung ax meets three tests. First the ax and its handle must be so securely joined that the two act as a single solid unit under any conditions of stress. Second, the bit(s) of the ax must lie in the same plane as the longitudinal axis of the handle. That is, when looking down along the cutting edge, you will see the center of the handle knob. (See Diagram 45.) This ensures that the ax is capable of hitting where, and along the line, it is aimed. Third, with the ax held edgewise against a straight surface, bit and handle knob both contacting that surface, the bit touches at its mid-point. This evidence of vertical centering provides equal protection against both overreaching and underreaching when chopping.

Instructions given in this chapter are for fitting axes with handles of wood. In hanging fiberglass or fiberglass-core handles in axes, follow the manufacturer's instructions. Just remember that every ax handle, no matter what it is made of or how it is made, must pass the three basic tests mentioned above.

Because you will seldom fit a handle to a brand new ax, the first ax-hanging chore will probably be removing the remains of the old handle from the axhead. Never try to pound the head off a handle, for the body of the ax is soft steel and hammering can damage it. Cut the old handle off close to the axhead. If the wedges in the top end are loose, pry them out if you can. If you succeed, straddle the ax over an open vise, and with a short piece of steel rod, punch the whole business back out the bottom of the eye.

Ordinarily, though, you will not be able to dislodge an old handle that easily. You usually must dig, drill, or punch the old wedges and bits of wood out one by one until the whole eye is cleaned. Where splinters of old handle are loose, it is often easier to punch them upward out the top of the eye. The eye flares wider at the top end. A straight rod works better than a tapered punch, which tends to get stuck. A narrow chisel may be of help to cut wood free, though with the steel walls hemming it in and steel wedges lurking

alongside, the keen edge of a wood chisel can disappear in a single wrong tap.

The easiest tool to use is an electric drill with a small bit. Then you can drill out the wedges and any wood in sight and punch the remainder through with the rod. Two cautions: Avoid hitting the wedges or the ax walls and particularly the narrow ends of the eye or the crevices between wedges and the walls. In these narrow spaces, the drills easily seize and break.

Descriptions have been written of how in an emergency it is possible to burn an old handle from a single-bitted ax. To protect the temper in the bit, bury the ax bit downward in mud or moist clay up to the eye. The exposed section containing the eye and poll will not be harmed by heat. Then pile hot coals around it until the wood of the handle is destroyed. Clearly, this trick should not be attempted with a double-bitted ax. About this system, a nagging thought is difficult to get rid of. If a man were so short of tools that he had to clean an axhead in this manner, he might also have some trouble hanging the new handle for the same reason.

Tools for fitting the new handle are the same as those for making a handle, the primary ones being the spokeshave (or drawknife) and the rasp. A large bastard file is also useful.

With the eye of the ax clean, try to fit the top end of the new handle into the bottom of the eye. If the handle is too large to enter evenly, bevel its top rim until it enters and will stick there. Then gently reverse the handle in your hands so that you hold the grip end and the axhead hangs at the bottom. Facing you is the flat surface of the end knob. It should have at least a 1/8" bevel around its rim. You will hammer that surface a good deal, so the bevel will keep the edges from chipping. Then holding the handle just below the knob, pound the flat surface several times with a hammer. Center your blows. Also be gentle until you are certain that the axhead will not fall off the handle. You should feel a slight sponginess of impact as the handle drives into the eye. The axhead must not rest against the floor or anything else. Merely let it hang suspended on the end of the handle.

At each blow, you will be able to sense the movement, or lack of it, of the handle into the head. When your hammer blows lose their sponginess and have more of a ring, you will have driven the handle into the eye as far as it will go with its existing dimensions. That distance may be quite slight, perhaps only a part of an inch.

Now reverse the handle again and look down along the bit to see whether it is centered on the end knob as shown in Diagram 45. If it is pointed to the right, you must reduce the handle thickness on that side along the line where the bottom of the eye rests. If the bit points to the left, the left side must be treated accordingly. If the line of the bit is aimed squarely at the center of the end knob, then both sides of the handle must be reduced equally, provided that both scrape the edge of the eye.

Next, check vertical alignment. Rest the ax bit downward on your workbench or other straight surface. Both the middle of the bit and the end knob of the handle should simultaneously contact the surface, as in Diagram 45. If only the lower half of the bit contacts the surface, the forward edge of the handle must be reduced along the line that the bottom of the eye rests. If it is the top half of the bit that touches, then the back edge of the handle must be reduced. If the bit contacts only at its center as it should, then both forward and back edges will need reducing, provided that both scrape the edge of the eye.

Having made these alignment checks, remove the handle from the axhead. Straddling the ax over an open vise, pound the handle back out with a short stick or rod. Do not pound the axhead itself. With the handle free, note the line of scarring that marks maximum advance into the eye. It is along this line and a little to either side of it that you must cut away a thin layer of wood as indicated by inspections of alignment. Where no scarring is evident, no shaving is needed. If there is no line at all, or too little to guide you, you did not drive the handle forcefully enough into the head, so pound it back in again and repeat the whole process.

To ensure a proper fit, slice the wood away in small doses. If you remove a lot at each fitting, sooner or later some spot will be too low. Then you could swallow one or more of the criteria for proper hanging of an ax, or you could get a new handle and start over. Or you could be lucky, and by seating the ax still farther down on the handle, work out of the spot that was too low. The process is tedious. Ten or a dozen fittings or more are not unusual to attain a well-aligned fit.

The farther you drive the handle into the eye, the more both lateral and vertical alignments become fixed. Sometimes the eye of an ax is not straight, and drastic cutting of the handle to one side or another is necessary to achieve correct alignment. This will make a weak handle. If you can do it, this is reason for returning the ax as defective.

How far down the handle you seat the ax depends on what you want for handle length. Most commercial handles are built with a shoulder and at least ½" of the shoulder should be retained below the final position of the head. Below the shoulder, the lateral dimensions of the handle begin to diminish. Although a loose axhead will usually work upward, this is not always true. Having some shoulder left beneath the head provides security against having the head slip downward. In the latter stages of fitting, driving the handle will curl surplus thickness of wood up away from the steel. This also helps provide a solid final seat for the head.

Before the last driving, saw a slot down into the top of the handle from corner to corner, and deep enough to reach the middle of the eye when the handle is driven home. This slot is to receive a wooden wedge when the handle is in its permanent position. The wedge should also be of good hardwood. Make it wide enough to loosely fit the long dimension of the eye and having an angle of thickness of about 8°. Length of the wedge should be at least 3" to give it enough body to hold together while being pounded in. Shape the lead edge of the wedge as you would an ax bit so it will not be too fine.

Driving the handle the final time, pound the end knob until your blows rebound sharply, the sound is resonant, and the shock uncomfortable to your hand gripping the handle. Strike only in the center of the knob. The punishment this knob can take is surprising, but it can split. Check the alignments a final time, and if all is as it should be, saw off the upper protrusion of the handle about ⅛" above the head.

Now tap the wooden wedge into the top slot so it is well-spaced and stands by itself. Then pound it home. With a wide hammer, you might keep the wedge from splitting, but preventing this is not easy. Pound as evenly as possible. If splitting occurs, hammer each piece in separately. Finally the wedge will crumble, but hammer home every splinter

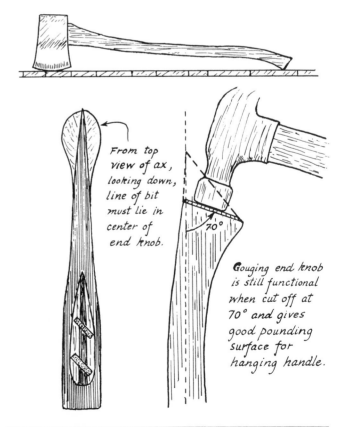

Diagram 45

Handle Alignment

When laid, bit down, on a flat surface, the _middle_ of the bit and handle must both touch.

From top view of ax, looking down, line of bit must lie in center of end knob.

Gouging end knob is still functional when cut off at 70° and gives good pounding surface for hanging handle.

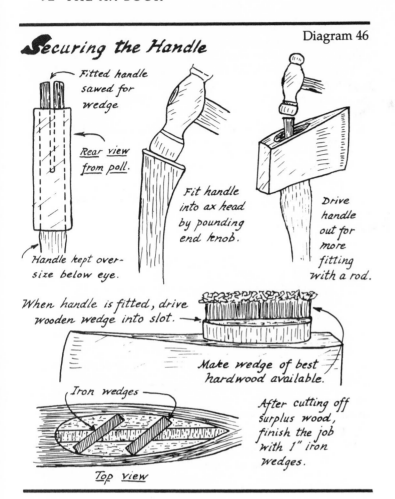

Securing the Handle Diagram 46

Fitted handle sawed for wedge

Rear view from poll.

Handle kept over-size below eye.

Fit handle into ax head by pounding end knob.

Drive handle out for more fitting with a rod.

When handle is fitted, drive wooden wedge into slot.

Make wedge of best hardwood available.

Iron wedges

After cutting off surplus wood, finish the job with 1" iron wedges.

Top view

you can. Inspect the bottom line of the eye. No withdrawal should be evident, but if there is, pound the end knob again to reseat the head where it should be.

Axes are seldom held securely by just the single wooden wedge. You should have on hand two soft steel wedges of the type that is about 1" wide by 1½" deep. Spacing them so they do not crowd each other, drive these wedges in diagonally across the wooden wedge. The first may drive easily, but the second will likely take some pounding. Now cut off the surplus ⅛" protruding handle and you have an ax you can trust. Finish the top with a file or grinder and rub it with linseed oil for several days until it will take no more.

Ax manufacturers used to warn against wedging too heavily because of the danger of bulging the eye. Without slighting such a warning, it can also be said that such cases are not common with modern axes. Having a loose-fitting axhead is also a danger. If you hang your ax as described above, the handle will stay there until you drill it out.

It is not rare to buy a brand new ax, use it a few times, and discover that the head is loose. This abomination is sometimes compounded by a capped wedge fitted on the end of the handle. Pry this out, or if you cannot, file or grind the cap off. Then into the exposed top of the handle, drive one or more of the steel wedges. Most hardware stores also carry a narrower steel wedge that may fit where the larger ones do not.

One of the ancient, but not honored, solutions for securing an axhead is to soak it in a bucket of water overnight. If your handle is basically sound, it will not be improved by soaking, nor will the ax. Wedge the handle properly and your ax will be ready to use anytime without waiting overnight for it.

25

Other Woods Tools

Versatile as the ax is, it cannot do everything. Even if your ax is the only cutting tool you use for firewood, a number of other tools are useful and some are essential. Being familiar with a few of the more common items, you can better select the ones you need.

In the broad category of "felling aid," the first vital item has been mentioned before, the combination-grit pocket sharpening stone for your ax. Unless you do not intend to be in the woods more than a couple of hours, always take this stone. But it can wear out pockets as well as sharpen axes. A convenient carrier is a plastic sandwich bag which can be replaced as needed.

Axes, particularly double-bits, do not travel well unless they are sheathed. Cut some rectangular strips of sidewall from an old tire, fastening them together on three sides, leaving the fourth side open to slip over the ax bit. Punch holes at the two inner corners for laces to secure the sheath around the handle. With a double ax, make two sheaths, lacing them to each other to protect both bits. (See Diagram 53.) Tie knots on the ends of the laces so they cannot pull back through the holes. This will not only save relacing. It will also save the double-bit sheaths from getting lost or separated.

Sheaths will fit better if they are made of three thicknesses of sidewall, the middle layer being a rim spacer to provide a roomier interior and a backstop for the sharp edge of the bit. Fasten the layers together with rivets, soft wire, or even clinched nails.

If you use a saw of any type in the woods, you will always need felling wedges. Modern ones are often made of plastic or aluminum to avoid damage to chain saws. Felling wedges are smaller than splitting wedges. (See Diagram 13.) They are driven into saw kerfs, either to open the kerf or to keep it from closing. You should always have at least two of them, or more if the trees are of any size or if you attempt any fancy correction of lean. With the wedges, you will also need a maul or sledge to drive them.

For splitting in the woods, take at least one 8-pound steel splitting wedge. In warm weather, or when the trees are over 10″ in diameter, three splitting wedges may save you working time. (See Diagrams 22 and 23.) Splitting means a maul, also in the 8- to 10-pound class. Making your own wooden wedges of both types is good economy, but this must be

remembered well in advance. Green wedges crumble easily.

The term "pickaroon" applies to two different tools. The one that was once common in the East was a long pike with a small hook at its end as well as a point. This was a riverman's tool when long logs were floated to the downstream mills on the spring runoff. That pickaroon is little used today. Both

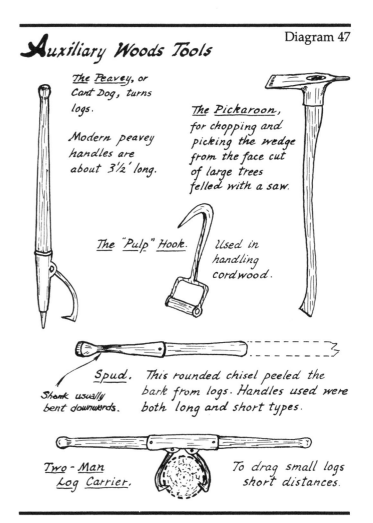

Auxiliary Woods Tools   Diagram 47

The Peavey, or Cant Dog, turns logs.

Modern peavey handles are about 3½′ long.

The Pickaroon, for chopping and picking the wedge from the face cut of large trees felled with a saw.

The "Pulp" Hook. Used in handling cordwood.

Spud. This rounded chisel peeled the bark from logs. Handles used were both long and short types.

Shank usually bent downwards.

Two-Man Log Carrier. To drag small logs short distances.

timber and pulpwood are transported almost entirely by truck.

The other pickaroon is a felling aid. In the western and Pacific timber areas it is also known as the "Pulaski tool." This pickaroon is allied to the ax, but designed for a different function. Though double-"bitted," it is customarily hung on a single-bit handle. The principal bit, instead of being parallel to the plane of the handle, is perpendicular to the handle. The opposing "bit" is actually a short pick. This pickaroon is for splitting apart and then picking out the wedge of wood made by a saw in face cuts. For small trees, you would have little use for a pickaroon. For the large trees, if you did not have the tool, you might wish that you did, for removing the face chunk without a pickaroon might be difficult, unsafe, or both.

For one man to try to push a tree into its lay with a pole may seem ridiculous, but as noted in Chapter 11, it is not. Naturally there are limitations. The tree must not be too large or too heavy. The lean to be overcome must not be too great, and the tree must be just about ready to fall. There must be no appreciable wind. For cases within that definition, the pickpole is a useful tool. Because of its length, it is not an especially handy one. From the viewpoint of use, though, the longer the pole, the better. Twenty feet is a practical maximum. A hardwood pole having sufficient stiffness would probably be too heavy, so you may have to use softwood. Years ago, you could purchase spike and ferrule kits for outfitting a suitable pole yourself. You can still make a pickpole by drilling the small end of a pole to receive a pointed rod. Let it protrude about 3". Several firm twists of wire will make a satisfactory ferrule to keep the end of the pole from splitting.

Roping a tree into the lay you want may occasionally be necessary for a tree having a lean toward buildings, water, highways, power lines, or anything else that must not be hit. The drawing force should usually be something more than your own unaided muscles. For using a vehicle, you should have at least 100' of ⅝"-diameter rope. One or more single block pulleys can also be useful to permit change in direction of pull. For attaching the rope to the tree you may need a ladder, climbing irons and belt, or a cord with throwing-weight to sling around the upper tree and enable you to draw the rope up and secure it. As noted in Chapter 11, the weight should have smooth contours so it can be retrieved by pulling it back. The throwing cord should be strong, ⅛" nylon perhaps 100' long.

The last felling aid is the jack fitted with studs on base and piston, also referred to in Chapter 11. Though a jack can be useful in correcting lean, remember that its complexity makes a jack less reliable than wedges. A hydraulic jack is convenient for both size and operation, but the screw type can be safer. Both of them must be fitted for the load they will have to carry.

Personal equipment may not be "tools" but can be important nonetheless. One modern item worth considering is the construction worker's hard hat. Woods are full of limbs and portions of tree trunk waiting to fall. These slough off otherwise sound trees quite frequently. Not all of them are noticeable. A hard hat will not stop everything, but it is more expendable than your skull.

Every tool creates its own set of calluses on the user. If you begin an activity too strenuously, calluses can start as blisters. Using an ax is no exception to this rule. Unless you use the ax regularly, you should wear leather gloves or choppers in any weather. You will accomplish more if you are not favoring your skin. When you harden up, then you can shed the extra protection. Feet also need protection. Steel-toed boots have prevented many woods injuries. There are valid arguments against steel toe covers, but the weight of evidence is with them when one is working with logs.

When you are using a chain saw, another highly desirable personal item is a pair of trousers with protective padding covering the front of the leg. The padding can be cut, of course, but the warning can save your leg.

Of processing tools, the first needed might be a peavey, or, as it is also called, a cant dog. Peaveys with handles of 3½' are suitable for most firewood work. As noted before, longer handles are no longer common. This log-turning tool has a stout spike in its bottom end. A similar tool with a sharp lip at the bottom instead of a spike can also drag a log. Known as a cant hook, it is usually a mill tool rather than one used in the woods. If you are without a peavey, a strong pole used as a lever can sometimes perform the same function, though scarcely as well.

No record of axes can neglect the broadax. Recently, modern broadaxes hung with modern single-bit handles have been marketed for wall decoration purposes at about the price of three ordinary axes. Though this is probably a good business tactic, it does illustrate how times change. The original purpose of a broadax was to hew level surfaces, usually logs into timbers. (See Diagram 48.)

The log being hewed, often secured by toothed iron "dogs," would be scored with the ax at intervals to facilitate hewing off flakelike chips. Then the hewer, standing alongside his work and swinging downward on it, would split off the scored sections. Accuracy was attained by marking the logs end to end with a taut chalkline, or charcoal-blackened line.

Of all ax designs, broadax designs have perhaps been the most varied. Broadaxes made for hewing in this century have generally varied from 3½ to 10 pounds, with bits of one-sided bevel ranging in width from 6" to 12". An offset handle was customary to permit the hewer to strike vertically at a line that was slightly to his side. It was skilled work, and dangerous. Hewing strokes were principally vertical, were not backed-up, were executed on the wrong side of the frontal zone (See Diagrams 7 & 8.) and terminated alongside the hewer's shins. It was not a job for the unskilled.

Steve Young of Concord, Maine, who helped edit this book, told of being a young boy listening to his grandfather and his grandfather's two brothers, still vigorous men, discussing their work. All three of them were woodsmen, all earned a premium over the ordinary woods wage because they were hewers. With broadaxes they converted logs into dimension timbers. They took pride in that. They were good and they knew it.

Steve's grandfather had seriously explained, "I hew to the line."

Great uncle #1 was unimpressed. "I take out the line," he retorted.

Great uncle #2, usually reserved, smiled cunningly, but his

voice was deliberate. "I split the line." he said.

That era is gone. Today in sawmills of our Northwest, two passes of an automatic saw can produce more timbers than all three of those professionals could have hewed in a day. Gone too is their skill, skill of a level nobody is likely to witness again anywhere.

A pulp hook is a steel hand hook used for handling cordwood. One of the better designs is about a foot long with a horizontal handle, as in Diagram 47. If you are hand-loading much cordwood, a pulp hook can be useful if the wood is wet, icy, or snow-covered. Otherwise, you can probably load more without using the hook.

Another tool you may encounter is the spud, used for peeling bark off pulpwood. The spud is a curved, round-nosed chisel mounted on either a long or short handle. Run beneath the bark of pulpwood in the early springtime, the spud peels bark with surprising ease. If you were accumulating logs for a cabin you would need a spud.

Though not usually a woods tool, the sawhorse, or saw-buck, is necessary for anyone who is doing much hand sawing. The sawhorse holds wood elevated for sawing. As shown in Diagram 32, designs are numerous. The most familiar one may be two stick criss-crosses nailed together side by side and about 2' apart. The wood to be sawed is held between the upper legs, and the whole business sits on the lower ones.

There are a host of different woods tools, past and present, that service the hauling and transportation of wood. Though most of these have been made only for large-scale timber operations, some transport items are of use to anybody gathering firewood. One of the foremost is chain. Chain may play less part in timber operations than formerly, but it is still important. If you haul a log, you will probably hitch to it with chain. Chain will easily crunch over rocks that would batter cable and cut rope on the spot. Even if you haul only behind a pickup truck, you should have at least a $5/16"$ chain 10' to 16' long with a slip hook on one end and a grab hook on the other.

Then there are two more items you might use. One is a set of log tongs. These are just a big edition of the old iceman's tongs. They would replace the chain for hitching to a log in hauling. The tongs would be easier to attach and detach, sometimes too easy. Until they are lodged in a log, tongs need tension to remain attached. Another item is a two-man log carrier. This stout handle, about 5' long, has a set of opposed peavey hooks in its center. By engaging the hooks in a small log, two men, one on either end of the carrying handle, can lift and drag off a log that neither of them could budge alone. If you work with a partner, the carrier could give you good service.

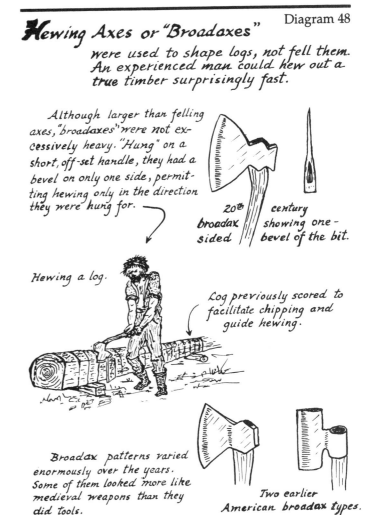

Hewing Axes or "Broadaxes"   Diagram 48

were used to shape logs, not fell them. An experienced man could hew out a true timber surprisingly fast.

Although larger than felling axes, "broadaxes" were not excessively heavy. "Hung" on a short, off-set handle, they had a bevel on only one side, permitting hewing only in the direction they were hung for.

20th century broadax one-sided showing one-bevel of the bit.

Hewing a log.

Log previously scored to facilitate chipping and guide hewing.

Broadax patterns varied enormously over the years. Some of them looked more like medieval weapons than they did tools.

Two earlier American broadax types.

Over rough roads, a high load of wood must be bound securely. Without additional aid, a man cannot cinch a load tightly enough. When you are using chain, a chain binder is just about indispensable. This is a hinged lever device with a grab hook on either end. With the binder in extended position, the hooks are separately engaged in the chain as far apart as possible. Then the lever is drawn up where it secures, shortening the distance between its hooks by about half. This usually will cinch the load. If not, hold the slack gained and repeat. For binding lesser loads, a twisted rope as described in Chapter 18 is also worth remembering.

26

Saws

In our uncertain world, the case for knowing how to use an ax to keep yourself warm can stand on its own merits. The higher that costs of fuel and precision manufactures soar, the clearer the merits of the simple ax become. The man who needs firewood can make his own decisions about the tools most efficient for him. What he needs is information about available choices so that he can make intelligent decisions about wood-harvesting methods. Many firewood users already own saws, most of them chain saws. For all these cases, the next three chapters are included to provide understanding of timber-cutting saws and to permit informed comparisons between saw and ax.

In the heavier aspects of gathering firewood, there is no question that saws can cut more wood faster than axes can. The other side of the story is in two parts. First, the ax can cut any wood that a saw can cut, and on lighter work can beat any saw. Next, manual saws cannot do everything that an ax can do. Perhaps a chain saw can, but compared with an ax, a chain saw is large, cumbersome, expensive, complicated, fragile, more costly, and more difficult to maintain. For the part-time saw user, the ration of time and money invested to firewood cut will usually be excessive when compared to that of the ax user.

All of this, both advantages and disadvantages, applies particularly to the chain saw. In our affluent society there are undoubtedly more chain saws than all other outdoor woods saws together. So although there is little need to plug chain saws here, mentioning some of the older types of saws may serve a worthy purpose. They, too, can still be useful.

The principle of the toothed saw has been recognized for centuries. However, modern history of the saw starts only after 1760 with the advent of rolling mills that could produce steel plate of uniform thickness. From the plate, strips were cut to make saws. In the United States, no saws were produced until after 1790. Even by 1846, more than a half century later, saws were not used in the woods.

But before the Civil War began in 1861, saws had appeared for bucking felled trees into logs more efficiently. By 1880, in Pennsylvania, saws were being used for felling trees. By the turn of the century, the ax was still indispensable, but it had become an auxiliary tool. The great trees were both felled and bucked with the saw. Paul Bunyan was on the way to join his ancestors.

It was the two-man crosscut saw that toppled the ax. Its semiflexible strip of steel usually was bowed slightly downward in the middle and had upright handles secured to each end. The handles were detachable and could be easily removed to let a saw escape endwise from a kerf that had pinched shut. With a willing man on each end, the crosscut saw was an efficient cutter. On later models, if the saw were properly sharpened, it could spew out whole streamers of chips that would hold together in falling like pieces of hot spaghetti.

Two-man saws were manufactured in a variety of lengths to fit the timber they would cut. Many saws used in the West were 12' to 14' long, and lumber operations among Pacific Coast redwood trees had saws as long as 18'. Operations in the rest of the United States did not need such lengths. In the East, 5½' to 6½' was common for a two-man saw. Crews needed about a 3' pulling length, so that plus the diameter of the tree made the length of the saw. For trees up to 3' thick, a saw 5½' to 6½' long was plenty.

These were pull-saws, not pushers. If a man tired on one end, it slowed both men, because in large part the return stroke could not be pushed back. The saw had to be pulled back from the far end. For all that, the pusher could give substantial aid to the man who was pulling. It was intimate, synchronized teamwork with each man instantly aware of every ounce of strength that his partner was, or was not, devoting to their joint effort. Sawing tested endurance more than bull strength. It was often a contest with exhaustion. Saw partners were necessarily compatible with each other or their relationship was shortly intolerable altogether.

On large trees the demanding rhythm of sawing might be sustained many minutes without a break. A casual observer would detect small sign of the implacable destruction being worked on the tree. The men would make little noise and, because they remained in place, relatively little movement. Other than their breathing, the only sound would be the harsh and repetitive hiss of the saw, first to one side and then to the other. Trailing the saw as it appeared on each side would be the exhaust of tiny chips. When it came, movement of the high top was always dramatic. Then followed by the crack, the swiftening rush, and explosive finality of the collapse to earth, each toppling was stark recitation of how so little could wreak so much.

In development, the one-man crosscut saw probably came before the two-man type. Later versions of the one-man saw ranged from 3½' to 5' or wider and were often somewhat heavier than the two-man saws. This made the one-man saw more rigid. It could be both pushed and pulled in the kerf. When felling wedges were driven into the saw kerf to hold it open or to help direct the lay of the tree, the 1" to 3" greater width of the one-man saw was a distinct disadvantage. The wedges could not be driven into a shallow kerf lest they hit the back of the saw and make it bind.

The principal handle was a looped wooden grip of sturdy design, much like that of a carpenter's saw. The far end of the saw was drilled to receive a smaller stick handle so the one-man saw could be used by two men. Or the stick handle could be attached just forward of the loop grip, allowing one man to saw comfortably with both hands at once.

Not infrequently, the far end of the one-man saw would flop from side to side during bucking in a perverse rhythm that prevented sawing. The traditional cure for this was to slip a chopper mitten on the stick handle to dampen the vibration. Occasionally this worked. The one-man straight crosscut saw was never a major felling tool. Though the two-man model required two men, its use was far more than twice as efficient.

The bucksaw was a wooden frame holding a thin, narrow saw blade in tension so that it could cut in either direction. Blade length was about 2½'. Factory designs of bucksaws usually provided a turnbuckle to provide tension, but a rope twisted with a small stick could serve as well, and often did. For cutting firewood on a home sawhorse, the wooden bucksaw was a reliable tool, but it was both too small and too awkward to be of great value in the woods.

After World War I, a new saw appeared from Scandinavia. Being particularly useful on the small timber of the Northeast, much of which was harvested for pulp, the new saw became known as a pulp saw as well as a bucksaw. But the most common name, bow saw, was also most descriptive. Its extra thin blade of only about 1" in width was held in tension by a tubular steel bow. Some models of these frames were one-piece and some were two-piece adjustable. Blades became available in lengths from 2' to 4'. These saws were light and handy to use. But beyond that, their fragile-looking blade dug in and cut as no saw had done before with so little effort. The bow saws were not large and their blades really were fragile, but the popularity of the bow saw swept like a wave over the Northeast and into the spruce woods of Canada. As household, garden, and camping items, smaller versions of the bow saw are still popular today.

It is risky to conclude that the unfamiliar lacks merit merely because it is unfamiliar. Americans have been particularly prone to falling into this trap exactly because so many things American have been so universally admired. When I first glimpsed a Japanese carpenter's saw, I laughed at its puny size, odd shape, and peculiar operation. After using one myself, I stopped laughing. The traditional Japanese-design saws are half the length of ours, have needle-pointed teeth, and cut on the pull stroke rather than with the long push stroke that we use with our carpenter saws. Not only do the Japanese design saws cut easier than ours, but they often have teeth on both edges, making two saws in one.

I once came upon a Japanese one-man woods saw with the long raked-back teeth for pulling, not pushing. The narrow

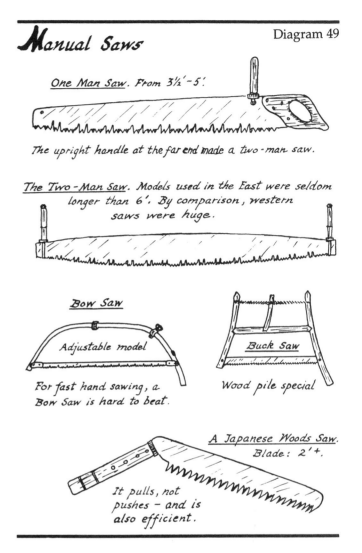

Manual Saws Diagram 49

One Man Saw. From 3½'-5'.

The upright handle at the far end made a two-man saw.

The Two-Man Saw. Models used in the East were seldom longer than 6'. By comparison, western saws were huge.

Bow Saw

Adjustable model

For fast hand sawing, a Bow Saw is hard to beat.

Buck Saw

Wood pile special

A Japanese Woods Saw. Blade: 2'+.

It pulls, not pushes — and is also efficient.

2' cutting edge ended in an offset stick handle. If it had not been for my prior experience with Japanese carpenter saws, I would have laughed a second time. As it was, I regretted that we had no such saws in America. I was unable to try that woods saw, but my guess is that it would have been amazingly efficient for one-man use.

In 1946, World War II being over, I had another job. I was a swamper's helper and was yarding logs with a team of horses. It was a small operation and, for those times, a backward one. As always, the tree fellers were the aristocrats of the woods. On that beautiful autumn day, I was lucky to be driving team. Usually I was only hacking brush and making twitch-trails, those side trails leading to the felled trees. So it was with the critical awareness of the underprivileged that the team and I surged into a clearing where the felling crew for that job were strangely inactive. They had something that I had never seen before, and I pulled up the team.

It was a two-man device over 4' long. Between the operator's handlebars on one end was perched a gasoline engine. The midsection was a deep bar on edge, and at the far end was a horizontal handle for an assistant. The crew held the machine balanced on a log in a half-cut kerf. A slice of bucked log lay beside it. A fact that occurred to me only later was that the log bridged a slight depression over an outcropping of ledge.

Not realizing that I was looking at the tool that would revolutionize tree felling, I made inquiries. Winding a pull-rope back on the starter reel, the crew chief informed me over his shoulder that this was his new chain saw. Then after I had asked twice, he also divulged that it weighed 84 pounds. He added with a snarl, "But look what it will do!"

I duly inspected the slice of log. By this time the chief was winding the pull-rope back on the starter reel for another try. By his manner and some coarse things he said, I gathered that this was more than just his second attempt to bring the machine to life. My boss was waiting for me, so I clucked up the team and passed on.

It was a dozen minutes before I returned, but I was in time just the same. Only at that moment had the saw crew commenced operations again, bucking that same log. Nothing fazed the saw now. Amid spurting sawdust, it roared through the log, and as the cut ends pinched in and settled, the saw began chewing into the ledge underneath. The change was abrupt. Darting sparks replaced the sawdust as if the Fourth of July had begun. This was accompanied by an immediate crescendo of cursing and counter-cursing, but the sparks continued. Even in the sunlight they were spectacular and must have shot several yards. More than anything else, the saw resembled a stuck rocket.

All this I only caught at a glance, for the whole atmosphere was more festive than my team had been trained for. As we swept swiftly through the clearing, I had all I could do to keep out of the way of my lunging load. Behind us there was still much noise and dancing about. We were well around the bend before the blat of the saw engine stilled. It was not until the afternoon of the following day that I finally heard it again. The men in that saw crew were innovative. They developed a better system somehow, for they went on to cut a lot of logs, and with that same saw, too.

Once launched as a portable item, even if not too portable, the chain saw developed rapidly. As its weight fell and capabilities grew, no great intellect was required to forecast the trend. Cost of labor was high and rising, yet fuel, machinery and parts were relatively cheap and plentiful. The tool that could cut wood fastest would be the one used. That was the chain saw. Within a decade after World War II, the chain saw had no competition left in the woods from other tree-cutting tools. It was a clean sweep from coast to coast. All other saws had joined the ax.

27

Sharpening Saws

To cut much wood with any tool, the tool must be sharp. Saws are certainly no exception to this rule. A dull saw is about as near to uselessness as you can get, and power or no power, a dull chain saw is the most useless of all. When an ordinary saw becomes dull, the dull teeth can still grind away in contact with the surface to be cut. But with a chain saw, the dull teeth become rounded up away from the surface to be cut just as the point of a ski is tipped up to glide over snow. A couple of doses of grit will do this to a chain saw. Then it actually will not cut at all until it is made sharp once again.

With chain saws, avoid the suburbanite self-sharpening models. The self-sharpening system is initially costly and continues to be so, for it scours away your chain too fast. To sharpen the production type of chain saw, you need round files of a size fitting the teeth of your saw chain, a file holder to maintain the file at the right depth on the teeth as you sharpen, a file handle, a depth gauge jointer which we will explain in a moment, and an 8″ flat mill file for occasional adjusting of the depth gauges.

Filing is about all there is to sharpening saws, but that is enough. Each of your filing strokes must be methodical and even. Holding the file in both hands, one hand on the handle and the other on the tip of the file, you should push the file firmly but smoothly against each saw tooth as you sharpen it. Lift the file off the tooth on your return stroke. Dragging a file back puts pressure on the tiny file teeth from the wrong direction, tending to break them and dull the file.

Between filing strokes, brush the file with your fingertips so you begin the next stroke with a clean file. Filings left on either the file or the work surface will get ground again on your next stroke, slowing your progress and dulling your file. As a round chain-saw file becomes shiny, turn it in its holder just enough to expose a fresh surface. Doing each of these little tricks routinely will help you file more quickly and nearly triple the life of your files.

For sharpening a chain saw, attach a handle and a file holder to a round file. Next, stabilize the chain saw somehow. The easiest way to do this is to clamp the chain-saw bar in a vise. This done, the teeth on top of the bar will hold steady while you file them. You will be sharpening only those teeth having the beveled sides of their cutting edges facing you. The curved inner bevel of each tooth must be filed at about 30°–35°. The file holder will have an inscribed line showing this angle. Keeping that line parallel to the chain-saw bar, and with the file holder resting on top of the saw tooth, file the curved edge of the tooth to be sharpened. While bearing downward on the file, also maintain pressure against the curve of the saw tooth.

There is still another factor to remember. You must keep the file level or, properly speaking, keep the file perpendicular to the vertical dimension of the chain-saw bar. Filing at that angle will give the saw tooth the proper profile of about 5° overhang from the vertical. If you canted the file upward, the tooth would be too dubbed off and would not cut well. If you tipped the file downward, the tooth would acquire too much hook. Not only would that make the leading edge of the tooth too fragile, but the saw would also tend to buck.

File each tooth until your fingertip can feel the slight beginnings of a wire-edge on both top and side edges of the tooth. If the chain is so visibly dull that the edges of a tooth appear rounded, be sure that the rounded appearance has been sharpened away before you consider the tooth sharp, even though you can feel a wire-edge.

Rotate the saw chain to expose other teeth whose beveled sides are facing you and sharpen them also until you have done them all. The beveled side of any saw tooth is its inner side. The edge of the bevel is the cutting edge. Note that all saw sharpening strokes always travel from the inner side of the tooth toward the outer side where the cutting edge is. However, at this point, the chain saw is only half sharpened, for every second tooth has its flat, outer side facing you. To sharpen these teeth, turn the saw around in the vise and resecure it. Now the teeth with the beveled sides facing you will be those whose flat sides were facing you before. All of these teeth are still dull, so sharpen them just as you did the others.

Just forward (in direction of chain-saw rotation) of the cutting edge of each saw tooth is a depth gauge, an elevated tip that rubs against the wood being cut and thus controls the depth of chip each tooth cuts. You should check the depth gauges about every third time that you sharpen the teeth. A good average depth-gauge clearance (below tooth level) for firewood is .025″. You check this clearance by using a depth gauge jointer, a metal shield of designated thickness placed on the chain surrounding the tip of each gauge. Any part of

Diagram 50

Understanding Saws

Bow Saw moving this direction →

<u>Cross-section</u> of saw in the kerf. "Set" (the bend at the tips) of saw teeth cuts a wider kerf than the body of saw, so that the saw does not bind.

.008"

How a Saw Saws:
Alternate cutting teeth, set and sharpened to opposite sides of the saw, make parallel cuts. The raker teeth then scoop out the severed wood chips, allowing the cutting teeth to sink even deeper on their next pass.

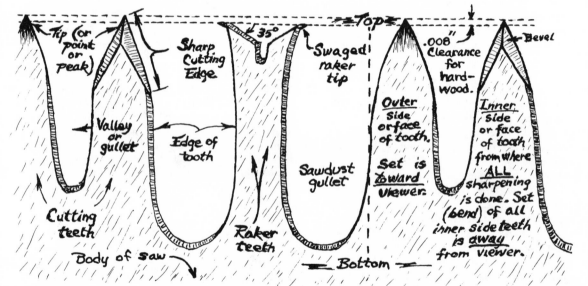

- Tip (or point or Peak)
- Sharp Cutting Edge
- 35°
- Top
- Swaged raker tip
- .008" Clearance for hardwood.
- Bevel
- Valley or gullet
- Edge of tooth
- <u>Outer</u> side or face of tooth. Set is <u>toward</u> viewer.
- <u>Inner</u> side or face of tooth from where <u>ALL</u> sharpening is done. Set (bend) of all inner side teeth is <u>away</u> from viewer.
- Cutting teeth
- Sawdust gullet
- Body of saw
- Raker teeth
- Bottom

<u>NOTE</u>: For sharpening purposes, saw teeth are always <u>uppermost</u>.

Styles of Filing Saw Tooth Tips

Middle ridge

Needle Point, the common form of a sharp tooth tip.

On larger saws, file off most of middle ridge for smoother sawing.

Rolling Point, very durable, but difficult to file.

Middle-Bevel Pt. Wider than the needle point and more durable.

the tip that protrudes is then filed off even with the hardened surface of the jointer. Use the flat mill file for this job. Afterward, the forward (in direction of chain rotation) corner of each gauge should be rounded off with the flat file so that the gauge will ride over wood smoothly without snagging. With each of these steps accomplished, your chain saw will be ready to cut wood again. Anyway, the chain will be ready.

Fortunately, chain saws sharpen rather easily, for they dull easily also. Irksome as sharpening a chain saw may be, you would do well to keep it sharp. To get any work done at all, a dull chain saw has to be forced, a hard way to treat an expensive tool. Not even a big meal and a night's sleep can do much for a cracked piston.

To sharpen the old, reliable, manual saws, the one- and two-man crosscut saws and the bow saw or buck-saw, it helps to know a few facts and terms first. The sharpening process is not difficult, but it is painstaking. There are five major steps and a number of lesser ones. Each must be performed nicely for every tooth. Because there are numerous teeth and each step may require several file strokes per tooth, do not expect to sharpen a saw in ten minutes. You may take longer. For that matter, only an idiot would attempt to guess how long it will take you to do your first successful sharpening.

But if you persevere, you can learn to sharpen a saw well in an hour and a half. If you are a methodical ancient-arts nut, you may even halve that time, or better, or even touch up a saw that is not too badly abused in 20 minutes. That is worth shooting for. You could even start a second business. Signs don't cost too much.

Saw sharpening starts with jointing, the filing of all teeth to a uniform length, including, on some saws, the rakers, the chisel-tipped teeth that scoop out the cut chips. Because jointing inevitably results in misshapen teeth, the next step is reshaping the teeth, together with the intervening valleys. After that there is setting, the bending of alternate teeth to opposite sides of the saw so that the saw will cut slightly wider than its body and not bind in the kerf. Then comes the sharpening proper, the actual keening of the teeth, including the rakers (the sawdust-clearing teeth), if any. The final step is dressing, the clearing of wire-edges and burrs from the outer sidewalls of the saw. In all, sharpening a saw is a skill you can boast of, even if only in private.

A saw is most often used with the teeth pointing down. But during sharpening, the saw itself is usually upside down, with its teeth pointing up. So for sharpening purposes, always consider a saw with its teeth uppermost, the tops of the teeth being their cutting tips and the bottoms of the teeth being their bases where they join the main body of the saw. The height of a saw tooth is shown by the peak of its cutting tip. A tooth is "high" or "low" if its tip is above or below other like teeth. The wide surfaces of a saw tooth are "sides" or "faces." The narrow surfaces are "edges" and, when so shaped, "bevels."

The "inner" side of a tooth is the side showing its two beveled edges slanting up to the tip. All sharpening is done from the inner side. On the "outer" side of a tooth, the bevels are not visible. It is the tip of the outer side that cuts the kerf.

Manual saws are different from chain saws in more ways than one. Manual saws have their pointed teeth set alternately to each side of the saw. This slight bend permits cutting a kerf somewhat wider than the body of the saw and prevents the saw from binding. Uniformity of both length and set of saw teeth is a critical matter. A dull saw will usually cut better than one with sharp but irregular teeth. If the teeth are irregular in length, you cannot start a kerf. If they are irregular in set, you will be unable to continue sawing long in a kerf that has been started.

The sharpening tools you need for the manual woods saws are a file handle; a flat mill file of 8" length for the crosscut saws and 6" length for a bow saw or bucksaw; both files to be of single-cut; $5/32$" and $1/4$" round files; a 12" steel straightedge; a single-edge razor blade; a fine grit sharpening stone (a round ax stone will suffice); and a saw set large enough for the saw you are sharpening. We will speak more of the set shortly.

Sharpening a saw is difficult without a vise. If you own a saw-sharpening vise, use it. If not, clamp the saw, teeth uppermost, in an ordinary vise between two boards. The saw teeth should protrude well above the boards. On the board facing you, bevel off the top edge down away from the saw teeth so it will not interfere with filing. And to help these boards grip the saw more effectively, shape them with a plane. On the side that will contact the saw, plane the entire center of each board until its middle is depressed and only about two thirds as thick as its ends. Then when the board is placed in the vise, only the thick ends of the board will initially contact the saw. As you close the vise, you will flatten out the hollowed centers of the boards, making both ends of each board strain tightly inward against the sides of the saw.

The first step in sharpening all manual saws is jointing them, making all their teeth of even length. To do this, lay the flat file without its handle (an old, worn file is best) along the teeth of the saw so that the end of the file is heading toward an end of the saw and the flat surface of the file is perpendicular to the body of the saw. If the file is tipped to either side, the teeth on the tipped-down side will be shorter and the saw will not cut straight. File holders for this job were once common items in any hardware store, but are no longer.

If you hold the jointing file with a hand on each side you can help keep it perpendicular to the saw. Run the file lightly along the line of teeth. Make sure the tip of the file leads, not the tang. Files cut only when moving in that direction. Continue moving the file over the teeth until the tip of every tooth shows at least a tiny shine, the jointing flat, where the file has squared it off. The inevitable exception could be a broken tooth. Then you might have to compromise. In most cases, to joint all cutting teeth down to the level of one that is broken off could be wasteful and excessive. But broken teeth excepted, the jointing operation must produce a jointing flat on all teeth. This not only assures you that all teeth are the same height. The jointing flat is an irreplaceable guide for uniform sharpening of the teeth.

Having jointed the cutting teeth, now joint the rakers. These are the sawdust-clearers and are slightly shorter than the cutting teeth. Rather than deepening the sides of the kerf as the cutting teeth do, the chisel-tipped rakers scoop along the bottom of the kerf, lifting chips after they are severed. Flanking each pair of rakers is an enlarged valley, the gullet, which stores chips until the saw clears the kerf, when the chips fall out. Sawdust clearing is essential to prevent clogging and to keep the saw from binding.

With the older saws, sawdust clearing had always been a problem, but the lumber industry had been living with it for many years. But when advantages of the new raker-tooth pattern became known early in this century, popularity of the pattern grew rapidly. Pairs of raker teeth faced each end of the saw, initially between groups of four cutting teeth. Soon there was little argument that clearing sawdust better meant faster sawing. This was particularly apparent in sawing green and wet wood, or in large logs where clogging was chronic. Further experimentation led to siting pairs of rakers between groups of three cutting teeth, and then only two. By the time the chain saw invaded the woods after World War II, the dominant tooth pattern for larger manual saws was the raker model with only two cutters to each pair of rakers.

Whenever the cutting teeth are jointed, the rakers (if the saw has rakers) must be jointed at the same time to maintain their correct depth below the cutters. If the rakers were the same length as the cutters, the rakers would lodge in uncut wood fibers and the saw would do little sawing. The difference in length between cutters and rakers should vary according to what the saw will cut. For hardwood or frozen wood, and ordinarily for firewood, the rakers should be .008″ (0.2 mm) lower than the cutters. For sawing softwood, the clearance should be .016″ (0.4 mm) because the cutters sink deeper into the softer wood.

A saw whose rakers were jointed for hardwood would be sluggish in softwood because the rakers would sink too deeply. A saw jointed for softwood would tend to clog in hardwood because the rakers would be too short to lift the chips for discharge. A compromise clearance for both hardwood and softwood would be .012″ (0.3 mm).

It is fine to quote clearances, but the figures are of little value unless you can use them. Before the chain saw made manual saw tools obsolete, you could procure a raker-jointing tool. Placed on the teeth of a saw, the device featured a hardened surface with a slot in it. If the rakers peeped up above the slot they were too high and you promptly filed them off even with the hardface. The tool was usually adjustable, and using one was simplicity itself. But today they are no longer to be found.

Saws having rakers are of little value unless the rakers are properly jointed. Fortunately, an alternate system of jointing them is possible, though more laborious than using a jointing tool. Lay the steel straightedge on the jointed cutting teeth, bridging a pair of raker teeth. A single-edge razor blade is about .008″ thick, or what you need to gauge the difference between the heights of cutters and rakers. Slip the razor blade (but not its thick rear rim) between the straightedge and raker tip. If the fit is too tight, file away the tip of the raker until there is a clean fit. Be careful. It is easy to file too much and to know too late. File straight across, that is, perpendicular to the plane of the saw. And do not let the file tip to either side. For on top of each raker, you must also have a level jointing flat, a shiny area of contrasting angle, for your guidance in later sharpening.

Two clean single-edge razor blades together make a usable .016″ clearance gauge for softwood rakers. Cut the thick rear rims off both blades without distorting their surfaces. For a .012″ compromise gauge, use a single- and a double-edge razor blade together.

What if the rakers are too low? If one or two rakers are low, forget them. If many of them are low, how low? Will they fit the .012″ clearance for hardwood/softwood compromise, or the .016″ clearance for softwood sawing? Should you accept them at all, or joint the cutting teeth down to fit the raker level?

Perhaps the last word on raker clearance has not been recorded yet. Nobody seems to have thought much about the subject for well over a generation. The advent of the chain saw stopped manual-saw development almost overnight. The figures given above were the most recent that I could find published by a saw manufacturer. Everything considered, earlier figures of another saw manufacturer did not substantially conflict. Other testimony of reflective individuals who had extensive experience maintaining saws as well as using them, verified about the same range of clearance.

But if the rakers of your saw are much too low, inadvertently or otherwise, before you rejoint and reshape the whole business, let me say that many other persons who might be competent authorities on the subject have advised various raker clearances, for hardwood alone, ranging from .016″ all the way to "three thirty-seconds." The latter is .094″, almost 12 times the manufacturers' recommendations. That last source, a professional, told me, "If you don't cut the rakers three thirty-seconds low, the saw will buck!"

With all the jointing done, restore the approximate pointed profile of any flat-topped teeth, but without filing the jointing flat. Do not sharpen any teeth. Just restore their original shape. The shape of the teeth is dependent upon the valleys or gullets between them and these must also be filed down to return original proportion to the teeth.

Use the correct-shaped file for whatever shaping you must do. Manual woods saws were, and still are, made in various tooth patterns, so specific rules for shaping any one of them cannot apply to all. Just determine what the original pattern was and maintain it. Recutting an old saw into a different tooth pattern is possible but not practical. In most cases, you need only the files listed previously. Some older bucksaw blades may require a large triangular file. For best results in some narrow gullets between teeth you should use a flat mill file with a rounded edge. However, round-edged flat mill files are no longer common either, so you may have to procure a smaller round file.

In filing out valleys and gullets, leave no sharp angles, for they may lead to formation of cracks there. Your files will last longer if you hold the handle low for the first stroke or two. After that, you may file straight in, perpendicular to the saw. This method is also substantially easier.

Gullets need to be kept large and square-edged to catch and store sawdust for discharge. You can trim and clear gullets faster and better with a round-edged gumming wheel. But this is a narrow abrasive wheel, so using a file may be safer unless you are experienced.

The next step is setting, the bending of alternate teeth to opposite sides of the saw. Setting ensures that saw teeth cut a kerf slightly wider than the body of the saw, allowing free running in the kerf. Set to the same side as previously set. More modern saws are also usually taper-ground, with the

Diagram 51

Saw-Sharpening Tools ~
for manual woods saws

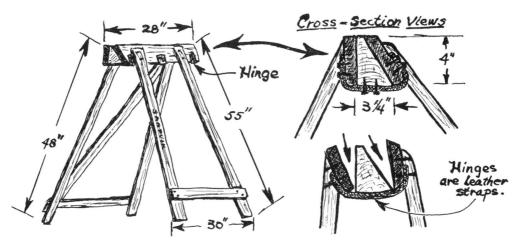

Cross-Section Views

28"
Hinge
55"
48"
30"
4"
3¼"

Hinges
are leather
straps.

Wooden Saw-Sharpening Vise can hold saw blade either upright or at an easy diagonal for sharpening. The more you bear down on the saw, the tighter the vise clamps. Cut off legs, if needed, to have vise at elbow-level.

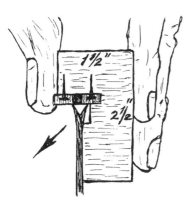

1½"
2½"

Cross - section

Wooden Jig used to hold file perpendicular during jointing. Thumb pressure & protruding nail heads behind the tang of the file hold it firmly in position while jig is held down & against the saw.

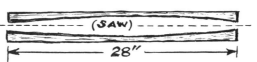

(SAW)
28"

Overhead view of boards having hollowed-out centers to steady a saw clamped in an ordinary vise.

4"

End View

6"

The Setting Iron, a strip of flat steel with a slot just wide enough to fit over a saw tooth. Turn the iron downward to set the tooth.

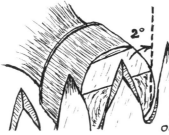

2°

An Impact Set Anvil you can make by grinding a 2° bevel from the upper face of an old hammer. Align each tooth properly on the line of bevel and hit the tip accurately with another (small) hammer.

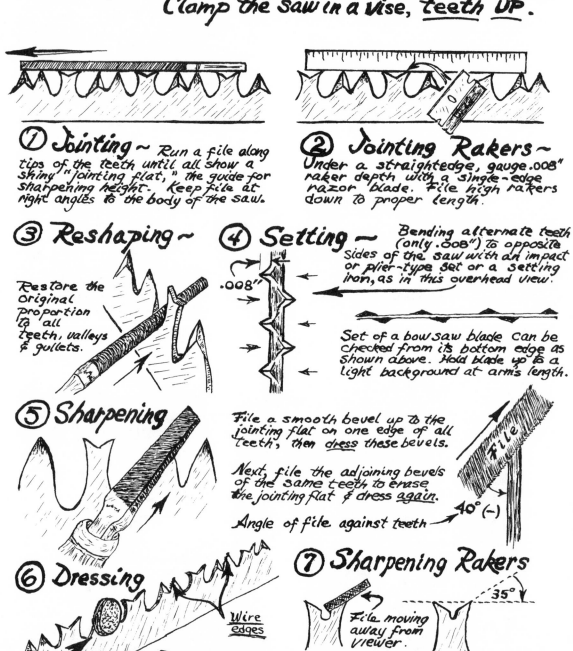

Diagram 52

Sharpening Saws: *Have good light!*
Clamp the saw in a vise, teeth UP.

① **Jointing** ~ Run a file along tips of the teeth until all show a shiny "jointing flat," the guide for sharpening height. Keep file at right angles to the body of the saw.

② **Jointing Rakers** ~ Under a straightedge, gauge .008" raker depth with a single-edge razor blade. File high rakers down to proper length.

③ **Reshaping** ~ Restore the original proportion to all teeth, valleys & gullets.

④ **Setting** ~ Bending alternate teeth (only .008") to opposite sides of the saw with an impact or plier-type set or a setting iron, as in this overhead view.

.008"

Set of a bow saw blade can be checked from its bottom edge as shown above. Hold blade up to a light background at arm's length.

⑤ **Sharpening**

File a smooth bevel up to the jointing flat on one edge of all teeth, then dress these bevels.

Next, file the adjoining bevels of the same teeth to erase the jointing flat & dress again.

Angle of file against teeth → 40° (–)

File

⑥ **Dressing**

Wire edges

Run a fine-grit sharpening stone lightly along the outer side of the saw TOWARD the sharpened bevels to remove the wire-edges.

⑦ **Sharpening Rakers**

35°

File moving away from viewer.

File the chisel-tipped rakers at correct angle and perpendicular to the plane of the saw until the raker jointing flat is erased.

body of the saw thinner than the tooth edge. This construction helps prevent binding somewhat, but even taper-ground saws must be set.

The amount of set needed is small. For a saw to cut hardwood or wood that is frozen, the amount of set need not be over .008″ (0.2 mm). That amount is applied to each side of the saw. The sides of a softwood kerf (not frozen) would be rougher, binding the saw more, so the set should be about .012″ (0.3 mm). These figures will help you little if you have no way to measure them. For the same void we have noticed before also applies here. The missing item in this case is a saw set gauge. You cannot buy these any more either.

But all is not lost. What must be remembered about set is that you should use as little as permits your saw to run freely in the kerf. You can break saw teeth in trying to give them too much set. Also, the more set a saw has, the more wood must be removed from the kerf. The extra effort adds up. And the more set a saw has, the more vulnerable the saw is to pinch damage in the kerf. Find by experience how little set your saw needs to run freely and do not apply any set greater than that.

In theory, you could set saw teeth with ordinary pliers, but because you could not bend tooth after tooth uniformly with pliers, some other tool must be used. It has long been recognized that saw teeth retain their set better if the set is made by sudden impact rather than by a relatively gradual bending strain, such as would be imparted by pliers. Generally, though, a bending device is easier to use than an impact set, though not always. Today, plierlike saw sets that do bend saw teeth uniformly are the only type usually found. These sets customarily feature screw adjustments to accommodate different sizes of teeth and different degrees of set. Before you buy one of these tools, make sure that it will actually set the teeth of your saw. Many plier-type saw sets are made only for use on carpenter saws and, adjustable or not, are too small to set woods saws.

Two other types of saw set are worth noting because they are not difficult to make. Both were once commercially available. Neither seems to be today. The first, a bending device, sometimes called a setting iron, is the simplest of all saw sets, a strip of flat steel with a narrow slot cut perpendicularly in from one edge. You can easily make one from a 6″ piece of old saw, or similar stock. The slot, which can be cut in with a narrow file, should be just slightly wider and longer than the thickness and length of the saw teeth you will set. To use the setting iron, fit its slot down over the tooth to be set, with the tooth centered between the edges of the slot and the tip of the tooth pointing to the upper end of the slot. In this position, the tooth is caught fast between the close-fitting edges of the slot. To set the tooth—that is, to bend it—just pull the appropriate end of the setting iron downward. As the setting iron moves, so will its slot and so will the captive tooth. Do not pull too much.

In similar fashion, the setting iron can easily bend teeth upward to eliminate too much set. You can learn to sense rather accurately a uniform amount of set by how far you pull down the handle end of the iron.

It is also not too difficult to make an impact saw set. For metallurgical reasons I am not qualified to explain, teeth set by the blow of a hammer hold their set better. With an impact set, the tip of the saw tooth is pounded down against a small beveled anvil so that the tooth tip is molded to the same angle of bevel. For firewood sawing, this angle should be about 2°.

Such an anvil can be made by grinding back the upper half face of an old hammer at 2° from the original flat face. If the original face is not flat, level that off first. Scratch a profile of the 2° bevel on a piece of sheet metal or flattened side of a tin can and cut it out carefully for your guide as you grind back the hammer face. When you finish, you will need only a small hammer to accompany your new setting anvil. A good tack hammer will suffice.

With impact sets, you do not need fierce pounding. With the tooth centered on the anvil, the line of set (where you want the tooth bent) must lie against the anvil's line of bevel. The tip of the tooth will overhang the beveled-off area. When hammered, the tip will driven down against the bevel. Just tap the tooth, accurately, but smartly. Note that with impact sets, to adjust the angle of bevel you must tip either the anvil or the saw. Some impact sets secure the anvil to a bench or table and feed the saw over it, tooth by tooth.

Hand-held setting anvils have been known and used for many years. Another usually available saw-set anvil that has been proven in use is nothing more than a railroad spike whose sharply tapering bottom end provides a convenient bevel on which to set saw tooth tips. Though the spike's angle of bevel is several times greater than saw manufacturers have recommended for optimum set even for softwood, the spike seems to have produced results found quite satisfactory. As with other facts connected with sawing wood and life in general, there are numerous favorite paths to approach the same goal.

A critical item for setting by any method is how far down the tooth the line of set, or bend, should be. Though this distance can vary with different saw-teeth patterns, it probably should never be more than ¼″ below the tip of a saw tooth. A better means of determining this distance is in relation to the beveled edges that sharpen the peak of the tooth. Slanting off on the inner side of the tooth, these bevels converge below the tip. For most cases, the line of set should be just above where the inner lines of bevel converge. This will produce set only in the upper tip of the tooth, but there is evidence that high setting is best. If you use the setting iron previously described, such a high set may not be possible, so you may have to select a point a bit lower.

That is all there is to setting. You place the set at the proper depth on the tooth, then close the plier-type handles, or pull down on the setting iron, or tap the tooth with a hammer. Set all teeth to one side of the saw first, then set the alternate teeth to the other side. Then look carefully along both sides of the saw from both ends to inspect for uniformity of set. If any teeth are set too much or too little, correct them or set them again. Surprisingly, you can even detect irregular set of bow-saw teeth by inspecting the blade from its rear, the narrow edge opposite the teeth. Hold the blade out at arm's length and examine each section of it for a regular pattern of alternately-spaced tooth points protruding from the line of the saw. Any that point out too far or too little need attention.

The actual sharpening of the teeth is next. Sharpening requires good light. Daylight is best. Where that is not possible, have at least two light sources, one overhead and one somewhat in front of you. The reason for this is that you must sharpen each tooth until you eliminate the jointing flat, the shiny spot left at the tip of each tooth from the jointing process. The jointing flat is the only guide you have for maintaining uniform height of the teeth. If you file too heavily and eliminate the jointing flat too soon, the tooth will be too short. The probability of filing all the teeth precisely as short is so minuscule it is not worth talking about. So if you file one or two jointing flats away prematurely, it is best just to forget them. Those one or two teeth will be too short to do much cutting. But if you file many more jointing flats off prematurely, you should seriously consider starting over, jointing, shaping, and even setting every tooth again. Doing that a couple of times will show you reason to rig yourself good lighting.

Woods saws are designed to cut when both pushing and pulling, so their teeth are sharpened on both edges. Each tooth should present an even-sided peak. It is neither necessary nor desirable to sharpen the edges of the teeth from tip to valley. Only the tip of the tooth, perhaps as little as .020" of it, performs the cutting, and that is all that needs to be sharpened. Of course to sharpen that tip, much more of the edge is inadvertently sharpened also. But having the rest of the tooth relatively blunt-edged, or partially so, is beneficial because the wider edges help sweep sawdust more efficiently from the kerf.

Sharpening is similar to setting in that you work on only one side of the saw at a time. As you face the saw in the vise, half of the teeth are set away from you. It is these teeth whose beveled inner surfaces face you that you will sharpen first. Only upon finishing with them will you reverse the saw in the vise and sharpen the rest.

To sharpen any one of the peaked saw teeth, its upper slopes, the cutting portion of the tooth, must be beveled with the file. All filing will be done from the inner side of the tooth as it faces you. You will file toward the outer cutting surface. All file strokes should be firm, even, and maintain the same angle of thrust throughout.

Attach a handle to your flat mill file. It is possible to use a file without a handle, but you can work far better with one. Taking the handle in your more dexterous hand, grip the file's tip with the thumb and fingers of your other hand. Use an 8" file for sharpening the one- and two-man crosscut saws and a 6" size for bow-saw blades. Some of the wide, old bucksaw blades may require a large triangular file, but if you want to saw much wood, retire the wide blade for a narrow bow-saw blade. Anyway, an old bucksaw blade is too valuable to saw with. If it is rusty enough and if you have an old, or a lye-dipped, genuine antique wooden frame to fit it, it is marketable anywhere for interior decor.

Ready to sharpen, the upper flat end of your file would rest on one of the upper, sloped edges of the tooth with the file handle below the level of the tooth and somewhat to the side. The angle of the file to the surface of the tooth should be about 40° or less. Your task is to refurbish and sharpen a beveled edge, or the remains of a beveled edge, that is already there beneath your file tip. There is nothing original about the sharpening process. You will merely be doing again what has been done before.

When the filing stroke is made from that position, it will cut a 40° bevel (or broader) on the upper, sloped edge of the

tooth. Filed deeply enough, the surface of the bevel will intersect the rear (the side facing away from you) face of the tooth, and that particular beveled edge will be sharp. You may notice a wire-edge on the outer rim of the bevel to prove it. If the stroke is not deep enough, it must be repeated until an even bevel reaches the line of the outer face. This represents sharpening only for one edge for one tooth, but all the others would be done similarly.

However, you may find a recognizable difference in filing a bevel to the left or to the right. The difference will be in you, not the teeth. On one side you will be able to file more easily than on the other. Before you do any serious sharpening, try a few light filing strokes to determine which side will be more difficult for you to file. If it is the left edge, for example, file the left-hand bevels before the right-hand bevels.

This arbitrariness concerns the all-important jointing flat. Being the only guide for tooth height, this jointing flat must not be filed away until the last gentle stroke completes the sharpening for that tooth. This means that the first bevel must still leave about half of the jointing flat visible for guiding you in filing the second bevel. Final expunging of the jointing flat must be a light stroke. If you cut too deeply, the tooth will be short. Therefore, the bevel you find easier to file well is the one you should do last. Where you have control, you will have power to be gentle. File your awkward-side bevel first.

It is necessary to back the story up a bit. When you are filing the bevels, wire-edges, or burrs, will commonly hang to the cutting edges. To eliminate these, the side of the saw must be dressed with a level-surfaced, fine grit stone. If you have no better, use the fine-grit side of your pocket ax stone. Run it lightly along the entire line of sharpened teeth, centered about midway on the face of the stone. Keep your fingertips back from the edges. The direction of dressing must be toward the sharpened edges. Do not get too eager doing this. You can easily grind away both tooth set and length. A single pass along the line of teeth should be enough.

The single dressing pass represents an economy as well as a precaution. The single dressing is possible only when all first bevels are filed first. The same is true for dressing the second bevels also. Nor can both bevels be dressed at once. The stone must oppose the bevel to dress off the wire edge. Dressing both bevels on a single pass would dress off half the wire edges, but would also brush the other half back in on top of the bevels. There they could be eliminated only by individual attention to each one.

After the first bevels are completed and dressed, file the second bevels as described for the first ones. Then dress them also, and those teeth are sharpened except for one refinement. The two bevels that converge at one of the sharpened tips form a middle ridge from the tip down to the top of the tooth's inner face. The tip will be less thick, and therefore cut better, if some of this ridge is filed away. That should be done.

Filing away the middle ridge creates the middle bevel. It is another job that requires finesse. The middle bevel must stop short of the tip by perhaps .025" (0.6 mm), about the thickness of a bow- or hacksaw blade. Its length should be about the same as the ridge was, which means that it must not extend far downward either. A longer bevel would be too deep, making the tip too thin for retaining set. Filing the middle bevel takes a fine file and light touch. Inspect after each stroke.

So far, we have assumed that a sharp tooth must be a pointed one, and the more pointed the better. Even in theory, neither item is altogether true. The pointed tip is formed by the converging bevels, the second bevel having gradually filed away the jointing flat until only a needle-point peak remains at the exact height of the former jointing flat. (If the work has been careful, we can consider the height to be the same as the jointing flat was. Our concern is sharpening saws, not measurement science.) The flaw in the needle-point peak theory is that this tip is too fragile. For most softwood it is satisfactory, but in sawing hardwood it is not nearly as durable as a rounded peak.

The rounded peak, or "rolling-point" tooth, cuts fast and easily, but its principal virtue is durability in maintaining its edge. It stays sharp longer because, being wider at the tip, it has greater resistance to shock and wear. The rolling point is really a little rounded-end knife, cutting easily in either direction. The disadvantage of a rolling-point tooth is that much more skill is required to form it and maintain it.

Don't try filing rolling-pointed teeth until you can sharpen the ordinary needle-pointed teeth well. Instead of having a straight bevel rising to the tip on each cutting edge, the rolling-point bevels rise in gentle curves. Filing smooth and curved bevels to a jointing flat requires much practice and excellent control. Usually there will also be considerably more file strokes required. Filing rolling-point teeth is not for the beginner.

There is a modified style of rounded-tooth tip for which the filing is far easier than for a rolling-point tip, though not as easy as for a needle-point tip. This is the middle-bevel point. Like the rolling point, the middle-bevel point has the strength of a broad, round-tipped silhouette, yet has a thinner section than the needle-point tip.

To form teeth that have middle-bevel points, file the first bevels carefully. If the jointing flat is large, file some away, but leave it moderate-sized. Dress the first bevels. One light pass should be enough. There will be two more dressings to come. File the second bevels *without* filing away the jointing flat. Leave enough to guide filing of the middle bevel. Dress the second bevels. Now with the smooth file, file the middle bevel as if you were filing only the middle ridge away, but continuing delicately until the jointing flat disappears. Do not tip the file to either side.

Left facing you will be two smaller ridges on either side of the middle bevel. File each of these ridges away right to the cutting edge with light strokes. Do not let the file wander on to the middle of the peak. After this, if you still notice any pronounced ridges, give them a feathered stroke of the file. If not, leave that tooth alone. Too many attempts at rounding could damage the peak. The profile of its rounded tip may not be perfect, but it will cut and it will last much longer than a needle-point tip.

A final dressing is needed for the tips. Unfortunately, to oppose the wire edge at the tips, this dressing will not be one horizontal pass, but a series of vertical passes. Centering the stone against the outer sides of the tooth tips, move it lightly downward, keeping only enough pressure against the saw to rub the wire edge from the tips. Repeat for the next group

of teeth until you have done them all. Dress each tooth only once unless you see that another individual pass is needed.

This completes the sharpening for all the cutting teeth whose beveled edges faced you as the saw lay in the vise. Now reverse the saw in the vise and treat the alternate cutting teeth in the same manner.

The last chore is sharpening the rakers which have not been touched since you left each one with a jointing flat at the proper height. Raker teeth come in pairs on one base, like the arms of a T, one raker pointing to one end of the saw and the other to the other end. In sharpening the rakers, first deepen the narrow gullet between their arms with a narrow round file. This will give you space to lower the raker shoulder with the mill file, slanting down from the tips of the raker at about 35°. Unlike a cutting tooth, the raker cuts across the kerf. Its final tip is a chisel-edge perpendicular to the plane of the saw. So in filing down the shoulders, file straight across to retain this facing. Then the pair of rakers look more like the ears of a horned owl than the arms of a T. On many saws, more filing must be done in the shoulder region than at the tips of the raker. Keep the top edge of the raker even as you file up the 30° slope to the jointing flat. Treat the raker with

---

Ax and Saw Sheaths   Diagram 53

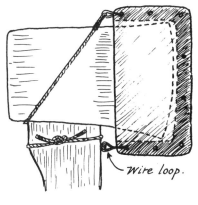

Sandwich-construction sheath. Middle rim of leather, rubber, lead, etc., protects bit.
Outer cover is the same, or of wood or sheet metal.
Rivet, screw, nail, or wire-stitch together.

— *Wire loop.*

Double Sheaths   *Tie to each other.*

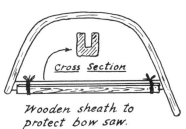

Cross Section

Wooden sheath to protect bow saw.

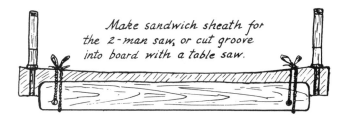

Make sandwich sheath for the 2-man saw, or cut groove into board with a table saw.

the same care you had for the cutting teeth. Let the last stroke erasing the jointing flat be nothing but a caress.

After filing the rakers, professional saw filers used to finish the raker teeth by swaging them. That operation was lightly hammering the upper edge of the tip so that the chisel edge assumed a more horizontal pointing than the relatively vertical position left by filing. Swaging usually required two to four hammer taps, first on the entire upper raker edge, then working out to the tip. The process gave the raker much better scooping action and made more efficient sawing. Swaging also reduced the height of the raker tip. The reduction used to be figured at .004″ (0.1 mm) and, to compensate, the rakers were jointed .004″ higher to start with.

There is no question that proper swaging is most desirable. At the same time, swaging also requires more than the usual amount of precision, skill, and experience. Unless you have the proper tools and practice on an old saw first, you might consider omitting the swaging from your sharpening agenda.

Early woods saws were much like carpenters' saws—larger, of course—but with one tooth immediately beside another. As the possibility of eliminating sawdust-clogging became better appreciated, various toothing patterns were designed to help the problem. The raker pattern described above has been the most successful of these. But a pattern known as "peg tooth" also deserves attention just because there are so many peg-tooth saws still in existence.

Peg-tooth saws have no rakers. The triangular teeth have spaces left between them to accommodate sawdust, and it is the teeth themselves that scuff sawdust from the kerf. The increased number of teeth give excellent results in sawing dry and smaller wood. Appropriate sharpening files for peg-tooth saws are the flat mill file for sharpening the tips and the round file for cutting out valley bottoms. Do not attempt to sharpen the entire edge of each peg tooth. Just give a full bevel to the tip area. That is all that is needed. Having some of the lower edges of the teeth relatively blunt helps carry out sawdust.

When you complete sharpening a saw, of whatever pattern, try it first in a softwood log. If wire edges still adhere to the teeth, the softwood will remove them with more kindness to your cutting edges than hardwood might.

Saw teeth are so easily dulled during transportation that making a sheath for the saw will save you much frustration and extra work. If you have a table saw, you can easily make a sheath by sawing a slot in the edge of a board of suitable length. Cover the saw teeth with this slotted board and you can stop worrying about what the saw will hit in your garage or the back of your truck. Drill a hole in each end of the sheath for a stout piece of twine to tie the sheath to the saw. Tie knots in the ends of the twine so they will not slip out of the board and become lost.

28

Operating with a Saw

Though this is a book of the ax, saws are not going to suddenly disappear. So to furnish comparative information about gathering firewood, some facts should be included about felling trees with a saw. The basic principles of felling are the same for both ax and saw. Hinge and kickback stop are essential to felling with either tool.

Some techniques of felling with a saw cannot be used with an ax. In outlining these points, I assume that you already know how to operate a saw, including the ubiquitous chain saw. So that will not be covered here. There are plenty of eager salesmen waiting to tell you, "See, all you have to do is flip this switch!" Just remember that an ax is easier to buy, maintain, repair, transport and use on light work than a saw is. That is principally true for just about any type of saw. An ax can do the heavier work too, but more slowly.

However, for operating in one spot with nothing going wrong, a chain saw can cut more wood faster than you could hope to cut with an ax. And for felling trees, the saw—any saw—has another advantage over the ax because of the manner in which the saw cuts. Instead of a sizable notch, the saw leaves only a narrow kerf in its trail. And in this kerf you can pound wedges. The added safety and control over lay gained by this wedging technique on the larger trees is one of the major advantages of felling with a saw.

Just as with an ax, in felling with a saw the face cut is made low and facing the lay or direction of fall. The face cut must still be a notch, not just a single saw kerf. When felling with an ax, the face cut is necessarily a notch. Felling with a saw, you must deliberately make the face cut a notch so that the hinge can fold without interference during the critical beginning of the fall. Naturally it is possible to omit performing the chore of cutting twice into the face to form a notch, but the omission is a foolish one. The larger the tree, the more foolish it is. It compromises both safety and accuracy of fall.

As noted in Chapter 10, the depth of the face cut can vary according to circumstances. When the two saw kerfs meet in the apex of the face notch, they will leave a broad wedge of wood which must be knocked out to open the notch. For small trees, you can probably knock this wedge out with the end of the saw. For a large tree, the slice may be so heavy that you will have to split it apart and pick it out. The preferred tool for the task is a pickaroon, a double-ended tool mounted on an ax handle. The head has an adzelike bit on one end and a small pick on the other. With one end or the other, or both,

you can dislodge the wedge in any face notch.

When using a chain saw, you can save a bit of timber in the butt of a tree at the expense of the stump. Instead of meeting the first cut of the face notch by sawing down at it through the valuable butt, it is almost as easy to saw on an upward slant through the wood of the stump. Besides keeping a

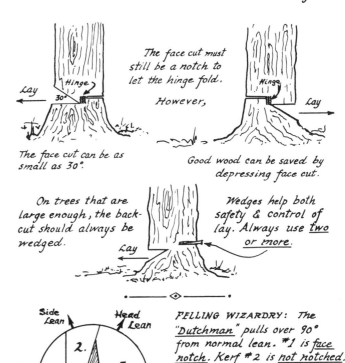

Felling with the Saw   Diagram 54

saw does have advantages.

The face cut must still be a notch to let the hinge fold.

Lay   Hinge   30°

However,

The face cut can be as small as 30°.

Hinge   *Lay*

Good wood can be saved by depressing face cut.

On trees that are large enough, the back-cut should always be wedged.

Lay

Wedges help both safety & control of lay. Always use <u>two or more</u>.

Side Lean   Head Lean

2.

Lay   1.   3.

Hinge

4.

(Cross Section)

FELLING WIZARDRY: The "Dutchman" pulls over 90° from normal lean. #1 is <u>face notch</u>. Kerf #2 is <u>not notched</u>. Side lean swings tree onto #2. #3 prepares tree for the fall and #4 forms the hinge to ensure further rotation into lay. The Dutchman is not for the novice.

square-ended log, this trick gives you a slant-bottomed notch from which the notch-wedge can be more easily knocked out. Whether cut up or down, the angle of the face notch should be at least 30° so that the tree can fall at least 30° before collision between the closing surfaces of the butt and stump. (See Diagram 54.) When a tree has fallen that far, its real lay is pretty much determined.

When the face cut is complete, move to the rear of the tree for the back cut. This will require only a single saw kerf. You specifically do not want a notch for the back cut, because in the single saw kerf, you can insert and pound wedges without any further preparation. On smaller trees, the back cut has insufficient depth to hold both saw wedges and saw. On average, the minimum size tree that is advantageous to wedge is about 18" in diameter. When felling trees smaller than that, depend upon some other method of directional control.

When felling larger trees, start wedges in the kerf as soon as the saw has cut deep enough to clear. Be sure the wedges enter solid wood beyond the bark. The felling wedges are much thinner than splitting wedges and their faces are normally scarred so that pressure in the kerf cannot spit them out. In cold weather, blackening felling wedges with birch bark flame may also prevent spitting out. Early wedging will keep your saw from binding and can also be good insurance against the possibility of the tree's tipping backward on top of you. Use two or more wedges and hit each of them in turn as you pound them into the kerf. That way, they will all carry the load together rather than any one of them doing it singly.

Bear in mind that the hinge and kickback stop principles are the basic means of control and safety in all manual tree felling, no matter how the tree is severed. All other techniques only supplement these two. Wedging cannot work miracles. Never double wedges vertically in attempting to double the lift. To attempt too much with wedges is to risk having them spit out. Then the tree, suddenly without support, could lurch backward, perhaps disastrously. With standard felling wedges, a ½" lift is about all you should expect. For an average 70' tree, that would move the top about 3' laterally. But considering that you seldom should be trying to redirect a heavy-leaning tree anyway, 3' of top movement could be enough, and might be difficult to attain in any other manner.

Any further redirection of such a tree would have to await the final shaping of the hinge. Just as when felling with an ax, remember that the falling tree will incline toward the thicker side of the hinge. A chain saw can cut pretty rapidly. Sawing on the hinge, if you want to know where your tree is going to fall, you had better keep intimate track of how much hinge remains intact on each side. Even an inch may make a difference. Listen for any movement. But because a chain saw is also pretty noisy, look up as much as you can. Movement is greatest in the top, and you are likely to detect it there first.

There is a masterly saw-felling technique known as the "Dutchman" that can often attain a lay of 90° and even more on one side or the other of the natural lean of a tree, provided that the lean is not too pronounced. (See Diagram 54.) This is remarkable. In using the Dutchman, the face notch is made toward the lay desired. Then a second kerf deepens the face cut, but only on the end toward the principal lean. This

addition is not notched out, and because it is cut under one corner of the lean direction, the weight of the tree will settle on that kerf about as soon as it is made. As the kerf closes, the top of the tree rotates out of its natural lean into a new lean nearer the desired lay.

The third step is to saw the back cut parallel to the face notch but leaving the hinge heavy and triangular. The final cut evenly deepens the face along the line of the original notch, reducing the thickness of the hinge to an even strip until the tree rotates a second time, falling then toward the face along the desired lay.

Obviously, the ax cannot perform this saw magic that has the tree settling its weight into a thin saw kerf. Both second and fourth kerfs must be done with some finesse, for the tree will immediately try to pinch them shut. Note also that the fourth and last cut is made with the sawyer on the forward side of the hinge. This is no place for a learner. The Dutchman is a marvelous technique for manipulating the direction of fall of the larger, and therefore the most dangerous, trees. It is not suited for most trees left in the East that usually have smaller girth.

Nor is the Dutchman a felling method for just anybody to experiment with. Involved in its successful completion are numerous separate judgments that fall under the classification of "art, not a science." The method is described here to offer a glimpse of what real felling proficiency can mean. But until one has gained that grasp of tree-felling artistry, one had better leave the Dutchman to professionals who have mastered it. There are not many of them.

Good tree-felling practice rarely excuses lodging one tree in another, but it does happen. Lodging also results from storms and other natural causes. Whatever the origin, felling a lodged tree is not an uncommon task. Doing it with machinery seldom involves more than severing the stump, then dragging the tree down with a skidder or other power source.

Grounding the tree without power can be tricky. It could be done with an ax but might be infinitely laborious. With a chain saw, cut the leaning trunk off the stump from the under side up, almost to the top side. Then withdraw the saw and above the scarf, use the saw to worry the remaining sound wood until the trunk falls off the stump. Be careful not to pinch the saw. If you are cutting 4' cordwood sticks, mark off the next cut and from the under side, again saw almost through. This time the weight of the tree will open the scarf as the new trunk butt plunges earthward. Pull your saw free in time. The first 4' stick may or may not be completely free. If not, cut it free, again being wary of pinching. Reduce the rest of the trunk similarly into 4' sticks.

With each stick cut off the trunk, successive butt ends thump to earth nearer the tree's lodged crown. Typically, the loosened crown does not move laterally but only downward as another butt stick collapses below it. At some point, the entire crown mass of branches and trunk remnant become vertical. The mass is never exactly balanced and will fall somewhere. If you are beneath it cuddling a chain saw, you had better have the situation pretty well figured out.

I once cut a lodged oak from which I later made five 4' cordwood sticks on the opposite side of the stump from the side it had been lodged. In its final dive, the crown had reversed direction. I am not proud of that. I tell it here only as evidence that lodged trees can be downed low-tech.

On heavy trees with large limbs, the chain saw is quicker in limbing. If a limb is free-hanging, cut through the bottom third alongside the trunk. Finish the job by sawing down from the top. Then the limb will drop off without tearing or binding your saw. If the limb is pushed upward, or helps support the tree, reverse the order of cutting. Slice the top third, or the side that the pull is coming from, then make the second cut from the opposite side, usually the bottom. Where a severed limb may swing against you, if you cannot change positions, first cut it in one or more pieces from the outer end, relieving its tension before shearing the remainder off alongside the trunk. Be careful when cutting limbs that may let the log roll or fall toward you.

As compared to bucking with an ax, the saw is quicker except on small wood, and the saw's narrow kerf wastes virtually nothing. Still, there can be problems. Bucking a log with an ax, you will never be stopped because your ax is stuck. But a stuck saw can occur almost routinely unless you use your head about where and when to cut.

With manual saws, you cannot undercut or sidecut a fallen tree unless it is lodged in another, and that should be seldom. This limits how you can use manual saws for bucking. Unsupported segments can be easily cut off a log, for the kerf will open wider as it deepens. But with logs supported on either side of a kerf, the kerf will often close as it deepens and pinch the saw. A manual saw can lose its set from being pinched. With chain saws, both bars and chains can be damaged in closed kerfs, and spare parts are not cheap.

Sawing small logs, you may avoid pinching by propping the log up, perhaps by pushing another chunk beneath it beside the kerf. A large log may have to be turned so that it rests on a new combination of supporting humps beneath to enable you to finish the kerf from the other side. The latter remedy is not a cure-all, for it is possible to get a saw pinched on both sides of a kerf.

To free a stuck saw, lifting the log with a lever may help. Occasionally the kerf can be opened with wedges. If all else fails, you can chop the pinching sides, or one of them, away with an ax. The best solution is prevention. Never let the saw get pinched. Somehow, move the log into a favorable position before you begin sawing. Often there will be simpler cuts to make first. With the size of the log reduced, the pinch situation will be easier to handle.

Bucking with a chain saw is marvelously easier because you can make side cuts at will and even make undercuts without turning the log. You can do this adjacent to the ground by pushing the saw through the log. That is not the best chain-saw practice, but it can be done. Use caution. Chain saws can get stuck, and nosediving into grit is always possible.

In bucking a free-hanging section with a chain saw, first make an undercut of about a quarter to a third of the diameter of the piece so as to prevent splitting. Then just slightly higher on the log, slice through the top side and the piece will fall off. The slight difference in alignment between top and bottom cuts is insurance that the cut-off piece will fall cleanly away. If the top lip of the falling piece were longer than the bottom lip of the log, they would lock. (See Diagram 55.)

Diagram 55

Limbing & Bucking with the Saw

Cross-section views of successive chain saw kerfs in _larger_ logs to keep saw from getting stuck.

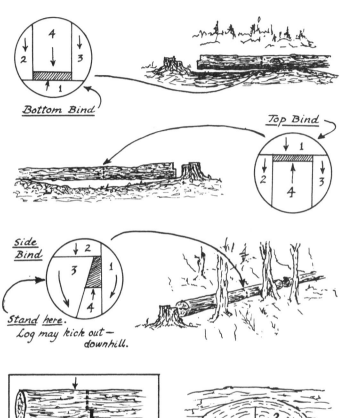

Bottom Bind

Top Bind

Side Bind

Stand here. Log may kick out— downhill.

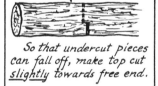

So that undercut pieces can fall off, make top cut _slightly_ towards free end.

Free-hanging heavy limb.

The larger the log, the greater the advantage of the chain saw for bucking. Using it as shown in Diagram 55, you can easily buck large logs with tensions that would unquestionably pinch out your saw unless you made the cuts in the order shown. This capability would permit bucking the largest logs in place. This is exactly what the small operator needs, for he would have difficulty turning huge logs in bucking them.

On the other hand, few woodlots will yield monster logs any more. If you have some, you would be well compensated to sell them for a better purpose than firewood. As with the description of the Dutchman, these diagrams are included to give you the basis for appreciating what harvesting trees can entail. _Basis,_ mind you; not mastery. There is a difference between reading and doing. Trees will not fit completely inside books, not by a good bit.

29

The Exercise Element

Fads have spectacular careers. Like spring flowers, they burst open with perfumed splendor. The public consciousness is captured. People gather to stare, simper, and inhale the delicious scents. But this stage does not endure with either flowers or fads. The moment comes when they no longer dazzle or smell so sweetly. They shrivel up and disappear. And by then, the spectators are usually weary of the whole show. They turn away and leave, seeking something new.

We can fervently hope that this will not be the fate of the current exercise fad. For few caprices that catch the public fancy are so salutary for participants as exercise. Too often our mechanized life no longer makes demands upon our bodies unless exercise is deliberately injected into our schedules.

Luckily, if you exercise regularly and sufficiently, you will be able to accomplish more. You will not tire so easily from normal exertion and you will easily rise to those extra needs of life that pop up with such regularity that they are really part of the normal pattern of existence. If physical exercise tires you, you are no different from anybody else. Yet even on the same day, regular, challenging exercise will make your waking hours more effective and your sleep more restful. This is an across-the-board phenomenon, for the mind is subject to the body. When the body is fit, the mind is more alert. An overtaxed body will be dulled by fatigue.

Children naturally exercise. Either they sleep or they move. It is also natural for grown-ups to demand of children, "Why can't you keep still?" Yet most of us would be better off if we could match active children step for step. Somewhere between high school and twenty-five years old, we stop moving so much. After that, we feel like moving less and less. Then, unless we force ourselves, or circumstances force us to keep going, we deteriorate. What you do not use, you are going to lose. Oh, it takes time, but that is the process, and time has a way of slithering by whether we watch it or not. When you finally cannot move at all, they cart you away.

What anybody needs while he is still able to enjoy it is movement, the exercise that keeps muscles supple, fat burned up, joints oiled, and the blood circulating. Then you not only can do more, but you want to do more. Movement generates movement, and you will feel as if life is worth living. You do not have to be a champion athlete to attain this level of well-being. What you must have is the discipline to exercise on a regular basis.

And like other traits, discipline in one aspect of your life will carry over into the others. In large part, you are what you make of yourself, and can do what you believe you can do. Confidence helps, and if your body feels equal to living, that helps create confidence. Everybody is after pleasure today. How worthy a goal that is does not concern us here. But if you do not believe that feeling fit is a distinctly pleasurable experience, you need only loll around without exercising a few years to find out.

That general level of health is related to physical well-being is indisputable. Not that regular joggers may not catch colds or the flu, for they can. Nevertheless, many debilitating, infectious diseases pick principally upon the infirm. When one is in good health and still contracts a disease, one is more likely to have a less severe case and to recover more quickly. Scourges commonplace in our civilization—ulcers, obesity, constipation, migraine, hemorrhoids, arthritis, hypertension, and heart disease, for instance—are much less likely to attack those who consistently exercise regularly.

Arguing whether this is a cause or effect is pointless. All body parts, systems, and functions are so interdependent that it is difficult to know exactly what helps what. Exercise appears to benefit anybody who uses it. Until this is proven wrong, you should embrace exercise as a way of life.

Research on the sustained effects of exercise is still too scanty to state that an exercise regime will make you live longer. From the other benefits of exercise, that conclusion might perhaps be inferred, but to date it cannot be proven. Of particular interest, though, are three rather isolated regions of the world where humans do live longer than elsewhere. One is in Ecuador, one in Russian Georgia, and the third in northern Pakistan. All three are in mountainous areas where life is agricultural and its culture requires the inhabitants to travel on foot up and down mountain slopes daily. In each of these enclaves, persons still able and vigorous at well over 100 years of age are not unusual. As of a few years ago, when the National Geographic Society published an article on these pockets of longevity, one man in Soviet Georgia was believed to be 167 years old. Diet may play a significant role in these astonishing life spans. But the fact that the demanding requirement to work the body every day is present in all three localities is also inescapable. It suggests that the body will last longer if one uses it more.

The body is a unit. What affects part of it is related to the rest. If you are vigorous, enjoy good health, and feel fit, you will look the part. And even without primping for a beauty contest, an image of vitality is singularly attractive nevertheless.

Two other lesser benefits of exercise are also worth mentioning. A body that is used more needs more nourishment to keep functioning. If you like to eat, that is good news. If you have any self-control at all, you can learn to draw the line beyond which additional food only packs fat about you. Another odd fact that will be useful for some is that vigorous exercise dampens the taste for things alcoholic. There, too, you must be able to discriminate between simple thirst and desire for alcohol. Of course, the opposite phenomenon is also true. Plentiful alcohol inhibits both desire and ability to exercise.

Exercise is not all honey and roses. Quite frankly, I resent time that I have to devote to it whenever I cannot get out of it. For a man who is busy with the million needs of life, taking time out for daily exercise can be a heavy burden. And that is not all. When you finally are performing your daily stint, it will usually be at least boring, and not uncommonly it may be painful. In other words, exercise merely for the sake of exercise is only for the fanatic or the unoccupied, no matter what the benefits may be.

There is a way out. Arrange your work schedule and other activities so that what must be done anyway can serve as your daily ration of exercise. Walking to work is a familiar example of this, though a fifty-mile commute could be a bit much. If you cut your own firewood, you have a ready-made solution, killing two turkeys with the same ax. There is plenty of exercise in cutting wood. You need only view it in that light and schedule it accordingly. Instead of ramming the wood-gathering task to earliest completion each year, perform a scheduled amount daily.

If your firewood needs are average, cutting and storing it may not provide all the exercise you will need over the course of the year, but it will help. There is exercise in virtually every element of gathering firewood, starting with getting to the woodlot. If that is too near at hand, or too distant, running back and forth with your ax may not be feasible. But for moderate distances, the run could be ideal, providing your neighbors do not take fright.

With the aim of stimulating your body, the principal advantage of the chain saw becomes a disadvantage. For admittedly, it does require more effort to fell and buck a tree with an ax than it does with a chain saw. So working with an ax and working your body out at the same time, you can savor the satisfaction of doing two jobs simultaneously. Furthermore, your exercise will no longer be boring, for chopping wood never is. That is, chopping is never boring to a man willing to do it.

In speaking of chopping so far, we have concentrated more on how you should do it rather than on the effort you must put into it. Now that the subject is exercise, it is fair to note that you should not attempt to hurry or you will be doing as much resting as you will chopping. Strike a moderate pace that you can maintain. The act of chopping involves most of the body and provides plenty of exercise for your heart and lungs as well as your arms and back. The same applies to manual sawing. Drawing one of these saws back and forth will tell you what kind of condition you are in. To see how you measure up against one of your friends, or vice versa, con your friend into sawing contest with each of you on opposite ends of a two-man saw. A couple of minutes will tell you everything. With a one or two-man saw, the only way to saw through a sizable tree without resting is to take it easy all the way.

Bringing your wood to the road for pickup is the best of exercise. In many cases, manhandling can save making numerous short vehicle trails. Lifting and carrying away a heavy stick is certainly exercise, as you will appreciate after a few yards. In lifting, bear the weight on your shoulder and avoid raising heavy loads by main strength of your back. With any really heavy load, keep your heels together and your back straight and erect. If you cannot lift a load in that manner, leave it alone. If it is a stick, split it or cut it. Otherwise, you will risk both rupture and back injury.

Cutting wood to size with an ax is time-consuming, as is also true of using a handsaw. But this very fact is opportunity for exercise. Splitting stove-length chunks can likewise be exercise, and it is virtually recreation, a game you can play as fast as you can safely select a new target from the pile. Stacking the cut and split pieces takes energy too. Remember that felling, splitting, cutting, and storing your own firewood, you will cumulatively lift about 24 tons for each cord. This figure does not include the effort necessary to transport the wood during each lift.

All the foregoing assumes that you do in fact need additional exercise daily. Unless your daily routine is different from that of most American men today, you will. By your appropriately spacing the wood-gathering chore, many of the normally tedious exercise hours can become not only bearable, but enjoyable. Then in the bitter winter there will be double reason for the crackling wood fire to warm you. And because of the time your greater energy saved from other tasks, you will be able to relax in front of it. It is a good feeling.

30
Your Woodlot

In comparing wood with oil and coal, it is currently fashionable to speak of wood as a "renewable resource." That application of the term is not altogether accurate. Wood is a harvestable crop. But to consider wood indefinitely renewable is deceptive. For as with most crops, there is nothing automatic about sustained production, not even of wood.

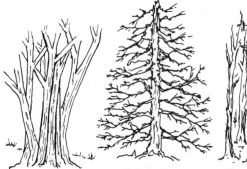

Woodlot Culls
Diagram 56

Cutting them for firewood will let new growth expand.

In a Clump: *Leave the best, take the rest.*

The Wolf Tree: *It has too many branches & takes too much space.*

Too Heavy Stands: *Thin them out. Leave the best.*

Trash Trees: *Cut the less desirable trees to encourage the better ones.*

Broken, Dead *or Diseased trees should all be taken.*

The Light Hog: *Perhaps a mature, beautiful tree ready for cutting. If it is getting old, it is best to cut it.*

Another common declaration is that a woodlot will deliver an average yield of one cord per acre per year. The inference is that this can also be continued indefinitely. Unfortunately, most of us do not have to travel far to find an acre, or more, that is not occupied, that could grow trees perhaps, but does not even yield a good crop of weeds. It all depends on how the lot is managed. If you are one of the lucky ones who have access to a woodlot, take care of it now so that it will still produce wood in the future.

The products of a woodlot, even a firewood lot, should be put to the "highest and best" use. Translated, that means that if you have marketable trees too valuable to use as firewood, sell those trees as logs if possible. If you do not own equipment to snake out and transport logs, you may have to shop around for somebody who does. If you can make a few choice logs, the prevailing timber prices may pay you well for your trouble.

Before deciding on this, you should determine several items. How many marketable logs do you have, and of what kind and size? How will you get them available for transportation? How much will this cost you or will you do it yourself? How will skidding logs affect your lot? How much will the sale net you, or how much will the custom lumber you take save you? All these questions are relevant. Firm dates for both cutting and pickup are also important. As noted before, the time of year can make substantial difference for both felling and drawing logs. Ground is easily chewed up in the springtime by logging operations.

Forgetting is easy. If you are reserving specific trees for sale or any other reason, it is best to identify them. Using cans of spray paint is an easy way to do this. Spraying a different color on the trees you will fell for firewood is also sensible. Blazing these trees is a good way to plan your work for the year. Another advantage of marking is that you tend to form standards for what you will cut before you become buried with immediate problems of felling.

Any mature tree should be cut. That does not apply to a dooryard tree that has utility in its beauty, setting, or shade-giving or screening qualities. But in the woodlot, a mature tree is one that has reached its probable maximum size and may soon deteriorate if left standing. Another factor is equally important. By capturing sunlight, moisture, and nutrients within its range, a large tree inhibits or entirely prevents development of young growth. Even the arresting wind-hammer of large branches or the constant push of trunk growth can crowd out other trees. And underground, there will be a concurrent and crushing battle of roots.

In some cases, you may wonder whether trees are mature, but if there are signs of rot, splitting, or major limb loss, or a top is broken, those trees should probably be culled. This not only preserves their value while they are still sound, but gives the young growth in the area a chance of its own. Trees that have been partially tipped so that they grow at a diagonal should likewise be taken, for they block an undue amount of light from the larger area below.

Where former fields or pasture have grown back into trees, it is not uncommon to find trees that are not particularly tall, yet have enormous spreading branches. These "wolf" or hog trees show the luxuriance of their unhampered growth in the open with access to sunlight all around instead of having to stretch toward open light as the long-stemmed forest trees must. Unless you favor the appearance of these squat forms, it is better to remove them in favor of young growth. Hog trees dominate a disproportionate amount of ground for what they are worth, which is not much. As timber, they are full of huge knots. As firewood, the same knots could grievously inconvenience you at splitting time.

There is vast difference in the amount of light that different kinds of trees need. Quite often, trees that are crowded out are of the same variety as those that win the race skyward. For firewood purposes, it is fortunate that many of the best fuel trees require less light when growing than their softwood cousins.

Sometimes smaller trees must be cut to accommodate larger ones. Underneath the cover of healthy and still growing trees there may be smaller trees alive but showing clear sign of losing the battle for light and nourishment. This will commonly occur when the luxuriant crowns of the taller trees have broadened to fill gaps between branches that formerly let sunlight shoot below. Indications of too little light are spindly growth and the live limbs being few, stunted, and clustered at the top of the crowded tree. Seldom does a tree survive long with this appearance. It is better to cull this defected growth while it is still alive and its wood is still sound.

As a rule, most trees rise in a single stem from one root mass. Evergreen trees are more likely to grow in this fashion. The broadleaf trees that generally make better fuels are frequently found growing in pairs, or even in clumps of four or more from the same root mass. Red maple is a quite common example of this. With available sunlight, nutrients, moisture, and growing space all being shared, no one of these trees thrives as well as it would if it grew alone. One or more stems may die before reaching maturity. These rot eventually, perhaps leaving the surviving stems with scars, open entrance to infection or growth handicaps that they may never overcome. Worse, the sum of the wood generated by a clump may never equal the amount of quality wood yielded by a single tree of the same root mass. So when thinning trees, leave the most vigorous specimen in a clump and cut all the others. If the best one is not harmed when the culls are felled, sometimes it will show remarkable immediate growth. Meanwhile, you will have the smaller members of the clump for firewood.

A different problem exists among single trees of equal vigor that are growing too close to one another. They must have adequate space to expand. If they are about eight feet or more apart, leave them to mature, unless they fit one of the culling categories just mentioned. If all trees in the area are not equally desirable, cut the ones of lesser value so that the better ones can thrive. Even though you favor hardwoods for firewood, do not cull all other trees indiscriminately. For instance, if you have a modest little stand of half-grown pine, it would be wrong to cut it in the hope that oaks might grow there instead. The soil, light and moisture conditions might not be favorable for growing oak even though you actually replanted the area with quality seedlings. Then, too, pine, white pine in particular, may be inferior firewood but will one day bring a fine return for its value as saw logs to cut into lumber. Eliminating a stand of half-grown pines would be a serious error, especially since they grow much more quickly than hardwoods do, sometimes by as much as 60%.

Much depends upon size. There is not much value in a sapling, but if a tree has about twenty years of growth, you should seriously consider letting it continue to maturity. Even with a less desirable variety—poplar or gray birch, for example, the decision to cut or not to cut a growing tree should always be a comparative one. If you urgently need a particular tree, take it anyway. But if not, ask yourself what harm there is in leaving it. If a poplar is competing for space with an oak, maple, ash, or similar, cut the poplar. But if the poplar is soaring above alders, leave the poplar and cut the alders.

An important element in nurturing a tree crop is simple care for young growth when felling. This should be routine, but often it is not. Felling is difficult, and the choices of lay are always limited. Protecting young growth may not be the first priority in selecting a lay, but neither should it be the last. Here, too, you will have choices. If smashing young trees is unavoidable, choose the lay where the young stock has the least future promise. A special case is culling a tree that will do more damage in falling than it is worth. Though this could be an argument for leaving that to rot, you could be sorry later for having ignored a budding hazard. A better solution might be trying some of the less common measures for controlling lay, such as jacking or roping the top. These might permit you to fell the tree where it would do little or no damage.

Among other things that we could profitably copy from Europeans is how to increase forest yields. In much of western Europe, forests have been manicured for generations, and their timber productivity per acre exceeds ours. Having far more forest land, the United States and Canada have never worried about timber shortages. In some areas, we are still cutting virgin timber. But not all North Americans are so fortunate any more, and on an individual level, it does make a difference how much wood we can squeeze from an acre. It could even determine whether we keep warm or not. To get the most out of a woodlot, you have to put time into it. What must be done is no secret. A successful gardener spends time planting, thinning, weeding, and trimming before he is ever able to harvest a crop. The same principles apply to a woodlot.

For trees to grow, they must have light and nourishment. It is not only rival trees that compete for food. Lesser growth

Trimming Standing Trees

Diagram 57

Be careful. The object is to preserve the trees, not destroy them.

For quick, clean pruning,

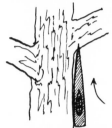

use an ax. Bounce the cheek of the ax flat-ways off the trunk as it heads for the branch, leaving the trunk uncut.

The end of the severed branch should be clean-cut, smooth, & leave bark unharmed. A rough cut will heal slowly – if at all.

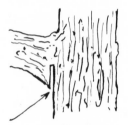

On heavy limbs, saw (or chop) at least the bottom third before finishing cut on top of limb.

On high limbs, use a polesaw, or even a ladder. Undercut if possible.

How many branches to trim will depend upon size, age, and the kind of tree. Young evergreen trees should be left with branches somewhat lower than on deciduous (broadleaf) trees. For a rule of thumb, trim the branches only from the bottom third of young trees, but make a point of keeping that bottom third trimmed for as long as you can reach it with a pole saw or any other pruning tool you have. This will be rewarded later with the greater amount of clear wood that did not have to twist around a branch, either live or dead. As the trees climb toward mature height, they crowd each other so that branches without enough light will wither, die, and eventually fall off. It is not unusual for forest trees nearing maturity to have branches only on their upper half or even upper third, but young trees cannot be trimmed that much without endangering them.

Trimming limbs on live trees is different from other woods operations, because instead of destroying a live thing, you are trying to preserve it. This requires care. The branch should be trimmed evenly with the trunk but without skinning the trunk. Doing this fast takes practice. Like all young things, young trees are tender and easy to injure. But on a healthy young tree, the wound left by a branch severed smoothly and close to the trunk will heal remarkably soon. Though not usual, these stub holes can sometimes be entirely hidden under a new sapwood layer in as little as three years. That will not happen if the stub of the trimmed branch is too long or the trunk is hacked because of cutting too close.

A saw would seem to be the best tool for limbing live trees, but that is not always true. In cutting, the teeth of a saw leave rough raking streaks that can shelter dirt and infection exactly as they would if the cut were in flesh rather than wood. The clean cut from a sharp ax will heal sooner provided that the cut is close yet leaves no scarring. For this work, a hatchet might seem ideal, but an ax is preferable. With a light ax on a handle of ordinary length, you have greater reach, more power, can use it one-handed if necessary, and can use two hands comfortably for steadiness of aim. An uncommon tool that is remarkably efficient is an extra heavy knife about 14" in length. The nearest commercial approach to a knife of this type is what is currently sold as a "Bowie knife," though most of them have points too light and handles too awkward for serious tree-limbing. You can make your own limbing knife from a section of an old crosscut saw blade. Because the stock is relatively light, keep the blade broad for greater weight. The ordinary machete or other knife of similar weight is far too light and also too long for cutting woody branches close to the trunk.

Pruning the larger live branches, cut the underside first. Strike or saw upwards at them alongside the trunk. This will keep the bark of the trunk from tearing when you next strike the base of the branch from the top and sever it. If your ax is sharp and the branch small, you may not need to make an undercut. Particularly on white pine, some dead branches can be easily broken off with the poll of a single-bitted ax without danger of scarring the tree. If the branches are small enough, the ax will not be hurt.

Striking with enough force to chop a branch off cleanly without injuring the tree is a trick. Instead of aiming directly at the crotch, make the cheek of your ax slap the trunk immediately above the crotch. In effect, the ax moves crab-

will also. So even though many smaller trees, bushes, shrubs, and even vines seldom keep larger varieties from light, they are forest weeds nevertheless and should be cut. With scrub growth trimmed back, seedlings of desirable trees will be more likely to survive. Every one of these that starts itself will save you the chore of replanting.

For either timber or fuel, a tree is more valuable when it grows high rather than wide because it will have more clear wood without knots. In forests, this type of growth occurs naturally as each tree stretches toward the sunlight. In the open though, a tree tends to grow outward as well as up because there is light all around. A major fraction of the tree will be developed in the limbs and branches rather than the trunk where the valuable timber would grow otherwise. Yet this lateral growth can be prevented. Whether a tree grows in the open or in the forest, you can aid both its growth and the quality of wood in the trunk merely by lopping off its lower branches. Deprived of these, a young tree will compensate by shooting upward, developing the tall, straight trunk so valuable for either timber or fuel. Pruning the lower branches will not hurt the tree unless you trim off too many branches or you botch the surgery.

wise, but because its principal motion is downwards, it ricochets off the trunk striking the branch at its base. With still more practice, this method is also useful in striking upward at undercuts.

A natural forest is a helter-skelter sort of place. Some part of it is continually dying, perhaps bruising or fatally injuring other trees in its fall. When a large tree topples because of storm or rot, it also blankets a considerable portion of forest floor. For a long time, little can grow from beneath its carcass. Of course it will finally all rot and young seedlings sprout from its ears, but that will not happen overnight.

To help a woodlot produce its maximum, you must be concerned with any element including forest trash, that interferes with the regeneration of young growth. Rot of an old tree is perfectly natural, but it is severe economic loss from any view except the longest term. If left long enough, any wood will rot and generate humus for future trees to grow in, but with large trees the entire process may take several decades. For the earliest return on woodlot investment, the object of good management is to prevent rot before it occurs. When a tree seems to have reached its prime, cut it.

Unfortunately, everything connected with tree-harvesting makes a monumental mess. In a well-managed woodlot, there would be few trees crashing to earth just because of decay, but there would be plenty of wood left on the ground nevertheless. Limbs trimmed from live trees, cut scrub growth, trash wood, casualties of felling, decayed pieces of no value, and, greatest of all, the limbs and tops of felled trees—all these are customarily left in the woods to rot. The industry word for the residue it leaves behind is "slash." It is useful here to expand the meaning of the word to include all wood from any source left to rot on the forest floor. We will exclude the product of modern portable chippers from that definition, since chipping machines are unlikely to be part of the small woodlot operation.

The smaller that slash is reduced in size, the less it will interfere with young growth and the sooner it will rot. With this aim, it is useful to focus your attention on how you will treat slash wherever it is. Stating that policy is essential if you have anybody working for or with you. Of the four major controls concerning slash, the first is diameter of stick, the minimum woodpile size being the maximum for slash. Naturally this assumes sound wood that is suitable woodpile material. All rotted wood is slash. Next, set limits on the maximum length of slash to be left without cutting it in two. Third, decide the maximum height that slash may project above the ground. Finally, will you pile the slash, windrow it, or let it lie where it was cut or fell? Slash that is finer and lies closer to the ground will rot more quickly, adding to the growth-nurturing humus. Properly done, this is quicker than either windrowing or piling the slash and leaves no mounds to blanket seedlings and crush young growth.

Taking as much wood as reasonably possible from each tree leaves little slash problem. For North American forests, this is a relatively new approach. However frugal our forebears were, they seldom applied it to the woods or to trees. Trees grew everywhere. There was no need to nurture the crop. When they wanted timber, they took it the easiest way possible. That normally meant taking straight trunks as far up as they were clear, leaving entire tops to rot in place. It was more economical to cut another whole tree than to worry marginal timber or fuel out of the top of the tree just fallen. So almost unimaginable quantities of wood were wasted. Yet because there was, or seemed to be, a surplus of trees, nobody cared or even gave the waste any thought. For the same reason, it seemed not to matter that the huge rotting tops inhibited new growth until they ultimately decomposed. Trees seemed to grow everywhere, so that also was another neglect that could be comfortably disregarded.

But times have changed. If you follow "Waste not, want not" as a reasonable slash policy, start with a maximum stick diameter of 1¼", about the thickness of a shovel handle. Put anything as thick or thicker into the woodpile. Whack apart any slash longer than 3' and do the same with any slash more than 1' above ground. With a sharp ax, this is but several minutes' work per tree. There is no need to pile or windrow this slash. With the larger wood taken away, the small pieces of limb present no obstacle to seedlings, and as the slash rots it adds to the vital humus.

Incidentally, using a chain saw to cut up slash is asking for trouble. The light pieces are unsecured on either end and the saw can easily hurl them toward you with amazing speed and crippling force.

Stump height is another item for a policy decision. There are about as many reasons for cutting stumps high as there are for cutting them low. How you cut them will depend upon your needs. A tree is thickest at its emergence from the ground, so to avoid waste, stumps should be cut as low as possible, taking the most wood where each inch really counts. Then along with the esthetics of not having high stumps, you will also not leave obstacles throughout the lot for other trees to break on in falling, or blocking what may otherwise be usable roadways. New growth is likewise somewhat enhanced, as low stumps rot more rapidly than high stumps merely because of less bulk.

There are three clear disadvantages to cutting stumps too low. Perhaps the worst one is that in the region of the swollen base of the trunk the interior grain is often curled and cross-grained from the influence of the roots below. Cutting the tree at that level harvests all the problems of contrary grain along with the extra wood. As firewood, that portion will not split as well. As timber, consequent warping or checking, once begun at that end, will tend to travel up the grain, spoiling what would otherwise be good lumber. Another disadvantage of cutting mature trees low is that you are more likely to encounter base rot in the heart of the tree. If what should be the strong midsection of the hinge is nothing but rot, you could be in trouble. A third disadvantage may seem easy to avoid, but it is a practical bugaboo of low-cutting in spite of that. The lower you cut, the more likelihood there is of grit and even rock somehow being in the line of cut. If you do not discover and eliminate it beforehand, a keen ax edge can become saw-toothed in a single stroke. It can be discouraging. The same disaster can happen to saws also.

All three disadvantages of low stumps disappear as the stump height rises. Cutting higher is easier because there is less wood to cut. A special case for high stumps is when the stumps will be removed, usually by bulldozing them out of the way. For that purpose, high stumps can save a lot of costly bulldozing time, for the high extension is a lever for the dozer to push against.

Diagram 58

Woodlot Harvesting Systems
Forest Management Applies to the Small Woodlot Also.

Cut the mature trees.
(Selective cutting)
Best for hardwoods.

Shelterwood Cutting.
Undesired trees cut.
Desired species left to seed
& shelter the young seedlings.

Clear Cutting: Done in strips or blocks, this system is not the bugaboo it has been painted. It is an economical way to both harvest and encourage desirable growth.

Every woodlot must have some kind of road network, even an exterior one, as when you bring wood to the edge of the lot for pickup. The fewer roads, the better. Roads can occupy a lot of tree-growing space. For a firewood operation, extensive roads should not be necessary. You will save much trouble and expense by limiting vehicle travel to periods when the natural ground can stand traffic. Frozen ground is best, and mudtime traffic should never be attempted off improved roads. Any kind of road-making is expensive, even if only of your own labor, and the better road you make, the more expensive it is. Never forget erosion. It is deceptively easy to skid logs over a slope in dry weather. But on the wrong hill, the trail that seemed only a slight scarring of the surface may have skinned the ground cover, permitting an impassable gulch to wash out later. Sometimes these victims of storms can be repaired only by major effort.

Barring fire, flood, blight, crippling windstorm, serious insect attack, overcutting, or being chewed by machinery, a woodlot should be able to regenerate itself and produce, decades into the future. Using careful selective cutting, you might have little need to replant. If you expanded into former fields or wished to improve your lots in areas of scrub, you would be wise to secure professional advice about available seed stock, hardiness, growth cycle, and economic factors of suitable tree varieties. Weigh those factors against your soil conditions, slope, moisture, tree cover, and exposure to sun where you wish to plant. Different species often prefer opposite sides of the same hill. Some flourish beneath others that mature sooner, thereby increasing your productivity by overlapping growing cycles, much as happens with selective cutting in natural forest. Seedlings of other varieties may thrive only when planted in their own separate areas.

A woodlot is truly an investment. It is worth sound advice on how to manage it for maximum return. Many states and provincial departments of forestry maintain staffs for this purpose. Keeping a woodlot productive may be a relatively new idea, but it is a good one. Your children, and after them, even their children, might appreciate it.

31

The Future

In recent years, Americans and Canadians have been widely criticized for being short-sighted about what lies ahead. If the complaint is valid, perhaps it does not reveal inferior intelligence so much as revulsion at facing specters already gestating. Certainly we live in a time of great change.

As always, though, the image of things to come is seldom easy to draw accurately. Crystal balls and tea leaves have often been as much aid as painstaking research and authoritative pronouncements in foretelling events. Yet trying to look ahead is only prudent for safeguarding the continuation of life. And based on knowledge of the past, we can scarcely overlook the likelihood of demonstrated cause and effect relationships being repeated in the future. If it can be shown that trends do exist, the task for those with the courage to look ahead is easier. A decision can be made that existing trends will probably continue, or probably halt, or something midway or even dissimilar will occur. Any one of these choices should be substantiated. And once made, the decision should be acted on. The rationale of this book is that knowledge of the ax is more than just a link to our heritage. That knowledge may still be useful so that life can go on.

One real-life scenario that seems to be unwinding in an unexpected direction concerns the material that we have been talking so much about—wood. By the close of the 19th century, coal had finally displaced wood as the fuel most used in the United States. As evidence that most people had their hearts in that conversion, the remaining wood fireplaces of that period were bricked-in and forgotten. Then on the heels of coal came oil. Concurrently, the marvel of electricity was harnessed, and especially with the help of natural gas fuel, usable energy seemed limitless.

After a couple of big bangs to end World War II, we suddenly had magic energy, power from nuclear fission. With a breeder reactor, it would cost us nothing. And coming soon, the barkers told us, was power from nuclear fusion which really was unlimited. For an encore, there was solar energy, and who knew what you could not do with that? The sun was big, really big.

It was a wonderful show—one of the best. After that, it was a bit of a surprise to find folks talking about wood once again. Before conjuring up a sense of *déjà vu*, we might take a look at where we stand, for nothing ever recurs exactly the same.

It has been said that when Europeans first came to America, a squirrel could have traveled the treetops from the Atlantic Ocean to the Mississippi River without touching the ground. Gypsy squirrels aside, that speaks of a lot of trees. Over half of the region of the lower forty-eight states was forest, including just about everything east of the Mississippi and much of the south-central region beyond. To the first white settlers, the total envelopment of the forest must have been sorely oppressive. Where the forest finally gave up were the prairies, grasslands that rolled past reach of the eye except where roving herds of bison might mask the view from horizon to horizon.

In the period of our early colonial history, the average depth of topsoil may have been as much as ten inches. It was an irreplaceable wealth cradling the luxuriant growth that rose out of it. In New England, white pine were known to have grown over 240' tall, a magnificence that was not puny even when compared to the later-discovered giant trees of the Pacific Coast. The broad arrow trees marked in New England for Royal Navy masts were 100' or more to the first branches and sometimes required up to a hundred yoke of oxen to haul them. Or consider a grapevine that faced early settlers of Ross County in south-central Ohio. That vine had a main stem over 5' thick before it divided into three branches, each of them over 2½' thick. Perhaps the grapes were sour, for the enormous vine was cut up for firewood. It yielded eight cords.

West of the Appalachians, the central hardwood forest was capable of producing cottonwood logs for dugout canoes 60' long. Even greater sizes of the marvelous white oak were common with branches beginning 70' up. One recorded white oak had a diameter of almost 11'. That the bountiful soil was so rich that it could resist decades of abuse is shown by a recorded Virginian observation that "substantial firewood" would regenerate itself in seven years. And that was in 1705, nearly a century after the first settlement.

But unremitting abuse can finally win. Our basic bank of wealth is the soil. In the United States today, our topsoil is about half depleted. On average, there are some 5" left. To be usable, it must be spread rather uniformly. Unfortunately, it can erode. When the surface is bared soil slips away with both wind and water.

Some years ago, afoot along U.S. Route 1 in northern Virginia, I paused to read a historical marker posted at a

Diagram 59

Tree Sizes – Then & Now

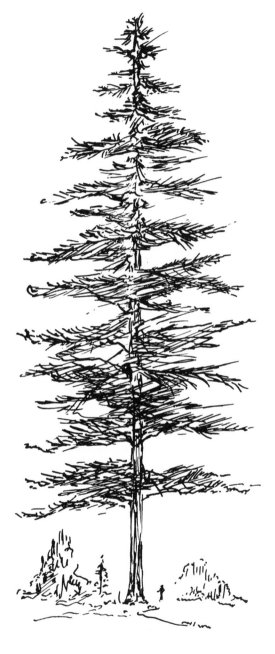

To Keep Wood a "Renewable Resource," We Must Care For Our Trees.

In Colonial New England, "Virgin" White Pine grew as high as 240'.

There, today, the sub-sequent growth is much respected if it ever reaches 90' to 100'.

culvert. It stated that in colonial times ocean-going vessels had traversed the route of the culvert with cargoes of tobacco for Europe. I stared, reading the marker a second time, but that was what it said. I peered over the hand railing. If the weeds in the turbid moisture below were any indicator, an ordinary canoe could just about ram through from one marshy side of the highway to the other. Something had filled that stream since it had floated tall ships to the mother country. Most likely the fill had been soil from the tobacco fields.

It would be wrong to point the finger upstream from a single culvert. To know that our soil has been ravaged almost everywhere, we only have to remember the brown winds of the Dust Bowl, to look upon any of thousands of deserted fields and stretches of scrub growth across the country, or to inspect the color of the Mississippi River as it pours central United States into the Gulf of Mexico.

We commonly associate soil with field crops, forgetting that in terms of modern civilization, the forests are also croplands and equally dependent upon the soil. Field crops are harvested annually. The harvest of wood must grow for years.

There are striking differences in forest productivity. Modern hybrid timber strains give great promise, yet much remains to be solved, including insect and disease resistance. Given the type of wood desired, basic productivity factors are the species of tree, climate, soil, and local growing conditions. All four of them affect age, quality, and size at maturity. Gone are the days of 1705 when the Virginian observer noted that "substantial firewood" grew back in seven years. Whatever his idea of "substantial" was, he had larger trees to compare against than we do today. Therefore, his "substantial" must have really been substantial.

Sweden has much forest land. Its production of paper pulp is largely from pines and spruces whose growing cycle is as much as eighty-five years. That compares with forty plus years in northeastern United States and as little as twenty-five years in the southern states. Climate, longer season for growing, and introduction of hybrid strains undoubtedly help determine these periods, but remembering the wondrously rapid seven years for "substantial firewood" in 1705, some other influence must also be at work.

Comparison of regional figures suggests depletion of nutrients in the soil, even if not diminution of the soil itself. The Swedish forests were being harvested at least several centuries before New England timber began to be exported to Europe in quantity during the 18th century. Commercial exploitation of southern pine forests began only after the American Civil War. These facts at least suggest that the longer a forest has been exploited, the longer its trees require for regeneration after cutting.

Slower-growing trees are not the only result of sustained assault on forestlands. Tree size also seems to be affected. Back-to-nature advocate Henry David Thoreau, after traveling through Maine timber country in 1846, related a story of two men lost in the woods. These men climbed a white pine "some two hundred feet or more" high to locate themselves. They succeeded, though one kept fainting at the height and had to be coddled and carried back to earth by the other.

Thoreau had not seen that tree, but he was an astute observer, even carrying a folding rule on his travels to take measurements. Virtually everywhere he went had already been cut over, but he spoke of seeing huge stumps and a deserted cull log five feet in diameter. His description of 42" Maine ax handles is also revealing. "The axe helves here were made to chop standing on a log, a primitive log of course—and were therefore nearly a foot longer than with us." This corresponds with the relationship already noted between ax handle length and tree size. In the century following Thoreau, the size of Maine trees decreased and Maine ax handles shrank to the size of the Massachusetts handles that had been familiar to Thoreau.

To use one of Thoreau's words, we no longer have "primitive" trees and they no longer grow to primitive heights. Anywhere in eastern United States today, an 80' tree is considered tall. A 110' tree is a marvel to gawk at and few people know where a 140' tree exists east of the Far West and Pacific Coast areas, even as a botanical curiosity.

It can be argued that eastern trees no longer grow larger because they are felled before they reach full height. That may often be true, but in general, most trees harvested either show classic signs of maturity or are as large as other trees of the same species that do show such signs. And at that stage, available records show that trees we now consider mature are often only a modest fraction of the size identical species formerly attained in virgin stands.

Again, at least part of the explanation seems to point to depletion of nourishment locked in the soil. Every time another cutting is carried off, that much is taken that was once in the earth. Wood is not an infinitely "renewable resource." It is not because the soil is not.

What does this mean for the future? As far as what one man can do alone, little. Even the combined resources of a great nation are probably insufficient to replenish ingredients that have been taken from the soil for generations. On lands producing annual crops, the status of the soil is even more easily measured in the mounting doses of fertilizer needed to sustain yields. Here, too, improved and hybrid seed has worked miracles, but cannot alter the basic fact that each crop from the ground reduces the future store by that amount unless nutrients are replaced.

In spite of the foregoing, two facts are clear. In terms of what our earth will yield, the United States is still the most productive country in the world. And however much the wealth in the ground has been dissipated, the remainder we still have is that much more precious.

The road ahead is unclear because the saga of the soil is not the only trend in progress. A more noticeable trend finds America, the richest nation on earth facing vast changes because of our consumption of oil. And even in the United States, as we all know, not everybody is equally rich. Not too long ago, a headline in the conservative *Wall Street Journal* announced, "Cost of Keeping Warm Poses a Real Hardship to Millions of Poor. . . . Some Get by by Eating Less." Studies in greater depth seem to prove the long-term hazards of burning coal, while the immediate hazards of nuclear fission energy give us gigantic fright. Capping all this, harnessing nuclear fusion energy, the nuclear breeder reactor, solar energy, or other alternative energy sources seems so costly, so difficult, or so far off, that the massive effort needed to master them may mean more joint sacrifice than we are willing to undergo.

Certainly there are more problems confronting our society than an individual can solve by himself, even excluding political and military problems, though both of those are just about incalculable exclusions. Nevertheless, some suppositions appear reasonable. We might expect that oil and oil-derived products will not get cheaper, and for reasons of scarcity or cost, we might have to conserve these items much more than we do now. We can also expect an even greater interest in wood for fuel.

Residents of wood country quickly turned their thoughts to wood fuel at the first indications of oil scarcity. This was natural enough. Yet I was startled when a friend who maintains his own little place of business at his home told me his heating plans. He had been searching for a furnace to take an entire 4' cordwood stick.

Idly curious, I asked him, "How many cords do you need a year?"

"Fifty," he said.

Fifty? Fifty cords of choice firewood for one small operation for a single year? He wanted to be free from the crippling prices of oil. Who could blame him? Yet the same urgency that millions of other Americans like him will feel can strip entire forests in record time.

Those who are fortunate enough to be able to cut wood to keep warm should be ardent conservationists on two fronts. In part, forests are always dying. They must be selectively harvested to conserve wood before it rots. If you have a woodlot, care for it as you would your bank account. For somebody, the woodlot that has been cared for may be a greater prize than the bank account. That somebody could be you. It could also be your children or, if there will be anybody still reproducing, their children.

For tree harvesting, I freely agree that a chain saw can cut large wood faster than an ax. Unhappily, there is not a great deal of really large wood around any more. And if you know how to use it, the ax is a potent tool. Remember that almost up to the American Civil War, all fuel and timber cut was felled with an ax. And in the uncertain future ahead, will you always find fuel for a chain saw? Or spare parts? Or even afford the saw itself?

Another statistic worth repeating is that in time past a good axman could fell, buck, and stack two cords of wood a day. Try that with a chain saw. At that rate, you would lay in a year's supply of wood for a small stove in a day and a half or, by the end of the week, more than enough wood to heat a good-sized house for a year. Can you spare time for that? The only real question is, are you willing to try to do it?

Even if only to live the good life, you owe it to yourself to acquire a decent ax. In his book *Woodcraft,* Bernard S. Mason said, "I like axes. I like to have one near me always to speak of simple things in a city-world of mad and whirling things. . . ."

There is a lot of meat in that quotation. All in all, I endorse it. Did Mason have the future in mind? None of us can see ahead of time, of course. But if I had to prepare for it, like Mason, perhaps, I would certainly pack an ax.

Glossary

AMERICAN AX—A distinctively blocky single-bitted ax of the American colonial period. Its short fore-end and favorable performance eventually led to manufacturing this design for export back to Europe.

ANGLO-AMERICAN AX—One of the four dominant single-bitted ax designs of the American colonial period. It was marked by a flaring bit and slight poll.

ANVIL—The bevel-surfaced stationary element of an impact saw set. When the hammer element pounds the tip of the saw tooth down over the edge of the bevel on the anvil, the tip is set at the same angle.

ASPEN—A common western name for the *poplar* tree.

AX—An efficient tree-felling tool that is sufficiently described elsewhere in this book. Of the word itself, the *Oxford English Dictionary* states: "The spelling *ax* is better on every ground, etymology, phonology, and analogy, then *axe,* which of late has become prevalent."

AXHEAD—Entire body of the ax itself, less handle.

AXIS OF LATERAL PIVOT—Axis running lengthwise through ax handle and head, about which the ax will swing to one side or the other as the chopper's wrist movement permits.

BACK CUT—Cut or notch made in the back side of the tree being felled. The back cut determines the shape of the hinge. The back cut is always made after the face cut and is always higher to prevent kickback.

BAR—The arm mounted on the front of a chain-saw chassis about which the chain rotates.

BARBERCHAIR—West Coast term for *splitting-up,* the tree breaking above the felling notch and the back slab of the trunk lashing out and upward to the rear of the tree. The cause is usually insufficient face cut or no face cut.

BEETLE—The two-handed wooden hammer used to drive wooden splitting wedges before steel hammers became common. The two faces of the beetle were usually bound with rawhide or an iron ring to prevent splitting.

BEVEL—(1) A surface tipped at an angle from another surface. (2) As applied to saw teeth, a bevel is an edge that has been sharpened so that it is no longer at right angles to the face of the tooth, in particular, the sharpened edge of the tooth that flanks and forms the cutting tip.

BEVELED EDGE—Same as *bevel (2).*

BIND—(1) To secure a load of logs on a vehicle or sled. (2) Having difficulty moving within a kerf because of lack of set, sawdust clogging or pinching. (Refers to a saw.)

BINDER—See *load binder.*

BIT—*Cutting edge of the ax, the blade. Bit* is also loosely used for the pointed end of any long-handled striking tool.

BLADE—*Cutting edge of the ax, the bit.*

BOLE—Another name for the *trunk* or stem of a tree.

BOW SAW—Light and relatively efficient one-man manual saw. Also called *bucksaw* or *pulpwood saw,* bow saws have been made to accommodate blades up to 48″. Construction is an arc of tubular steel holding a thin saw blade in tension between horns of the arc.

BROADAX—Broad-bitted ax used to hew or smooth logs, making flat surfaces by chopping along the grain of the wood, as opposed to severing the grain as a felling ax is used. Broadaxes have been made in a greater variety of designs than any other type of ax.

BUCK—To cut a fallen tree or log into shorter segments.

BUCKSAW—Usually refers to a one-man, wooden-framed saw holding a light saw blade in tension. 30″ blades were common, with tension maintained by a turnbuckle or a twisted rope. *Bucksaw* may also be used to refer to the bow saw.

BUTT—Poll end of an axhead, or the larger or stump end of a log or fallen tree.

CANT DOG—Generic term for a peavey. The cant dog always has a spike on the bottom end.

CANT HOOK—Similar to a *cant dog,* but has a sharp lip or "crow's foot" at its bottom tip to oppose the hinged, spike-end arm, or "dog." This permits dragging small logs. The cant hook is usually a sawmill tool.

CHAIN BINDER—Same as *load binder.*

CHAIN SAW—More noisy, expensive, energy-consuming, difficult to maintain substitute for the ax. Its saw teeth rotate on an endless, powered chain.

CHEEK—Convex rise of the ax bit to the rear of the cutting edge. Curve of the cheek should be gentle and smooth but never flat.

CHIMNEY SHELF—Same as *smoke shelf.*

CHOCK—Large wedge or similar obstacle placed in front of a log or wheel to prevent rolling movement.

CHOP—To cut with an ax, almost always across the grain of the wood being chopped. To cut with or along the grain of the wood is to *hew.* See also *split.*

CHOPPERS—Leather mittens made roomy enough to accommodate removable woolen liners. Choppers are practical for any outdoor winter work.

CHOPPING BLOCK—Traditional term for a block upon which short pieces of firewood are split. Any short section of log that will sit upright upon the ground and present a level top surface will make a good chopping block. A Y type of chopping block will support pieces to be split that would otherwise fall over.

CHOPPING PLATFORM—Two short logs joined side-by-side to provide a rugged trough in which to chop split firewood pieces to use-length. The chopping platform is virtually essential for gathering stovewood without a saw.

CLIMBING IRONS—Strap-on spurs that permit climbing trees without too many branches.

124

COAL—To fissure and break apart in chunks as firewood does when it becomes incandescent in burning. The process is distinctive of better hardwoods.

COME-ALONG—A light hand-operated winch.

CONSTRUCTIVE AXIS OF LATERAL PIVOT—Axis about which the ax will swing to one side or the other as the chopper's lateral wrist pivoting permits. On curved-handle axes, this axis lies in prolongation of the lower grip portion of the handle to a point at the rear of the entire axhead, thus allowing considerably more deflection than with straight-handled axes.

CONSTRUCTIVE FORE-SECTION—Fore-section of an ax as measured from the bit of the ax to the constructive axis of lateral pivot. On curved-handle axes, this distance may be twice as long as on straight-handled axes.

CORD—Quantity of wood measuring 4' × 4' × 8'. However, the quantity of solid wood within that space depends on how the wood is cut, split, and stacked. The real amount can vary greatly.

CORDWOOD—Wood cut in 4' pieces, usually as bucked or limbed from the tree.

CORNER—End of the cutting edge of the ax.

CORNER CUTTING—Reducing length of the hinge by cutting its ends on each side of the back cut.

CREOSOTE(S)—Complex products of wood combustion deposited from cooler fires in stoves, flues, and chimneys. They range from 100% liquid to hard, coal-like coatings. Creosote buildup is the cause of chimney fires.

CROSSCUT SAW—One- or two-man frameless felling and bucking saws of about 5"–8" width and as long as required. Some West Coast crosscut saws were as long as 18'. The two-man saws were generally quite flexible and were successively pulled toward each operator. These saws have been superseded by chain saws.

CUT—(1) To chop, saw, or hew. (2) Ax notch or saw kerf. (3) A *cutting*. (4) Gully, ravine, or small valley (of terrain).

CUTTING—Trees felled from a particular forest area, or during a particular period.

CUTTING EDGE—(1) Lead edge of an ax, saw, or saw tooth. (2) Loosely used, the bit or blade of an ax.

DEFLECT—To change the direction of a blow or stroke in motion.

DEFLECTION—Amount of divergence between intended line-of-cut and the actual impact; the chopping error.

DEPTH GAUGE—An elevated tip on a chain saw just forward of each cutting tooth that rides against the wood being sawed. Being slightly shorter than the tooth, the depth gauge controls the depth of chip cut by the tooth.

DEPTH GAUGE JOINTER—A hardened metal shield of designated thickness placed on a chain saw during sharpening to surround the tip of a depth gauge. Any part of the tip that protrudes is filed off to make the tip the desired height.

DOG—Steel arm with a right-angle spur at its end. The arm is often hinged, such as that used on a peavey to grab a log for turning. A common use of a stationary dog with a spur on both ends was to secure a log during hewing.

DOUBLE—*Double-bitted ax*. Also simply called a double ax.

DOUBLE-BITTED AX—Most efficient design of ax because of its straight handle. A second inherent advantage is that the double is two axes in one. The latter reason makes the double-bit more dangerous for learning and casual use.

DRESS—To run a fine-grit, hand grinding stone lightly along the side of a saw to rub wire-edges off saw teeth after sharpening. Direction of dressing must be toward the sharpened edges.

DRY—(1) To season firewood. (2) Refers to wood ready for burning. (3) Refers to a sharpening stone that does not require either water or oil on its surface while in use. The pocket ax stone is a dry stone.

DUTCHMAN—Ingenious method of felling large trees with a chain saw, it may sometimes permit controlling lay for more than 90°. The technique is comlex and dangerous.

EDGE—(1) Same as *cutting edge*. (2) The narrow surface of a saw tooth as distinguished from the wide surface, which is a *side* or *face*. When so shaped, the edge may also be termed a *bevel*.

END KNOB—The flared end terminating the grip portion of an ax handle.

EYE—Slot through the axhead in which the handle is inserted and affixed.

EYEBALL—To assess the direction in which a tree leans without any visual aids or instruments.

FACE—(1) Side of a tree toward which it will be felled. (2) Side of the tree in which the face cut is made. (3) The broad side of an ax bit. (4) For a saw tooth, the same as *side*.

FACE CUT—The first notch cut into a tree, always toward the direction of fall. The face cut is always a notch and must always be lower than the subsequently made back cut. The face cut is also known as the *under cut*.

FALL—To cut down a tree. The more specific term is *fell*.

FEATHER-EDGE—The steel rind that clings to the edge of a sharpened ax. The most practical method to eliminate a feather-edge is by stropping.

FAWN FOOT—Sharp projecting toe of some single-bitted ax handles. Its tip is a useless hazard that is best cut off.

FELL—To cut a tree down. Even beavers can fell large trees. But to fell them where intended without breakage of tree, equipment, other trees, or persons is "an art, not a science."

FERRULE—Binding about the working end of a tool handle to prevent splitting. Usually made of a metal sleeve or, as a makeshift, of wire.

FILE HOLDER—(1) A chain-saw sharpening device that, clamped to the round sharpening file, rests on top of the chain, maintaining an even cutting depth for the file. (2) Same as *jointing file holder*.

FLUE—Smoke passage leaving a stove or fireplace. A flue must be kept free of accumulated creosotes. *Flue* may include stovepipe and chimney.

FORE-END—Same as *fore-section*.

FORE-SECTION—Forward portion of the axhead as measured from the axis of lateral pivot to the bit. The shorter the fore-section, the more accurate the ax.

FRONT—Same as *frontal zone*.

FRONTAGE—Same as *frontal zone*.

FRONTAL ZONE—Area to the chopper's front, bounded on the sides by parallel lines running forward from the outer edges of the chopper's feet. For safety, no sideward or diagonal strokes should ever be directed at a target within the frontal zone.

FUEL—What you must have to keep warm. If yours is wood, it will cost you less and give you something enjoyable to do besides.

GERMAN AX—A rather longish, straight-topped ax of the American colonial period. One of the four dominating patterns, the German ax was common in the mid-Atlantic region.

GLUT—A wooden wedge with its top bound with rawhide or an iron ring to prevent splitting. Before the general advent of steel wedges, the glut was used to split logs in cracks opened by an ax or an iron starter-wedge.

GRAB HOOK—Hook used on the end of a chain so that the chain can be looped and shortened at will. The narrow slot of the grab hook will engage any link and stay as hooked on that link only.

GRAIN—The relatively fibrous character of wood in the direction of growth.

GREEN—Referring not to color but to the natural moisture contained within freshly cut wood before it has seasoned.

GRINDER—Electrically driven power grinder. Its high speed makes it a poor tool to sharpen axes upon as they are likely to be "burned."

GRINDSTONE–Old-fashioned natural sandstone wheel turned by hand crank, foot pedal, or, if modernized, by electric motor. In the latter case, speed should not exceed 40–60 r.p.m. Grindstones should always be used with water.

GRIP–Lower end of the ax handle, particularly including the end knob area.

GULLET–A deep or enlarged valley separating the teeth of manual saws, especially the valley on each side of the raker teeth. Purpose of the gullet is to carry sawdust out of the kerf.

GUM–To cut, deepen, or sharpen the edges of the gullets.

GUMMING WHEEL–A narrow, rounded-edge abrasive wheel for use on a power grinder to gum sawdust gullets.

GUNSTICK–Two slender, straight sticks hinged together at one end as with a pair of dividers. The apex of the gunstick points the facing of the under cut when the legs are placed in each corner of the face notch.

HACK—(1) To chop inexpertly. (2) Northeastern term for the *tamarack* tree.

HAMMER SET—Same as *impact saw set.*

HANG—To mount an axhead on an ax handle.

HARDWOOD—Arbitrary term for the wood of deciduous (broad-leaf) trees. Not all hardwoods are equally hard. Some hardwoods are much softer than the harder softwoods. Poplar and basswood are two examples.

HEAD—Same as *axhead.*

HEAD LEAN—The dominant direction in which a tree leans. The term makes sense only when used in reference to the preselected lay, the direction of fall.

HEART ROT—Core rot of a tree trunk, often growing upward from the roots. Heart rot can complicate felling if the middle of the butt is not sound enough to form a proper hinge.

HEARTWOOD—Dense, inner core-wood of a tree. The heartwood is dead and kept from rotting only by the outer layers of the tree which are live. Heartwood of some trees is noticeably darker in color. It is usually more brittle than the outer sapwood.

HEAVY LEANER—Tree that has a pronounced lean, or one that is noticeably tipped. A heavy leaner can usually be felled only in its direction of lean.

HEEL—Upper corner of an ax bit.

HELVE—Older term for an ax handle, especially a single-bitted handle.

HEW—To chop wood along with the grain, as when forming a square timber from a log by using a broad ax.

HINGE—The narrow section of wood within a tree trunk between the face cut and the back cut that remains unsevered at the moment the tree falls. The hinge is the principal means for controlling direction of fall, which will be perpendicular to the hinge, though "pulled" to its thicker end, if any.

IMPACT SAW SET—A saw set that bends saw teeth by hammering the tips over a beveled angle on a special small anvil. Any small hammer can be used. The set anvils have been made in numerous designs, hand-held, bench-rest, and for stump or log mounting.

IMPACT SET—Same as *impact saw set.*

INNER—Designates the side of a saw tooth from which the sharpening is done and from which the beveled cutting edges are visible, the same side of the tooth where set of the tooth bends away from the viewer.

JOINT—To file all saw teeth to the same length by running a file along their tips from one end of the saw to the other while the file is kept perpendicular to the plane of the saw. Jointing, the first step in sharpening a saw, must leave a jointing flat on the tip of each tooth.

JOINTER—Same as *jointing tool.*

JOINTING FILE HOLDER—A device for holding a flat file perpendicular to the plane of a manual saw while jointing the teeth.

JOINTING FLAT—The squared-off area on the tip of each tooth of a jointed saw. The jointing flat is an essential guide for sharpening teeth to a uniform length.

JOINTING TOOL—(1) Occasionally, the same as *jointing file holder.* (2) Same as *raker jointing tool.*

KEEN—To make keen, to sharpen. Also to wail or lament bitterly. The etymological connection here is seldom perceived by the uninformed until they attempt to sharpen a saw.

KERF—The cut made by a saw or ax. As the ax kerf deepens it becomes a notch. A kerf is sometimes also known as a *scarf,* though the two are not synonymous.

KICKBACK—(1) Referring to a tree being felled, to plunge backward off the stump toward the chopper. (2) The act doing the above. Kickback is a lethal hazard. Cause of kickback is failure to provide a kickback stop to arrest the rearward push of the falling tree.

KICKBACK STOP—Small wall of stump wood formed along the line of the hinge by cutting the back cut slightly higher than the face cut. As the tree breaks off in falling, its weight on the floor of the face cut is held in place by this wall, making rearward movement impossible.

KINDLING—Pencil-to finger-thickness sticks, twigs, or similar. The secondary-level fire starter, the first being tinder, which is finer and easier to light.

KNOB—Short for *end knob.*

KNOT—The hard, twisted-grain base from which a branch grows from a tree trunk or stem. When improperly hit, a knot may chip an ax bit.

LARCH—The *tamarack* tree, also known as *hack.*

LATERAL CHOPPING—Chopping strokes that are delivered horizontally or diagonally instead of vertically. Lateral chopping should never be directed at targets within the frontal zone.

LATERAL PIVOT—Voluntary or involuntary turning movement of a chopper's wrists to either side. Lateral pivoting will change the line of impact of the descending ax.

LAY—Intended direction for a tree to be felled.

LEAN—The direction a tree is naturally inclined from the vertical. For tree-felling purposes, lean is always viewed relative to the lay of the tree. From that, the dominant direction of lean is the *head lean,* the lesser direction is the *side lean.*

LIMB—To clean the trunk and major branches of a fallen tree of their limbs. The process of limbing should cleave the knots off even with the trunk.

LINE-OF-CUT—The line being chopped with an ax or, if a notch, the line running through the fold of the notch. Both notch and line must be level.

LINE-OF-CUT EXTENSION—Visualized prolongation of the line-of-cut past the chopper. The line-of-cut extension coincides with the chopper's frontal-zone boundary on the side he chops toward. The outer edge of his foot on that side should be against the line-of-cut extension, but not on the far side of it.

LOAD BINDER—Device for binding a load of wood securely to a vehicle or sled. A *chain binder* is manufactured item of hooks and a hinged lever to draw up and hold slack in a chain. Chain binders come in various sizes to fit any weight of chain. Also known as a *log binder.* A workable substitute binder can be devised from a stout rope loosely tied across the load through which a lever (a stick) is thrust and twisted to draw up and slack and hold it. The lever is secured in the load to prevent untwisting.

LODGE—With a tree, to become supported by another object and be unable to fall to the ground. The supporting object is usually another tree.

LODGE-DRIVING—After partially preparing a tree for felling, to finish the job by felling another tree against it so that both trees fall together. Lodge-driving is not necessarily a stunt, but is always hazardous and more mess to clean up afterward.

LOG BINDER—Same as *load binder.*

LOG CARRIER—A straight-handled tool with opposed, hinged spiked-end arms, or "dogs," at its middle so as to be able to grab and drag small logs as a two-man load.

LOG DOLLY—Two-wheeled device for attachment to a log so the log will roll rather than drag.

LOG TONGS—Heavier version of the old iceman's tongs for dragging logs.

LUMBERING—Any wood-harvesting operations, including those for firewood.

MANUAL SAW—A saw that must be operated by hand rather than by an engine. The principal manual saws used in the woods are the one- and two-man crosscut saws and the bow saw.

MATCH CUTTING—Felling by cutting the sides of a trunk away in successive alternate increments on either side. Decreasing hinge material is left on the side opposite the operator. Match cutting is dangerous and used only when no other technique is feasible.

MAUL—Long-handled hammer with wood-splitting bit also. Modern steel mauls are manufactured in weights of 4 to 10 lbs. In the heavier weights, a maul is a versatile and most useful tool. A century or more ago, another tool of the same name was used to drive gluts. That *maul* was cut and shaped from a young hickory tree, the smoothed-off root mass being the clublike head of the maul and the thinned-down trunk of the tree the handle.

MIDDLE BEVEL—The bevel formed by filing away the middle ridge between side bevels just below the tip of a saw tooth on its inner side.

MIDDLE-BEVEL POINT—A relatively strong and durable style of saw-tooth tip because of being rounded rather than needle-pointed. In forming the middle-bevel point, the jointing flat is finally erased only by filing away the middle ridge.

MIDDLE RIDGE—The vertical ridge between edge bevels on a saw-tooth tip extending downward from the peak to the top of the inner face of the tooth.

MILL FILE—A flat, rather smooth-cutting file commonly used to sharpen saws.

NEEDLE POINT—The common style of tooth tip filed on manual woods saws. The needle-point tip is not really as peaked as a needle but has a sharp silhouette formed by convergence of the edge bevels flanking the tip.

NOTCH—Open kerf made by opposed ax strokes that lift chips for deeper penetration. Also, the result of converging saw kerfs, as with the face cut.

OUTER—Designates the side of a saw tooth which performs the cutting, but on which no cutting edge bevels are visible, the same side of the tooth where the set of the tooth bends toward the viewer.

OVERREACH—Same as *overshoot.*

OVERSHOOT—To strike beyond where intended, or to strike the handle before the ax hits at all. The latter is a common scourge of handles during limbing.

PARBUCKLE—Use of ordinary rope to gain 2-to-1 mechanical advantage loading logs. The ends of a rope secured in its middle are run under and around ends of a log, then hauled in, rolling up the log in the loops.

PASS—One continuous movement of a sharpening stone in one direction.

PEAK—The uppermost portion of the tip of a saw tooth (as viewed during the sharpening process).

PEAVEY—The *cant dog,* a spiked-end pike with a curved, hinged dog attached to grip logs so as to roll them short distances. The peavey is named after Joseph Peavey of Maine, its 19th-century inventor.

PEG TOOTH—Style of manual woods saw tooth that has pronounced valleys between teeth, but no rakers. The peg teeth themselves scuff sawdust from the kerf.

PICKAROON—(1) Axlike tool, but with the bit at right angles to the handle, as with an adze. Instead of a poll, the other end of the head has a short pick. The pickaroon is used to chop apart and pick out the face-cut wedge of larger trees felled with a saw. On the West Coast, the pickaroon is known as the Pulaski tool. (2) An older tool, also known as *pickaroon,* was the extra-long-handled riverman's pike used in the East when timber logs were floated downstream in flood waters of the spring runoff.

PICKPOLE—Extra-long spiked pole used to help push smaller trees into the lay desired.

PINCH—To bind a saw in its kerf by side pressure of the pieces that are being cut. Pinching occurs when the log or tree settles into the cavity made by the kerf. Pinching can damage the set of manual saws. It can also send chain saws to the repair shop.

PLIER-TYPE SAW SET—A type of set that bends the tooth tip over an anvil by action of levers worked in the hand, as with a pair of pliers.

POCKET STONE—Round, two-grit ax-sharpening stone. The ax's best friend.

POINT—The cutting tip of a saw tooth.

POLL—The heavy rear butt section of a single-bitted ax. It should not be used as a hammer.

POPLAR—The *aspen* tree, also known as *popple.*

POPPLE—Same as *poplar.*

PULP—The trees or the wood cut from them that will be used for making paper. These trees are usually softwoods.

PULP HOOK—One-handed hook used to aid loading cordwood by hand.

PULP SAW—Same as *bow saw.*

QUARTER SAW—To saw a log toward its center to obtain plank or boards with relatively straight sections of the tree's annual rings. Quarter-sawed stock is least subject to warping, making it suitable for handles, etc.

RAILROAD SPIKE—Short, heavy, square-shanked spike used to secure railroad track to the wooden ties. Bevel of the taper at bottom end of the spike has long been used for an anvil to set saw teeth upon.

RAKER—Same as *raker tooth.*

RAKER GAUGE—Device to measure the difference in height between raker teeth and their adjacent cutting teeth.

RAKER JOINTING TOOL—A saw-sharpening device laid on the tips of jointed cutting teeth flanking each pair of rakers and having a hardened surface with a slot that is placed above the rakers. If the tip of a raker protrudes above the hardened surface, it is filed off. The raker jointing tool is usually adjustable to allow for different raker heights.

RAKER TOOTH—A chisel-edged, sawdust-scooping tooth slightly shorter than the cutting teeth. Raker teeth are placed in pairs between groups of cutting teeth so as to loosen and lift sawdust for discharge from the kerf in the gullets. Of each pair of rakers, one faces each end of the saw.

ROLLING POINT—A long-lasting, fast-cutting style of rounded-tip saw tooth formed by sharpening the bevels flanking the tip in gently rising curves. A rolling-point tip is difficult to form, requiring much experience and skill to form well.

ROOT MASS—The roots supporting each individual tree or clump of trees.

ROUNDED PEAK—A saw-tooth tip of the rolling point or the middle-bevel point types.

RUN—To saw crookedly. (Refers to a saw.) The usual cause of running is longer teeth on one side of a saw than on the other as a result of improper jointing or sharpening.

SAILOR—Section of rotten or detached wood still suspended in a tree but which may "sail" down on anybody below without warning. Mature trees are all too likely to harbor sailors.

SAPWOOD–The live wood of a tree just inside the bark layer. The layer that brings the tree moisture and nutrients from the ground. The sapwood is often lighter colored and less brittle than the inner heartwood.

SAWBUCK –Same as *sawhorse*.

SAWHORSE–Any device to hold wood off the ground for sawing. Most commonly made in the form of two sets of crossed sticks nailed somewhat apart, the distance to suit the wood to be cut.

SAW LOG–Log that will be sawed into lumber at a sawmill rather than be used for either pulp or firewood.

SAW SET–Device to bend alternate saw teeth to opposite sides of the saw so as to cut a kerf slightly wider than the body of the saw to prevent binding. A saw set may be an *impact set,* a *setting iron,* or a *plier-type set.*

SAW SET GAUGE–Same as *set gauge*.

SAWYER–Man who saws, especially in a sawmill.

SCARF–Dialectic (northeast) term for kerf, though the two are not synonymous. *Scarf* refers to the tapered part of a log that results from an ax-cut notch and, by association, is sometimes applied to the notch or to any ax or saw cut.

SEASON–To dry green or wet wood. Under optimum conditions, firewood may season in a couple of months. Usual seasoning time is about a year.

SECTION–Short for *cross section*.

SET–(1) To bend the tips of alternate saw teeth to opposite sides of a saw so that their kerf will be slightly wider than the body of the saw and allow sawing without binding. (2) The bend given to saw teeth by setting as in (1) above. (3) The device that bends the teeth as in (1) above.

SET GAUGE–A small, four-legged device that, laid against the side of a manual woods saw, measures the amount of set in a saw tooth.

SET HAMMER–The movable element of an impact saw set.

SET STAKE–Same as *anvil*.

SETTING IRON–The most simple saw set, consisting of only a narrow slot filed in one edge of a strip of steel. When fitted down over the tip of a saw tooth, the slot holds the tooth so that pulling down on the setting iron will bend (set) the tooth.

SHAPE–To file the edges of saw teeth and their intervening valleys so as to restore original proportion and size.

SHEATH–Protective cover for the cutting edge of an ax or saw.

SIDE–Same as *face (4)*. The broader surface of a saw tooth as distinguished from the narrow surface, which is an *edge* or bevel.

SIDE LEAN–The lesser direction in which a tree is tipped when viewed in relation to lay. The major direction of tipping is *head lean*.

SINGLE CUT–Method of finishing the surface of a file so it will cut more smoothly.

SKID–To drag a log or logs. Also a log or timber upon which other logs are rolled, dragged, or stacked.

SLASH–Limbs, tops, and other residue of felled trees that are left in the woods.

SLIP HOOK–Hook having a mouth wide enough to ride down the chain it grasps. A slip hook permits tension to cinch a load together tightly.

SLOPE–The angle of inclination of the cutting edges of a saw tooth as they approach the tip of the tooth.

SMOKE SHELF–Same as *chimney shelf*. A shelf area above the back of a fireplace that provides space for a cold air turnaround. Continual rotary traffic of cold air within the chimney is essential to sucking smoke up the chimney on the upward leg of the somewhat heated air current.

SNAKE–Same as *skid* (as a verb).

SOFTWOOD–Arbitrary term for the wood of conifers. In large part, these are evergreen trees. Not all softwoods are especially soft. Some softwoods are considerably harder than some hardwoods. Long-leaf pine and larch are two examples.

SPLIT–To knock wood apart along its grain.

SPLITTING-UP–Same as *barberchair*. The breaking of a tree above the felling notch and the back slab striking out and upward to the rear of the tree. That represents danger enough, but the tree that splits up can do even more. As the tree hits, the broken trunk and its rearward extension can completely bounce off the high stump in any direction. It is one of the most dangerous and unpredictable of woods hazards. The cause of it all is usually insufficient face cut, or no face cut at all.

SPUD–A round-nosed chisel with either short or long handle used to peel bark off logs. The nose curves downward to enable following curve of a log.

STAND–Adjacent trees considered as a unit, either of trees or of timber.

STEM–Same as *bole*. The *trunk* of a tree.

STROP–Leather strap used to eliminate the feather-edge from an ax or other keen-edge tool. Also the act of stroking the tool on the strap.

STUD JACK–Jack for use in tree-felling with pointed studs welded to both piston and base to prevent kicking out of the kerf when under pressure.

SWAGE–To lightly hammer the tips of raker teeth so that the tips turn and slightly hook toward their end of the saw. Swaging greatly increases the sawdust-scooping efficiency of the rakers.

SWAMP–To perform the auxiliary chores of tree-felling, including road-making, brush-clearing, limbing, and sometimes bucking.

SWAMPER–Man who swamps.

SWAMPING AX–Ax having a less keen edge than a felling ax, so as to withstand the knots encountered in swamping work.

TAMARACK–Common name for the *larch* tree, which is also known as *hack*.

TANG–The slim tongue at the bottom end of a file that is inserted into a file handle.

TAPER-GROUND–A method of manufacturing saws so that the teeth are thicker than the body of the saw. The purpose is to prevent the saw from binding in the kerf. This construction helps, but even taper-ground saws must be set.

TIMBER–Wood generally, though usually on the stump.

TINDER–Fine material used to ignite kindling to start a fire. Newspaper, if dry, makes excellent tinder.

TIP–The *peak* of a saw tooth, the portion that does the cutting.

TOE–Lower corner of an ax bit.

TRADE AX–A European tree-felling ax, originally of French design and manufacture, used extensively in trade with the Indians well into the 18th century.

TREETOP SWINGER—Use of tandem garage door springs to snap a tree into its proper lay.

TWITCH–Same as *skid*. To drag log(s) to a yarding area for loading and, sometimes, bucking. *Twitch* is also used as an adjective as in "twitch-trail" or "twitch-chain."

UNDER CUT–Alternate term for *face cut*.

UNDERREACH–Same as *undershoot*.

UNDERSHOOT–Same as *underreach*. In using an ax, to fall short of the intended line of impact, an occasional cause of serious accident.

VALLEY–The intervening space between saw teeth.

VERTICAL CHOPPING–Chopping strokes with little or no lateral movement. Vertical chopping is performed only in the frontal zone. The three types are: (1) Chopping that is backed-up. (2) Chopping that is not backed-up. (3) Chopping done below the level of the feet.

WEDGE–Narrow strip of material, usually steel or wood, that tapers to a thin edge at one of the narrow ends. Used for pounding into cracks and kerfs for the heavier splitting and felling. In firewood-harvesting operations, several types of wedges are used:

(1) Wood and soft steel wedges for securing the handle in the eye of the ax. (2) Felling wedges for insertion into saw kerfs for both felling and bucking. To avoid damaging chain saws, felling wedges are often made of plastic or aluminum. (3) Large splitting wedges of either steel or wood. *Wedge* is also the term for the notch-wood sawed from a face cut.

WET – Refers to wood having moisture throughout, but from soaking or weather, not from its natural internal sap. Wet wood will burn only to the extent that it dries out.

WIDOW-MAKER – Same as *sailor*. Any piece of hung-up wood waiting to fall down upon a careless chopper below.

WINDROW – (1) To pile slash in rows. (2) The row itself.

WIRE-EDGE – Similar to, but much coarser than a feather-edge. The wire-edge is the steel residue pushed to the outer edge of the bevel in filing saw teeth. The wire-edge must be rubbed off with a fine-grit stone moved along the side of the saw toward the sharpened edges.

WOODPILE SHINGLES — Interlocked plywood shielding an exterior woodpile from the weather

WRIST PIVOT – Turning motion permitted by the wrists, voluntarily or otherwise, that causes deflection of the ax in its line of impact.

YARD – (1) To gather logs into a loading, or loading and bucking, area. (2) The loading area itself.

YELLOW PINE – Generic name for the southern pines, principally the loblolly, longleaf, and shortleaf pines.

YOKE – A team of two oxen.

Bibliography

Conway, Steve. *Timber Cutting Practices.* 2d ed. San Francisco: Miller Freeman, 1973.

Curtis, Will and Jane. *Artistry in Iron.* Ashville, Me.: Cobblesmith, 1974.

Defenbaugh, James Elliott. *History of the Lumber Industry of North America.* Vol. II. Chicago: The American Lumberman, 1907.

Furnas, J. C. *A Social History of the United States, 1587-1914.* New York: Putnam, 1969.

Johnson, Allen J., ed. Auth, George H., assoc. ed. *Fuels and Combustion Handbook.* 1st ed. New York: McGraw-Hill, 1951.

Kauffman, Henry J. *American Axes.* Brattleboro, Vt.: Stephen Greene Press, 1972.

Ketchum, Richard M. *The Secret Life of the Forest.* New York: American Heritage, 1970.

Mason, Bernard S. *Woodcraft.* New York: Barnes, 1939.

Mercer, Henry D. *Ancient Carpenters' Tools.* Doylestown, Pa.: Bucks County Historical Society, 1960.

Morison, Samuel Eliot. *The European Discovery of America: The Northern Voyages.* New York: Oxford University Press, 1971.

Orton, Vrest. *The Forgotten Art of Building a Good Fireplace.* Dublin, N. H.: Yankee, 1969.

Panshin, A. J., and Carl de Zeeuw. *Textbook of Wood Technology.* 3d ed. Vol. I. New York: McGraw-Hill, 1970.

Sandvik Steel Works Co., Ltd. *Sandvik Forestry Saws.* Stockholm, Sweden, 1957.

Simonds Mfg. Co. *Simonds Cross-Cut Saw Plan.* Fitchburg, Mass., 1915.

Sloane, Eric. *The Seasons of America Past.* New York: Funk & Wagnalls, 1958.

Sloane, Eric. *A Reverence for Wood.* New York: Funk & Wagnalls, 1965.

Sloane, Eric. *The Second Barrel.* New York: Funk & Wagnalls, 1969.

Smith, David C. *History of Lumbering in Maine, 1861-1900.* Orono, Me.: University of Maine Press, 1972.

Snow & Nealley Company. *Catalog #66.* Bangor, Me., 1 November 1948.

Thoreau, Henry David. *The Maine Woods.* New York: Bramhall House, 1950.

Tocqueville, Alexis de. *Democracy in America.* Translated by George Lawrence. Garden City, N.Y.: Doubleday Anchor, 1969.

Wackerman, A. E., W. D. Hagenstein, and A. S. Mitchell. *Harvesting Timber Crops.* 2d ed. New York: McGraw-Hill, 1966.

Index